D0321550

THE ROAD FROM WEMBLEY

JOHN STONEMAN

THE ROAD FROM
WEMBLEY

Matador
9 De Montfort Mews
Leicester LE1 7FW, UK
Tel: (+44) 116 255 9311 / 9312
Email: books@troubador.co.uk
Web: www.troubador.co.uk/matador

ISBN 978-1848760-295

A Cataloguing-in-Publication (CIP) catalogue record for this book is available from the British Library.

Mixed Sources
Product group from well-managed
forests and other controlled sources
www.fsc.org Cert no. TT-COC-2082
© 1996 Forest Stewardship Council

Typeset in 11pt Bembo by Troubador Publishing Ltd, Leicester, UK
Printed in the UK by The Cromwell Press Ltd, Trowbridge, Wilts, UK

Matador is an imprint of Troubador Publishing Ltd

For Mum, Dad and Vanessa, and with thanks to James

Foreword

I remember it like it was yesterday. A boiling-hot, August Saturday afternoon at the start of the 1996-97 season, my first in semi-professional football. I'd made my debut for Arnold Town, of the Northern Counties East League Premier Division, as a late substitute at Denaby United on the previous Bank Holiday Monday, and was handed my first start as we travelled to Northern League club Ryhope CA for an FA Cup Preliminary Round tie. I've played most of my career as a centre-half, so you can probably understand why Ray O'Brien, our general manager, gave this headless 18-year-old, masquerading as a right-sided midfielder, an old-fashioned roasting at half-time. 'I'll show him,' I thought as I made my way back out onto Meadow Park to start the second half. Within two minutes I had, a right-foot half-volley from the edge of the box scorching into the top corner for the winner to set up another away tie at Gretna – yes, the same side who would play in a Scottish FA Cup Final less than ten years later.

It was the first of twenty goals I would score in more than five hundred senior Non-League matches before I retired at the end of 2007-08. I recall thinking at the time: 'Whatever happens to me now, I can always tell my grandchildren that like the legendary Eric Cantona (scorer of the Wembley winner in the previous final) and Norman Whiteside (whose goal against Everton in 1985 is the first Wembley goal I can remember) I had scored in the greatest cup competition in the world.' It was a truly wonderful feeling, but one which would eventually be surpassed.

Fast forward eleven years and I'm playing at Wembley in the FA Cup. Boiling hot day again, but unfortunately it's August, not May, and I'm running out at Vale Farm, the home of Combined Counties club Wembley FC. I'm now a twenty-nine year-old 'veteran' playing for Ryman Division One North club Ware in another Preliminary Round tie. It would be the start of the road to my finest achievement in football, and one which would bring me into contact with John Stoneman, who had had this wonderful idea to follow his own road from Wembley to Wembley. Magically for me, having dispensed of our lower league opponents by four goals to one, Ware FC and I would be a major part of John's story.

For twelve seasons my ambition had been to play in the First Round Proper of the FA Cup. I'd watched the highlights on *Match Of The Day* every year, wondering what it would be like to see myself on the small box in the corner of the living room. As the size of the TV grew, so did my yearning for that bit of personal cup glory. Something I had to write about every season from other players' perspectives as a reporter on *The Non-League Paper*. Since 2000 when I joined the newspaper, the ink in my pen had been envy green.

With this season's memorable cup run, when we were three-one up in the fourth, and final qualifying round with ten minutes to go, I can honestly say it's the first time I've ever had tears in my eyes while a game was in progress. I knew I would never get a better chance to get there. I was welling up at the thought of appearing at the same stage of the competition as double European Cup winners Nottingham Forest and Leeds United, Champions League semi-finalists as recently as 2001.

Watching the draw on the BBC in our packed clubhouse was surreal. The only space available for us players to sit was on a small patch of carpet right underneath the big screen and although there was disappointment that neither of the 'giants' came out with us (nor Notts County, my club), we drew a full-time professional outfit in Blue Square Premier club Kidderminster Harriers. I'd been trying for so long I wasn't about to start complaining about the opposition once I'd got there!

All the things I'd reported on in the past started to happen to me. The game, once again on our threadbare pitch, was made all-ticket with a capacity set at three thousand. We had to buy tickets and get the cash from our family and friends. I needed twenty four. We went into the club on the Monday morning before the game to film our attempts at the 'Crossbar Challenge' for Sky TV's *Soccer AM*. The local network Anglia TV came to my home to film me working on the day job, as they did captain and central heating engineer Danny Wolf, winger-cum-plumber Scott Neilson, and then all of us at our Thursday night training session. Setanta Sports had given me a camera to do a four-day video diary around the game, while *The Sun*, *Guardian* and local rags were present to ask the kind of questions I reel off to other players at the same time every year. Having the boot on the other foot, and the notepad and pen in another's hand, was fantastic.

On top of this we were given new training kit to wear on the day, the kit suppliers sent us a commemorative strip to wear with our names on the back and even local cafes, fish and chip shop and Tesco got in on the act, supplying us with breakfast, supper and energy drinks because they wanted to get behind the lads. For days my head was in a whirl and it was difficult to get focused on this game against a side four divisions our senior. If we'd have been going to the City Ground or Elland Road, I imagine I wouldn't have slept for a fortnight.

Walking out at a stadium where we personally know every inch of concrete on the far terrace, only to see it covered ten-man deep, was unreal. I had waited my whole career for this moment and we didn't disgrace ourselves. The atmosphere, compared to the kind of low three-figure crowds we usually play to, was electric, but unfortunately yours truly gave a free-kick away as we entered the final quarter-of-an-hour and ten-man Kidderminster scored from it. Within a couple of minutes it was two and game over – but at least I managed to make it into shot on *Match Of The Day*, James Constable's 25-yarder flying past me, as one of my mates put it in a text message that night, 'standing with my hands on my hips.' A lifetime ambition achieved!

I hear people say the FA Cup has lost its allure. Rubbish. As I write, I've just watched the final between Portsmouth and Cardiff City. Try telling Harry Redknapp he'll have to play a weakened side in the competition next year to concentrate on booking a Champions League spot in the Premiership. The 2007–08 FA Cup has been the year of the underdog; one which in my opinion rekindled many football fans' love with the greatest cup competition in the world. Take it from someone in the game's grass roots who has it to thank for his greatest football memories – it really is, bar none.

Stuart Hammonds
(Ware FC defender and reporter on *The Non-League Paper*)

Introduction

As Cardiff and Portsmouth are led out onto the famous Wembley turf for the 2008 FA Cup Final, I have to pinch myself to be sure I'm not dreaming. It's been an incredible journey. An eleven-month pilgrimage. I've travelled over two thousand miles, spent nearly a thousand pounds, watched over seventeen hundred minutes of football, and so far seen sixty three goals. I've also fulfilled an unexpected, lifelong ambition.

I've seen some of the best players in the world, visited some of the game's most-hallowed arenas and witnessed some of the biggest upsets in history. I've also seen some real stinkers, at stadiums which are barely worthy of the title watching players whose pre-match build-up is a doner kebab, five pints of lager and half a packet of Marlboro Lights.

I've been an unlikely ball boy, a backseat manager, a reporter, photographer and in equal measures a frustrated and delighted fan. I've sworn, cheered, sung and jeered. I've experienced the adrenaline rush of the last-minute goal, the sudden, all-encompassing misery of the late winner and the slow, lingering death of the plucky but outclassed minnow.

I've built bridges with my friends and family, built friendships with complete strangers, stood frozen in the same place for seven hours and raced across a continent to make it to a match on time.

But more importantly I've rediscovered my love of football. That magical, wonderful game. So simple in its premise and yet so complex in its execution. Something that I had lived and breathed for, taken for granted and then with disillusionment discarded.

And now, right now, sitting here in this glittering stadium, which is heaving with the heat and passion of ninety thousand expectant fans, I'm about to witness the culmination of all of those events. I feel both elated and numb in the same breath. Delirious at the achievement and despondent that beyond this magnificent climax looms a large void that I will have to somehow fill.

It all started back in July of last year. For some reason, and I honestly can't remember why, I found myself sat in my study at home, perusing the pages of the Football Association website. One of the links on the page caught my eye, a link which announced the fixtures for the Extra Preliminary Round of the 2007–08 FA Cup. I was amazed. It seemed like only yesterday – actually it had been just two months – since the previous final was fought over by Chelsea and Manchester United, and yet here it was again. The new competition would begin in August, linking the seasons in the span of just one summer. There were a record number of entries, seven hundred and thirty one in total. But the teams at this stage were completely unrecognisable from the familiar league clubs. They had curious names like Glasshoughton Welfare, Norton & Stockton Ancients and Jarrow Roofing Boldon CA.

It reminded me of the old milk advert from my childhood where two Liverpudlian boys were sitting at a kitchen table discussing the prospect of playing for Accrington Stanley…

'West Allotment Celtic?'

'Who are they?'

'Eggz–actly.'

It made me think about my own childhood. To the first FA Cup Final that I had watched on television aged eight, to the legion of underdogs I had seen perform miraculous feats of giant killing, to all of the thrilling, memorable ties that the competition had conjured up year after year. I felt warm and nostalgic for the Football Association Challenge Cup. The most famous knockout competition in the world. It had been a constant in my life. Always there waiting for me like an old friend who you meet for a couple of times each year.

It has been argued that the cup has lost some of its magic in the last decade, particularly when it threatens to be overshadowed by the Champions League. But the one thing that the FA Cup guarantees me which the European showcase can't is a sense of belonging. The Champions League is an elite club which few of us ever get a chance to join. If you're fortunate enough to follow one of the top four then you probably have a different opinion, but for me the Champions League is a competition where I rent out my loyalties like a mercenary to whichever English team is playing, without ever really caring.

The FA Cup is different. We are all in it. We all have a crack at the title. We may not fancy our chances of winning, but we all get that chance to participate. There are no limitations with this dream. No exclusive membership based on the depth of club chairmen's pockets. In fact although the likelihood is that we *won't* win it, the dream is available to hundreds of clubs up and down the country. And maybe, just maybe, this year will be our year.

As I sat in front of the computer screen, I realised that this was the reason why a record number of teams had been mesmerised by the dream. Why hundreds of Non-League clubs would be battling for the right to progress. Each step further into the competition bringing fresh challenges from stronger, faster, better teams. Each round navigated offering the monetary rewards which could underpin the finances of these little clubs. The FA Cup is like the Holy Grail, a mythical quest seemingly out of reach, promising great riches but where the journey itself is the actual reward.

I made a snap decision. I fancied that quest. The road to Wembley was starting and I wanted to be on it. To travel this great river from its bubbling source in ramshackle stands and renovated cow fields, meandering up and down the country as it increased in depth, power and pace until the final outpouring at the magnificent footballing cathedral of the new Wembley Stadium.

But where to take my first step? Which of the one hundred and seventy one Extra Preliminary Round matches should I attend?

And then I saw it. Tie number 104. Haringey Borough V Wembley FC. Surely my road to Wembley must start from Wembley?

1979
The Beginning

I first discovered the FA Cup in 1979 – the year of Arsenal, Manchester United and Alan Sunderland's moustache. I was seven years old and football mad. Despite living in an east London, West Ham heartland, I'd been persuaded by my older sister Sarah that I should support Arsenal on the strength that they had a player called 'Chippy' Brady. And the previous Christmas, Santa had brought me an itchy, red and white, long-sleeved jersey with Liam's number on the back. So completely unwittingly I found myself with a vested interest on cup final day.

On the morning of the game I had settled down on the swirl-leaf patterned, green carpet floor of our front room to watch the build up on our new colour television. The cup final was shown on both major channels, BBC1 and ITV, and I'd plumped for the latter, mainly because I'd always preferred the cheesey *World of Sport* over the stoical *Grandstand*. By my side was *Roy Of The Rovers* magazine – bought for me by my Great Auntie Ena – and I had carefully filled in all of the players' names into the cup final edition pull-out section.

Casting my mind back to that day, I don't specifically remember the television showing the players arriving in their coaches at the old twin-towered stadium or walking the pitch in their new cup final suits, but of course I know these happened. I don't remember the crowd singing *Abide With Me*, or the frustrating tedium of watching that marching band in the red jackets and bearskins, but I know these also happened.

And when the magnificent moment finally arrived at a quarter to three, and the two teams emerged from the yawning mouth of the famous Wembley tunnel before marching out around the dog track, I've no clue which resident royal was on hand for the introductions and a rousing chorus of *God Save The Queen*. But I know these all happened too, because these were the timeless rituals of the FA Cup Final, back in an era when that sunny Saturday in May was the most important date in the footballing calendar. It *always* happened like that.

Until the 1979 cup final I had never been a great watcher of football. I had always preferred to be actually kicking a ball in the playground or back garden. My seven-year-old attention span couldn't even make it through the edited highlights of *The Big Match* on a Sunday afternoon without wandering off. But that cup final was an epiphany for me. I was glued to the set. Again I can't remember the specifics – it was after all nearly thirty years ago. But I remember that things started well for the Gunners fans – and yes they were Gunners then, not Gooners – and that twice I had to fill in goal times in the Arsenal column of the *Roy Of The Rovers* wall chart.

With just five minutes left on the clock, United looked comfortably beaten to me and I naively thought that the yellow and blue ribbons – with Arsenal wearing their away strip – would already be laced onto the trophy. But then things started to go wrong. United nicked one back, then minutes later grabbed an equaliser. I remember experiencing for the first of what would be many times in my life that nagging doubt in the pit of your stomach that only football can muster. That gnawing ache born from the knowledge that a tide has turned and things are all slipping away.

By then I was in a confused state. My seven-year-old brain lacked the capabilities to deal with this cruel mistress who had promised so much and then threatened to snatch it all back. Surely my maiden cup final was not supposed to end like that? I'd followed the rituals. I'd written out the player names with no mistakes. I'd been as neat as a small boy could manage. I'd resisted the urge to skip the second half and go out into the back garden to recreate the Arsenal goals. So why were United so intent on ruining my first ever cup final? It just wasn't fair.

I didn't have time to sulk though. With literally seconds to go, a ball was swept across the face of the United goal and as goalkeeper Gary Bailey frantically scrambled to reach it, there was a dashing cavalier in a yellow and blue shirt with a curly perm and a seventies 'tache, on hand to toe poke the winner. Alan Sunderland. The burst of adrenaline and flood of relief was like a drug. In that instant I was addicted. It had been a magical, fairy tale final and like all good fairy tales it had delivered a happy ending. I had taken my first step on a long and winding road shared every season by football followers the world over. The road to Wembley.

August 2007
The Other Team On White Hart Lane

So, Haringey Borough versus Wembley. First things first, research. If you fail to prepare then you're preparing to fail. I know that Haringey is a London borough, and I think it's north of the Thames but frankly that's all I know.

Back in the days before the internet, finding out information about these small clubs was nigh on impossible unless you were part of the in-crowd of Groundhoppers – a cult which make trainspotters look veritably gregarious. The Groundhopper spends his Saturday afternoons (and of course midweek evenings) travelling around small grounds watching obscure matches from eclectic sounding competitions such as the Essex Senior League, the South West Peninsular League or the Midland Combination.

Armed with a carrier bag and a well-thumbed copy of *The Football Traveller*, they arrive at minor stadia like thieves in the night, log team sheet changes and goal times on separate scraps of paper to keep their match day programme pristine, order a Bovril at half time, and are always standing by the exits come the ninetieth minute ready for a quick dart at the final whistle. Suffice it to say that like an anorak-clad bush telegraph, Groundhoppers used to be the only ones who knew all about the locations of these obscure park pitches and their back of a fag packet fixture lists.

But of course the internet has changed all this, and now most clubs have got websites – which range from world-class publications to clunky, obsolete tomes – but most of which have at least basic details about the club. My first port of call was *Wikipedia* which told me some interesting details about Haringey Borough and its history. The club traces its roots back to 1907 and so was in its centennial year. However when they first formed they were known as Tufnell Park FC, had a ground in Holloway, and in the decades that followed played in the London, Athenian and Isthmian Leagues right up to the second world war. After the cessation of hostilities they lost their ground in Holloway (unlucky) and moved to Edmonton playing as Tufnell Park (Edmonton) FC, although they dropped the

Tufnell Park and the brackets in 1963 and continued for ten seasons as Edmonton FC before losing another ground (careless).

Meanwhile the original Tufnell Park reserve team, which had splintered off in 1909, had been playing as Wood Green Town at a stadium called Coles Park, but they had dropped into a thing called 'intermediate football', which I assumed was not good. The two sides then amalgamated to form Edmonton and Haringey FC, before becoming plain Haringey Borough.

There was a link at the bottom of the *Wikipedia* article for the official club website, so I hopped on over, and found lots of information about the club and directions to get to the ground. Now I was getting somewhere. It transpires that Haringey Borough *still* play at Coles Park and that this is just off White Hart Lane, yes *the* White Hart Lane of Tottenham Hotspur fame.

The directions read: *"Haringey Borough's main ground is Coles Park Stadium. The entrance is on White Hart Lane some five hundred yards west of the junction with the Great Cambridge Road and opposite the Bridisco factory. The nearest underground station is Wood Green on the Piccadilly Line. From there bus W3 (destination Northumberland Park) passes the ground. Five minute journey."*

Next I turned my attention to Wembley FC. Now I know that you are probably thinking that technically speaking I was doing this the wrong way round. That I should have waited for a season when Wembley were playing at *home* in the Extra Preliminary Round rather than away. After all, this book is called *'The Road From Wembley'*, not *'The Road From Haringey Borough'*, but hey, life's short and I had already checked on the FA website for the next match – the Preliminary Round – and seen that the winners of Haringey and Wembley would have a home tie against some team called Ware. So put that one down to poetic licence and let's move on.

From *Wikipedia* I learned this about Wembley. The club was formed in 1946 by a group of football fans who thought it wrong that the area which contained the National Stadium did not have its own football team. The club's motto is *"A Posse Ad Esse"* ("From Possibility To Reality"), and their nickname is The Lions. No mergers, no renaming, just a history in deliciously-named leagues such as the Delphian and Corinthian and more recently the Isthmian. They now ply their trade in the Combined Counties Football League Premier Division. I also learned that the link for the Wembley FC website didn't work. Shame.

Next I needed to study the form. The history and magic of the FA Cup is full of supreme acts of giant-killing heroism. When Ronnie Radford hit a thirty-yard thunderbolt to help propel Non-League Hereford United past the first division

Newcastle United in 1972, this was the stuff of legends purely because of the great gulf between the teams. It was also the stuff of great Parka legends due to the sheer number of khaki-clad kids that emerged in the subsequent pitch invasion witnessed by the BBC cameras.

But for Haringey Borough versus Wembley, I had no clue as to which team was playing the parts of David and Goliath. More internet research took me to a magnificent Non-League football website called *Tony's English Football Site* (www.tonykempster.co.uk). This weighty website lists all of the teams and leagues which make up the 'Non-League Pyramid'. From Tony Kempster I learned that basically it works like this. At the glittering top of English football you have the star-studded clubs of the Premiership. Below this you have the three divisions of the Football League and then the single highest level of Non-League football the Football Conference, although they now call this the Blue Square Premier.

At this point things start to get regionalised, starting with the Blue Square North and the Blue Square South and then sprawling out into lower leagues the length and breadth of the country. Promotion and relegation usually happens between all of these leagues, although because of the geographical structure and dependent on the quality of stadiums, teams are sometimes shuffled sideways or stay put rather than moving up or down. The different levels of the Non-League Pyramid are known as steps, with the Football Conference being Step One, Conference North and South are Step Two, working right down to the smallest geographical regions at Step Seven, which apparently is that 'intermediate football' thing where Wood Green FC loitered before their amalgamation.

Haringey Borough from the Spartan South Midlands League Division One were at Step Six and Wembley from the Combined Counties Premier were at Step Five. So far that season Wembley had won one and drawn one, while Haringey had a win from one outing. So it was my beloved Lions who were shouldered with the tag of giants ready to be struck down by a blow from the evil Haringey. You may notice that I had already decided where to throw in my allegiances.

I went to bed on the night before the big Extra Preliminary Round kick off with an air of expectancy. The minutes of planning were coming to an end. The following day I would take my first step on *The Road From Wembley*.

Saturday August 18th, 2007:
Extra Preliminary Round
Haringey Borough V Wembley

I set off for Haringey Borough at 1pm from my home in Braintree, Essex, and travel down the M11 towards London. Although I don't know where Haringey Borough's Coles Park Stadium is, I'm vaguely familiar with the North Circular and just need the car's sat nav for the final few turns. Despite this being the middle of August, it is a horrible day and grey clouds are scudding across the sky. The traffic on the North Circular is heavy, which I put down to a combination of the broken-down cars I pass on the way and supporters heading towards Tottenham's ground for a Premiership match against Derby County.

It takes a little over an hour before I turn right off the A10 into White Hart Lane – heading the opposite way from Tottenham – and I keep my eyes open for either a set of floodlights, or the Bridisco factory mentioned in the directions page on the club's website. Eventually both come into view. A set of fences run along the roadside leading to a small opening into the stadium, which is guarded by an octogenarian hobgoblin beside a traffic cone. I pull off the road and open the car window.

'Is this Haringey Borough?'

Hobgoblin, stammering slightly: 'Y,y,yes. Five pounds.' I thrust a twenty pound note into his hand and he fumbles for some change from his wallet.

'Any chance of a match programme?' I ask inexpectantly, but he gives me a nod, and as he gropes around in another bag, I look through the entrance into Coles Park Stadium, as dilapidated a sporting venue as you could wish for. Ahead of me are a long line of parking spaces which run along the top end of the pitch. To the left lies more car parking, a bedraggled grandstand and a group of temporary-style buildings which appear to be the clubhouse and changing rooms.

Hobgoblin hands me a flimsy, green and white striped programme with the club's badge on the front and I drive slowly into the car park. I have plenty of choice. I settle on a space at the bottom end of the car park at one corner of the pitch, figuring that this is the least likely place that my car will get hit by the ball, unless of course one of the two teams has a player who can emulate former England international Geoff Thomas when he hit that horrendous shot at Wembley which scythed off the corner flag.

Safely parked I have a chance to review the situation. Never have I been to a football match so sparsely populated. With just an hour to go before kick off, Coles Park Stadium is almost deserted. A small throng of about six people have followed me in, one of whom is wearing a Wembley baseball cap, so I peg them as the Wembley FC Travelling Support. Three portly middle-aged gents in suits are walking the playing surface and I hazard a guess they are the ref and his line-os.

The stadium is in the middle of a large area of allotments, which in turn are bordered by housing. Across the road in White Hart Lane, the Bridisco factory looms down over the main car park. Bridisco it transpires is an electrical equipment distributor. A white-posted perimeter fence runs around the pitch, and six floodlights stand around the ground, looking about as effectual as a set of torches glued on to a telegraph pole. The pitch has obviously only recently been cut. You can tell that by the tufted piles of mown grass which scatter the surface. The grandstand is a corrugated iron and concrete affair optimistically split into four sections of sixty six seats each. The players' tunnel is a gaping sore directly beneath one of these sections. All around the border to the allotments are giant telegraph poles from which hang swathes of netting which at one point were presumably destined to protect a Row Z clearance from ending up in the carrots, potatoes and lettuces. Time has taken its toll however and now the netting is all tangled around the poles, billowing in the strong wind which races across the pitch straight up into the grandstand.

By now a few hardy souls have chosen their seats but I decide to go in search of refreshment, so I walk down the far side of the pitch, around the bottom end and over toward the clubhouse. Inside are a group of about eight tables, one of which is littered with assorted biscuits and a cardboard sign for 'Club Officials Only'. I walk up to a counter that is emitting the smells of bacon and chip fat. It is manned by a pair of middle-aged women looking overworked despite the absence of any queues.

'What can I get you?' asks Woman One.

'What have you got?'

'Anything you like,' she replies.

'There's an offer you can't refuse,' says Woman Two.

'He can have whatever he likes as long as he pays for it,' says Woman One.

'That's what she says to all the blokes,' says Woman Two, with a wink and a laugh that would put Barbara Windsor to shame. I can see that this double-act could go on indefinitely so I intervene.

'What have you got *to eat?*'

'Bacon roll, sausage roll, burger roll, cheeseburger roll.'

'I'll have a cup of tea.'

'Sugar?'

'No thanks luv, I'm sweet enough.' Amid much cackling a mug of tea arrives, a strong-looking brew with lumps of spoilt milk swirling around the whirlpool left from a vigorous stirring from Woman Two's teaspoon.

'I think your milk's gone off,' I say and hand back the mug.

'That's not the only thing round here,' says Woman One.

'Blimey, you can talk,' says Woman Two. I rattle a two-pound coin on the counter and harrumph impatiently.

'Sorry about that luv. Go and sit down and I'll bring a fresh one over.'

I look around the gloomy room for a seat. There are about fifteen people already inside, all men and all of a type. Exactly the sort of people you would expect to see in a dilapidated stadium on a grey day in August. The Wembley Travelling Support are in one corner, talking loudly about the plight that Spurs will find themselves in if they fail to beat Derby that afternoon. The table reserved for Club Officials now has one middle-aged man swilling Scotch out of a plastic cup. There are no free tables so I decide to attach myself to a silver-haired man sitting with another who looks to be in his late teens. They are both perusing the green programmes handed out by Hobgoblin and swigging cans of Carlsberg bought from the bar that runs beside the serving hatch.

'Is this seat taken?' I ask, knowing it isn't.

'No go ahead,' says Silver Hair just as Barbara Windsor's step-sister brings over a healthier-looking cup of tea. I sip it and take a proper look around. A TV in one corner is pumping out a grainy edition of BBC Rugby, so obviously the Haringey Borough Entertainment Fund doesn't run to a satellite subscription. The walls look as though they are thirsting for a coat of paint, and in a bid to cover this, they are festooned with pennants from clubs who have previously visited this corner of north London. Bury Town, AFC Sudbury, Felixstowe & Walton FC, and with a delicious irony, a pennant from some outfit called Leyton Pennant. There are also a number of international clubs who I have never heard of. I hope for their sake that they have come from an eastern block country.

As I survey the scene, I ear-wig Silver Hair and Teenager.

Teenager: 'Look if they get through this round we will have to go to Ware. Saturday 1st September. Preliminary Round. Haringey Borough or Wembley V Ware.'

'No that means that they will be at *home* to Ware,' says Silver Hair, 'ideally we want Wembley to win so we get a different home ground in the next fixture.' My ears prick up. This sounds familiar.

Teenager: 'Do you think the BBC will be here?'

Silver Hair: 'Well if they do it, they usually start with Wembley and then follow them through. We may see them.' The BBC? What? I can't hold back my English reserve any longer. Have to speak to them.

'Excuse me, I couldn't help overhearing your conversation. It's just you don't sound like you support Haringey or Wembley, so I was wondering what you were doing here?' Silver Hair looks at me and pauses for a split second. I can understand his reservation in a room like this. Most of the people in here are obviously quite mad. Eventually he replies.

'Well it's the FA Cup you see,' he says, 'every year or so I like to follow it from the early rounds. So we've come here today to see Wembley…'

'… because you have to start the FA Cup with Wembley,' I finish for him, smarting inside. So much for my brilliantly original idea. Suddenly everyone in the room appears to be potential publishing threats.

'Yes,' says Silver Hair, 'and I used to live in Crouch End when I originally moved down to London, so I'm interested in the area.'

'And you said something about the BBC being here?'

'Yes whenever they cover the FA Cup from the start right through to the finish they usually begin with Wembley.' Recovering from the initial shock, I pry further, testing…

'So will you be going all the way to the final?' Silver Hair gives a friendly smile and I experience a strange change in my attitude, from competitiveness to comradeship.

'I'll see what happens. I don't normally go all the way through. Especially when the later rounds are on television. When you start having to travel up and down the country it can get very expensive. Are you planning to do it?' I nod.

'I hope you've got plenty of money.'

'Don't say that,' I say, winking conspiratorially, 'my wife already thinks I'm mad coming here for this. I haven't even considered the money it might cost.' Silver Hair smiles and I sense that the conversation has run its course. I swig down my tea.

'Right,' I say, 'I'm just going to see if they are going to announce the teams. I

might see you again. In fact, it sounds like we will definitely see each other again.'
I walk out of the clubhouse and look at my watch. It's a quarter to three. A car
screeches into the car park and nearly runs me over. A stressed-looking man jumps
out, reaches into the back of his car for a kitbag and athletically rushes off to the
changing rooms. Nice pre-match build-up.

I stand by the main grandstand looking up at a battered old speaker hanging
down from the roof, wondering if at any point it will crackle into life. My problem
is the team lists in Hobgoblin's programme. It announces 'Today's Teams' as 'From:'
and then has two great big squad lists without shirt numbers. I have no clue which
player is which, and this threatens to devastate my attempts at some accurate
reportage. As I stand there, I'm approached by a man holding a TV camera and I
bristle.

'Are you anything to do with Wembley?' he asks.

'No,' I say, 'who are you?'

'TV production company. ZigZag Productions. We're here to follow the
development of the FA Cup from the early rounds right through to Wembley.
We've come here today to see Wembley...'

'...because you have to start the FA Cup with Wembley,' I finish again,
scowling. He misses the anger and starts scanning the ground looking for a target.

'There are a bunch of Wembley fans in the clubhouse, you should try there,'
I mutter grumpily. Looks like I have some proper competition now. I'm still
waiting by the silent speaker when muffled hollers of 'Come on then lads,' 'Let's
have it,' emerge from the changing rooms and the two teams come out through
the tunnel. Haringey in yellow shirts and green shorts and Wembley in red/white
shirts and red shorts. Both teams trot out onto the pitch led by a short referee and
his two portly linesmen – identifiable as the gents walking the pitch on my arrival.
I glare up at the loudspeaker but it stays quiet so I stalk off to find a viewing
position. I decide to take up a place behind the Haringey goal. I'm the only person
there. The grandstand has filled and a headcount puts the attendance at between
forty and fifty people, (The official attendance would later appear on Tony
Kempster's website as sixty two).

At just past 3pm the diminutive referee bellows for 'Skippers please,' and after
a quick toss-up and change of ends, blows his whistle and the match gets
underway. The occasion of an FA Cup tie is apparent as both teams are clearly up
for the game. The opening skirmishes lead to some ferocious tackling and an early
yellow card for the Wembley number eight. The visitors' superior skills see them
dominant in possession and within five minutes they are awarded a penalty, much

to the chagrin of the Borough team. The penalty is to be taken at my end of the pitch and I stand poised with my camera to capture the first goal of my Wembley campaign, but the penalty-taker shanks it into the fence behind which I am standing and an extra from the *Jeremy Kyle Show* wearing the green of Haringey bellows 'Justice' into the face of the crestfallen striker.

But then five minutes later, Wembley do break the deadlock, after some good work on the edge of the box by their number ten who picks up the ball, shimmies inside two Haringey defenders, before drilling the ball into the back of the net. My first FA Cup goal. I check the digital screen on my camera, pleased to see that I've more or less got it.

The game restarts and the Wembley attacks continue. One shot loops over the goal landing in the car park just five yards from where I am standing and I realise I have a chance to get a touch of the match ball. A nod from the goalkeeper dispatches me to retrieve it. An FA Cup match ball. Fantastic! I'm holding my camera so can't pick it up, so I try to ball-juggle it up Ronaldinhio style. Unfortunately I'm not Ronaldinhio and while I flick the ball up off the ground, an over-enthusiastic hump with my right foot ends up pumping the ball back over the fence, right over the goal and straight out of the penalty box. I see the goalkeeper mutter 'Twat' at me as he in turn has to do a spot of retrieval, but I'm delighted at getting a touch.

Again the game resumes and as I watch the action, I notice a man walking toward me wearing a green blazer and carrying a clipboard. I accost him as he walks past and ask him if he knows the teams. He turns out to be the Haringey Borough Club Secretary and I'm delighted when he produces the official team sheets for me to copy into Hobgoblin's programme. It turns out that Paul Shelton was the scorer of the first goal on my cup odyssey.

Wembley's lead is extended before half time when right back David Taylor hits a deep cross into the Haringey box which due to a defensive mix-up finds itself nestling in the back of the net before anyone can react. Haringey are stunned and finish the half looking like a team staring the earliest of FA Cup exits in the face. I retire to my car as some rain starts to fall and I learn from the radio that Derby are getting gubbed three-nil by Spurs just ten minutes down the road. But I take solace that despite the fact that it's threatening to piss down, despite the fact that the writing's on the wall for the Rams to go straight back down to the Championship this season, despite the fact that I've got another forty five minutes of this mediocre fare to endure, my beloved Wembley look set to progress.

But in the second half, you get one of those classic examples of Goliathan arrogance. Wembley emerge back onto the pitch with the attitude that all they need to do is see out the remainder of the game. They are all Fancy Dan footwork, and laughs and jokes when their passes and tackles go awry, and slowly but surely Haringey get wind of it. The home team start to press and the chances and attacks mount. Halfway through the second period, a ball is played through and while Wembley scream at the linesman to flag at a player running back from an offside position, Haringey find themselves through on goal. A shot is parried by keeper Lee Pearce, but rebounds out to Haringey substitute Mark Maher who rifles home from the edge of the box. One-two.

Wembley realise that they have been coasting and try to shift gears for the last ten minutes, but Haringey's tails are up and they are already playing in top gear. They press for the equaliser. I start to sweat. The last thing I want is extra time with the traffic of the Tottenham exodus to navigate.

Haringey's tricky forward Ronardson Akubuo Obinna (yes, really) whips in a left foot shot which leaves Pearce flinging himself across the goal to parry away. If you saw the considerable bulk of Pearce you would commend the feat. He is the human equivalent of parking the team bus in front of the goal. I'm now willing the referee to blow for full time, as is the Wembley bench. But with just minutes remaining, Obinna finds himself again in space in the Wembley box and this time he makes no mistake in lashing it home. The Borough players go wild. I'm sure the crowd may have done as well, but we are too far away from each other and they are too few for me to hear. Finally the referee blows his whistle and the two teams stand around on the pitch shaking hands. I stand around too wondering what happens now. Do we have extra time or go straight to penalties? It slowly dawns on me that it will be neither. The two teams slump off the pitch and my spirits slump as I realise that we are going to have to do it all again. We are going to a replay.

Haringey Borough 2 (Maher 75, Obinna 88)
Wembley 2 (Shelton 10, Taylor 30)

Attendance: 62
Money Spent So Far: £5 (Entrance + Programme)
Miles Travelled So Far: 90

1980
He's Only A Poor Little Gunner

I always wanted to play football. My parents have a picture of me toddling around our back garden aged two, wearing a great big nappy and with a football at my feet. From these formative steps I moved on to the highly-competitive matches which were held every break and lunchtime at school between the boys in my class. Whether winter or summer, come rain or shine, we would always be playing football. We would start off by picking two captains, then this pair would duel out a game of 'Jumpsies' to see who got first pick.

Jumpsies for the uninitiated goes like this. Two boys stand ten yards apart and jump towards each other in turn. When you think you can perform a leap which will take you past the feet of your opponent you go for it. Succeed in making the leap and you get first pick. Fail and it's a relatively simple task for your opponent to achieve the winning hop. Regional variations include 'Toesies' and 'Heelsies', the different marker point which need to be passed by the successful leaper. To choose who would be captains, we would perform a round of 'Big Spuds' with our clenched fists.

When the formalities had been performed and the teams picked, assuming there was any playtime left, we would make two goals out of a netball post and a pile of jumpers or Parkas and set about it. I read somewhere recently that some of today's safety-conscious schools are banning football matches in playgrounds. To be fair, I can understand why. The maelstrom of arms, legs and flying challenges that those games could generate were an absolute hazard. Knees would regularly be scuffed on the playground concrete and blubbing victims sent off to the sick room, where the ladies on reception would apply a curious yellow unction and attach a dab of cotton wool. Then with a tear-streaked, grimy but determined face, the suitably patched-up victim would emerge back onto the playground and re-enter the fray. Quite frankly the dinner ladies would have served better if they'd sat on the touchlines chewing gum with a bucket of water and a magic sponge.

More in danger though were not the protagonists of the daily battles, but the poor unfortunates who while happily going about their business playing a gentle make-believe game, stumbled unwittingly onto the field of play. With no concept of tactics, positioning or reading of the game, they ran a rough gauntlet, particularly when the last-ditch tackles were flying in, or a twenty-yard thigh stinger was unleashed.

We were typical boys, raging with juvenile testosterone, and so flashpoints often flared. With no formal goal structure to aim for, close call decisions were strongly debated. Was it over the imaginary line, over the imaginary bar, over or inside the pile of Parkas? Devotion to one's cause often led to disagreements which were argued physically rather than mentally. The matches, the break times and the battles all merge into one in my memory, leaving nothing more than a hazy recollection of endeavour. However one particular event does stand out starkly in my mind and naturally it is one of my less illustrious hours. Why is it that the human brain is often so good at remembering a person's lows, rather than their highs?

In a typically hard-fought and close match I was playing alongside a boy called Franco Fucci. With a name like that, he should have been a large Italian Adonis with long dark hair constrained by a headband, a Roman nose and a technically-gifted touch. In reality he was actually the smallest boy in the year, with spindly legs and a complete lack of ability. He did have the Roman nose mind. After Jumpsies, Franco would always be one of the last boys picked, and this occasion would have been no different. When it came to the unfortunates who were last in the selection process, it became less a choice of what he *can* do, and more of what will he do wrong? What danger does he pose to your carefully crafted line up? Captains would often offer the two remaining duffers to their opponent knowing that they could be used as fifth columnists to undermine the opposition.

On this occasion, Fucci was my duffer. I'd stuck him out of the way on the wing, but eager to get some action he had drifted inside, like Wayne Rooney coming short. With the scores level (probably twenty-all), and my playground bell body clock ticking, I was bearing down on the opposition goal with goalkeeper John Fowley at my mercy, when Fucci strayed into my path. We collided and the ball spun away. The chance was lost and the opposition picked up the loose ball and promptly went down our end and scored a winner. I was furious and vented my anger with a well-aimed kick on Fucci's backside. It nearly lifted his small frame off the ground and he turned towards me with tears welling up in his eyes.

'I'm telling,' he said in a quavering voice, then turned and stalked off up the playground. *I'm telling.* The two words that sent fear racing down your spine. The playground has many unwritten laws. A Sicilian code of Omerta exists among school children. You don't *tell*. Not unless it's really bad. If Fucci was able to get to the teacher on duty the recriminations would be terrible. This after all was probably the childhood equivalent of ABH. It could lead to only one thing, a summons to Sister Theresa the nun who was headmistress of our school. A fate worse than death, particularly as my mother worked as a teacher at the school and the story would soon get back to her. I had one chance and that was to convince Fucci to change his mind, in the time it took him to make the playground walk of shame. I can still remember the dread that raced through my young body as I spent half a minute pouring apologies into my unfortunate, sniveling victim. I can't even remember now whether he did tell or not, so I assume that he didn't, but I remember that fear. Still today, now aged thirty six, I sometimes wake up in the small hours of the night with the words 'Please don't tell, Franco,' ringing in my ears.

My footballing fervour needed an additional outlet and in the winter of 1979 I joined my first Sunday morning club, a team called Roma, which played its games in the Echo League – a much vaunted boys competition covering Essex and east London which has been the spawning ground for the likes of Sol Campbell and Ray Parlour. Whether we had an affiliation to the Italian capital giants, or whether it was just a play on the name Romford where we grew up, I'll never know. But the Roma Under Eights team had the distinction of being trained by the former Spurs legend Les Allen, thanks to the fact that his boy Bradley was the side's star striker in the team.

I went training with Roma for the first time after my Dad got a small company car and so was able to take me along to the floodlights at Oldchurch Park in Romford. Two weeks later on Sunday February 24th 1980, I was in the team, stuck in central defence because I was tall, and playing my first ever match against a team called Preston, not the North End variety. I can remember coming on in the second half as a substitute in a three-one home defeat, on a junior pitch behind Hornchurch Stadium, the home today of Ryman League Premier AFC Hornchurch. It was even more memorable because a young Clive Allen, son of Les, brother of Bradley, was watching. Little did I know then that Clive would *actually* be playing in a cup final for QPR in just a few short years.

The following week I got a flavour of my first win as we stuffed a team called Heath Park nine-nil. I know all of this as the result of being the son of an accountant father, a natural-born book-keeper. A few years back my dad presented me with a book he had kept showing a list of every football match I had ever played in as a boy. From 1980 to 1990, neat rows of entries logging dates, results, goals scored, even the times when I had been voted 'Man of the Match'. It was a case of 'John Stoneman, this is your footballing life.' It's one of my most treasured possessions. In my first season I played in ten games, was Man of the Match once, won eight, drew one, lost one.

Meanwhile in the world where twenty two small boys weren't chasing a ball around a pitch, at the end of the 1979/80 season, cup holders Arsenal were back at Wembley for the third season on the trot, trying to emulate the success of the previous year. This time around they faced West Ham United, at that time playing in the old second division. A theoretical mismatch as lively as the cup final had seen in recent years. Living in a London borough on the Essex borders, I was smack in the middle of West Ham territory, and while I didn't agree with my Derby County-supporting father on his choice of club to follow, we were totally in agreement in our choice of club to loath. I hated West Ham with one of those totally irrational passions that only the male of the species seems able to muster. Maybe it was because nearly everyone in my school supported West Ham and I wanted to be different. Maybe I was allergic to claret and blue. Whatever. It was out there and I couldn't repress it.

In the build up to the 1980 cup final, the biggest banter between the two sets of fans revolved around an appalling song which had entered the pop charts in October of 1979 and stubbornly resisted all efforts to expel it for fifteen weeks. It was recorded by a group called The Ramblers, a *nom-de-plume* for a bunch of children from the Abbey Hey Junior School in Manchester.

The lyrics were inane:
I'm only a poor little sparrow (aaah),
No colourful feathers have I (it's a shame),
I can't even sing,
When I'm nesting in spring,
The turnips don't grow very high.

The tune had been adopted by the rival fans, the lyrics adapted thus:
He's only a poor little Hammer/Gunner,
His face is all tattered and torn,
He makes me feel sick,
So I hit him with a brick,
And now he don't sing any more.

This was to be heard ringing around east London schoolyards during every break time as the overwhelming numbers of second division Hammers fans taunted the smaller but superior first division Gunnerites. I was as loud and proud as anyone, despite the fact that we were outnumbered, because we had the security of being the higher division team. Surely this was no contest and class would out?

Come the big day in May, the ritual was played out. Marching bands, check. Coaches arriving, check. *Roy Of The Rovers* wall chart filled out neatly, check. I went into this one knowing that just ninety minutes stood between me and a whole bag-load of crowing come Monday morning in the playground, when Arsenal's superiority would be manifest by a constant chorus of '*He's only a poor little Hammer.*'

But despite the rituals being observed, this year there were nagging doubts. This time there was more riding on the result than last season, when I had come into the cup final wide-eyed and naïve. The gnawing sensation in the pit of my stomach, which I developed when Man United had equalised last season, was with me throughout the build-up and the whole of the first half. And then when Trevor Brooking headed, yes headed, the Hammers into the lead, I began to get very edgy.

I started to test out some new rituals mid-match. If I threw this empty packet of crisps into the bin in one shot, Arsenal would get an equaliser. Perhaps if I go out into the back garden with my football and manufacture a fictitious equaliser myself, then that would do the trick. But of course nothing did. West Ham went on to become the last lower league team in history to win the FA Cup and I had to face a raging torrent of abuse in the playground on Monday morning. Halfway through one of the most miserable school days of my life, a boy who played alongside me in the school team, Mark Gooding, said: 'I don't know why you support Arsenal, you should support Tottenham like me. We've got Glenn Hoddle.'

'What colour's the kit?' I asked.

'White shirts and blue shorts.'

'All right then.'

And so my defection was complete. I suspect that when closet Communist Dons turned the heads of idealistic Cambridge scholars in the fifties and sixties, it was much the same process. But if it was good enough for Pat Jennings and later Sol Campbell to make the North London switch then it was good enough for me. A Tottenham jersey was obtained as a present in the Christmas of 1980 and my transformation was completed when I grew too big to squeeze into my Liam Brady Arsenal shirt.

August 2007:
What's The Point Son?

The Sunday morning after my trip to Haringey Borough found me in reflective mood. The realisation that this was hardly the most original of ideas, plus the warnings from Silver Hair that it could take over my life and finances for a season had blunted my enthusiasm. The doubts were compounded by two things. Firstly a conversation with my father and then one with my wife. I had telephoned my Dad on Saturday night and told him with enthusiasm of my adventure in north London and my plans to document the FA Cup journey and in so doing create an international bestseller. His response was typical of the discussions earlier that day.

'Not that old chestnut,' he said, 'it's been done. Loads of people have done it. Brian James for one. I used to have his book back at Avenue Road.' Fifty Six Avenue Road in Harold Wood, a small suburb of London right on the Essex border was where I had grown up. My Dad had a study upstairs which was crammed full of books, files and folders and even an old jukebox that he had saved up for and bought with his first ever pay packets when he qualified as an accountant.

'I think I threw it out when we moved down to Hamworthy,' he continued, 'but I definitely had it. It was called *Journey To Wembley*. He was a reporter for one of the papers. The *Daily Mail* I think. Followed every round and wrote about the teams. It was good. I'll see if I still have it, but I don't think I do.' I started to think of some arguments about why that didn't matter but before I could, he piped up again, his voice tinny and crackly on the end of a poor line: 'And it'll cost you a for-tune.' He dragged out the word fortune for emphasis. 'You might have to go all over the country. And tickets won't be cheap for the big matches. If you can even *get* them. Cup final tickets are like gold dust. Get the papers tomorrow and I bet you one of the broadsheets will be doing the same thing. Or the BBC.' I told him that I'd seen some film cameras at Haringey Borough.

'There you go then. Being done.'

'Yeah but a book's different to a film,' I replied indignantly.

'Brian James was on expenses. You won't be. What's the point son?' I didn't reply at first. The crackle of the bad line the only noise between us.

'I'm not sure,' I said finally, 'I'll just see how it goes.' I wished I hadn't mentioned it to him. His arguments were all valid. And put his way it seemed like a completely pointless exercise. My wife Vanessa was even less enthusiastic when I called her later. Her parents had retired four years ago to a cottage in the middle of France and she was visiting them during the summer holidays with our three children – Eden, Evie and Jonathan.

'So what have you been doing today then?' She asked, after I'd finally got through. Her parents' cottage was in the middle of France and also in the middle of nowhere. I was amazed that they had electricity when we'd first been over to see it, let alone communication.

'I went to a football match.'

'Where?'

'Haringey Borough.'

'*Why?*'

'Because they were playing Wembley in the FA Cup.' She paused, I could tell that in her mind my answer had not addressed her question and the silence was her providing me with the rope I needed to hang myself.

'It was the first round of the FA Cup today.'

'*And?*'

'And I thought it might be a cool idea to go and see it. A real match. You know. Proper teams. Grass roots, jumpers for goalposts, that sort of thing.'

'So what was the score?'

'Two–all, they're having a replay on Tuesday.'

'Oh and you're going to that as well are you?' I could sense her brain working eight hundred miles away. Probing my words. I decided to try my luck.

'I've had a great idea for a book. I'm going to go to all of the different rounds of the FA Cup following the winning team right the way through to the final.'

'Oh is that right?'

'Yeah, it'll be great…' This was the point of no return. She would either think it a good idea, at which point I had her blessing, at least temporary blessing, or I was about to get it in the neck.

'This is so typical of you. Where exactly are you going to find the time? And who do you expect to look after the kids while you are swanning off to football?'

'They can come with me,' I said unconvincingly, 'if they want to.'

'So this is going to be your latest obsession then is it?' I could hear the exasperation in her voice. Ten days cooped up with the outlaws had made her edgy. Although to be fair I think the conversation would have resonated thus had we been in the same room.

'I don't know, I mean, no.' I fumbled for soothing words. 'Look, I'll just see how it goes.' I tried to change the subject. 'How are the kids?'

'Evie and Eden are watching frogs in the garden pond and Jonathan has lost the game for his Nintendo. He's driving me mad. He's fallen in the pond twice today already. Have you cleared up the house yet? You know we're back on Friday. That kitchen better be tidy when I get home and I don't want to come back to piles of washing.'

'No, of course not.' The conversation petered out with me promising to have the house in showroom condition for her return. I could understand her irritation. Like many men, my life has been littered with a series of obsessions none of which have been particularly productive from a career or family sense. It started with school when I decided to take up the violin to the chagrin of my parents. A few weeks of squeaky caterwauling later and my rosined-bow was dispatched to the loft. I had a brief sojourn in my teens and early twenties, when an unhealthy fascination with World War Two led to hours spent playing war-based games of all shapes and sizes. In my late twenties, after my first child Eden was born, I had an early-life crisis which led to me spending a summer playing for a baseball team each and all-day Sunday, and then playing football through the winter while Vanessa was left bringing up baby. Then I became involved in the relaunch of a motorcycle speedway team in Hertfordshire, and my position as press officer for the Rye House Rockets meant more time away from the family homestead, midweek and at weekends. More recently I had disappeared off for hours at a time training to run two marathons in mediocre times. She had a point.

Her idea of filling the spare time between the hours of the working week was much more productive – family trips, home decoration and improvement. I had her suckered for a while when the family trips I agreed to go on usually conveniently coincided with a speedway fixture, but I'm like the invisible man and she soon saw straight through me. So blathering excitedly into the phone about a searing footballing opus which would have me travelling up and down the country and hunched over a laptop for great periods of time, while she was stuck with three kids on her own in France, was probably not the best idea. She didn't give me both barrels there and then, but I could tell the shotgun had been cocked and that the safety was off. I would have to tread carefully. That's of course if I went through with it all. Like I said, the initial enthusiasm for the project had worn thin. It seemed like the world and his dog were either writing, photographing or broadcasting the Road to Wembley. And those that weren't had already done it. I slumped in my chair on the Sunday morning after the Saturday before, clicking from website to website, looking at all of the examples of what had been done and I felt deflated. I realised there was only one thing to do to arrest this malaise. I showered, got dressed and headed out to another match.

When I had scanned through the list of Extra Preliminary Round fixtures, I'd noticed that just like the later rounds when the big boys are playing, the fixtures were spread out from Friday night through to Sunday afternoon. While the majority of matches were played on the Saturday, there was one fixture that Sunday which stood out by a mile. The first ever all-Asian team FA Cup match between Sporting Bengal and London APSA, to be held at the Mile End Stadium. Both teams were bidding to become the first ever Asian team to make it through to the Preliminary Round and one of them was destined to succeed.

The exotic spice of this match was too much to ignore so I set off for east London ahead of the 3pm kick off, arriving to a tumult of colour and excitement. Video cameras were dotted around the athletics track which circumnavigated the playing area to capture this historic event, while the grandstand was packed with nearly four hundred supporters, the second highest attendance of the entire round. Only Dinnington Town versus Maltby Main had attracted more Extra Preliminary Round support with over six hundred paying punters, and this due to the attendance of the Sky cameras and an appearance by the FA Cup trophy itself.

With the giant skyscrapers of Canary Wharf in the background and the waft of Asian cooking spreading out from the hastily-erected snack bar, the two teams delivered a hard-fought contest. It was tense and tight. The crowd seemed equally split between the two sides and roared on every chance. I was swept along by a thoroughly entertaining match which ended in a nil-nil draw, despite the presence of extra time which for some reason manifested itself on this occasion but hadn't at Haringey Borough.

The endeavour on the pitch had been matched by the enthusiasm of the crowd. For the hundreds of people tightly packed into the main stand at the Mile End Stadium this had already been an FA Cup Final. All of the traditional cup final emotions had poured out, the tense atmosphere heightened by the sudden death nature of a cup tie, players in extra time rolling around on the floor with legs pointing skywards like oil derricks trying to relieve the cramp of two hours of non-stop action. I left east London with a big grin on my face. From an early round FA Cup novice, I'd now notched up two games in two days and over two hundred minutes of action. My cup fervour had returned. I'd show them.

Tuesday August 21st, 2007:
Extra Preliminary Round Replay
Wembley v Haringey Borough

I set off for my first trip to Wembley at around 5pm, wanting to get there early so that I can take some pictures and get myself set up. The car gobbles up the miles down the M11 and onto the North Circular Road and despite the fact that once again the grey clouds are lying low and heavy in the sky, my heart is soaring with excitement. It feels very right making my first journey to the borough of Brent on this FA Cup tour.

When you talk about Wembley to football fans they tend to fall into two camps. There are those that think it is the epicentre of all things football. A Mecca for the game. A fabled destination steeped in footballing history and revered the world over. Then there are those who think it is a miserable hole in north London with terrible transit links. Sitting in the Tuesday night commuter traffic, scuttling forward an inch every ten minutes, I'm in agreement with the latter. The North Circular is the original Road To Hell. It makes the M25 look like a cakewalk. Expanding and contracting from three lanes to one and then back again, it is littered with traffic lights and wholly unsuitable for the weight of traffic that attempts to traverse it. There is little to do but sit and shuffle the gear stick from neutral to first and back again. Some light relief comes in the form of a sign I spy as I pass a pest control shop called Protex which sports a large sign out front of the premises stating that the Protex Pest of the Week is the 'Brown Rat'.

I'm starting to regret my decision to follow Wembley FC as I struggle through the compacted traffic, but then as I climb the flyover out of Brent Cross, the magnificent National Stadium with its towering arch appears before me for the first time and it literally takes my breath away. So much so that I completely miss my turning and have to travel a mile and a half up the dreaded road before I can get off. I seem to remember that you caught the odd glimpse of the twin towers of the old Wembley from the North Circ, but you cannot miss this, it simply dominates the skyline like a huge modern-day cathedral.

The sight of the National Stadium lifts my traffic-laden spirits. I must be getting close now. However it takes another half an hour before I reach Wembley FC's ground, thanks to the bus lanes populated by leviathan, eighteen metre red buses and the London commuters all of whom are as aggressive as a red ant with a hangover. In fact I'm starting to get edgy that I might miss the 7.45pm kick off as the clock ticks through ten past seven and I'm still a mile away. I pass a fabulously juxtaposed signpost which points one way to 'Wembley National Stadium' and the other way to 'Vale Farm Sports Centre' and then the traffic eases and I turn right off the Harrow Road and into Vale Farm itself. Wembley FC's ground is annexed to a large sports complex which includes playing fields and a leisure centre, so parking is no problem. I walk up to the turnstiles and peer in at the man behind the Perspex.

'One?' He asks.

'Yes please.'

'Five quid.'

'Got any programmes?'

'We should have, they'll be here in a minute.' I hand over a tenner, get my change and then shuffle through the kind of turnstile that they probably have at the back entrance to the Old Bailey. Defendants and Concessions Only – Five Pounds. Immediately through the barrier I walk straight into a clutch of middle-aged men, shuffling carrier bags and hopping anxiously from foot to foot. They are all looking furtively at the back of the head of the man behind the Perspex and muttering to one another. Groundhoppers, I figure, waiting for the programmes. I earwig the two nearest.

Hopper: 'I don't so much mind them not having a programme, as long as they announce the teams.'

Hopper's Mate: 'I was at Warminster the other week and the referee let me go into his room and copy them down off the team sheet.' Just then the programmes arrive and a collective sigh of relief is emitted. But we've figured without the Old Bailey turnstiles. They're designed to stop people getting in, so much so that the Groundhoppers can't get out, and Perspex Man's attention is strictly eyes front dealing with the queue of three or four who are waiting to come in. It all becomes too much for Hopper. He flaps a ten pound note to a man on the other side of the barrier and implores him to buy two programmes, adding with desperation: 'I don't mind how much they cost.'

'Pound each,' comes the reply, at which point we all fish in our pockets for a golden nugget and flourish it through the turnstiles at our startled saviour. He buys in bulk and we all snatch the pink photo-copied contraband he stuffs back through the bars. We flash relieved smiles briefly at one another and then are all suddenly aware of a sense of embarrassment and scatter in different directions like crows from a field.

Programme on board I have a chance to survey my surroundings. Now Vale Farm is what I would call a properish football ground. It's enclosed on all sides by concrete fences that are close to the side of the pitch, leaving just enough room for a combination of terraces and narrow stands. The main grandstand runs almost the length of the far side with four rows of seats. Behind me on the near side are the changing rooms and more terracing backing onto the clubhouse, although you can't seem to get from the clubhouse into the ground. To do that you need to come back out into the car park and pass through Checkpoint Charlie.

I glance at my watch which shows five minutes until kick off. I quickly look for the nearest tannoy and march over to it, defiantly daring it not to spark into life with the team changes. Like its colleague in Haringey however it remains silent, refusing to pipe out even the tinniest of background music. I don't like my chances. My attention is distracted by a bellow of 'Up for it today Borough!' and the clump-clop sound of boot-clad teams emerging from the changing rooms and marching across the concrete runway that takes them to the pitch.

There are faces I recognise in the two teams from Saturday. I'm delighted to see Lee 'Team Bus' Pearce has once again been parked in front of the Wembley goal. And there are also faces I recognise on the terraces. The Wembley Travelling Support are all here, swollen in numbers in fact by the home fixture. Even Hobgoblin has made the trip around the North Circular and very dapper he looks too in a green jumper and tweed blazer. Who says bad guys from *Lord Of The Rings* can't dress sharply? I also scan the crowd for Silver Hair and am disappointed not to see him anywhere. Less disappointing though is the absence of the monkeys from ZigZag Productions. Pah, Soho lightweights. I'm just congratulating myself on this when the buggers appear through Checkpoint Charlie, obviously flustered, but whipping out their camera the minute that referee Mr J Panconi blows his whistle and the game gets underway.

The home side line up to attack the goal nearest to me so I walk around to stand beside it. I figure that this is where the action is most likely to be. Wembley showed signs on Saturday that they are actually quite a cultured side. Maybe it was the bobbly Haringey pitch that was against them, because on this surface they look head and shoulders above Borough. They ping the ball around with aplomb, playing little passing triangles which leave the men in green and yellow chasing shadows. Ten minutes in and Paul Shelton cuts apart the Haringey defence and is brought down in the box for an early penalty right in front of me, in a bizarre reconstruction of Saturday's match. The point isn't lost on a man walking past me who says as much.

'It's like déjà vu all over again,' I reply.

'Well let's see if we miss this one.'

I'm surprised to see the same penalty taker, now identified as Jumo Mitchell, step up for the spot kick. I'm also surprised that there is a penalty so early on in the game. A point exaggerated by the fact that I am now trying to fish out my camera while juggling the cheeseburger and chips I've purchased not two minutes earlier on my way past the snack bar. I step up to the barrier beside a snapper from the local paper, wafting the smell of onions over him while trying to look professional. I just manage the delicate balance of holding all three, camera to my eye, when the bleeding referee steps right into shot just as the penalty is taken.

'Bloody referees, always getting in the way,' I grumble to the snapper, but unencumbered by junk food he's already five paces away, happily getting a referee-free picture of Wembley breaking the deadlock. I take solace in my grub and walk around the top end of the ground to sit in the stand opposite the changing rooms. I am really enjoying the freedom you get at these pitches. You can go where you please, changing your perspective of the match on a whim. It's refreshingly different from the experience at the big league grounds where you are allocated your seat and stuck with it.

There are about twenty people seated in the grandstand, dotted around like scarecrows. The ZigZag Monkeys have commandeered a prime position on the halfway line. See No Evil has the camera glued to his eyeball, Hear No Evil waves his fluffy microphone around while Speak No Evil does the interviews. Right now he's talking to a tallish man with glasses. I take a seat and earwig. It transpires that Tallish Man comes from something called the Non-League Paper, which I assume is some sort of Groundhopper magazine.

'Yes, we're a small independent TV production company. ZigZag Productions. We're here to follow the development of the FA Cup from the early rounds right through to Wembley. We've come here today to see Wembley…'

'… because you have to start the FA Cup journey with Wembley,' finishes Tallish Man, nodding. I scowl to myself.

Just then Mr J Panconi blows his whistle for half time and the teams go in with the Lions dominating but still only one-up. If Saturday was anything to go by then we could be heading for extra time and penalties, which would be quite amusing but which could lead to a very late night. I'm torn between the excitement of a shoot-out and an early dart.

The clutch of scarecrows in the grandstand have all risen and started shuffling around the ground toward the snack bar and I follow along happily, procure a cup of tea and decide to watch the second half from the opposite side of the pitch. I saunter past the dugouts and spy the Club Secretary from Haringey Borough who gave me the teams on Saturday standing beside the Club Chairman who is the spit of Theo Paphitis from that telly programme *Dragon's Den*. I can't help thinking that if some entrepreneur pitched Haringey Borough to him, he was sold a pup. I walk over and ask Club Secretary if he can give me the visitors' line-up.

'Mind if I write on it?' He says, grabbing my programme.

'No go ahead,' I reply and he scans down the team line-ups, adding numbers to names, crossing out here and filling in there, before pointing out his counterpart on the Wembley staff and ushering me off to him for the home side. Good job he does as well otherwise I would have no clue that a towering header from Bradley Scott eight minutes into the second half extends the Wembley lead. Scott being a late replacement for Marc Talbot. OK so they are just a bunch of names that none of us know, but the accuracy of the reportage is the key here.

The second goal settles any Wembley nerves and you get the feeling that had they gone in at one-nil on Saturday then they would not have taken their foot off the gas in the way that they did. There is no complacency here as they frustrate and subdue any Haringey attacks and always look dangerous on the break.

I take shelter from some light rain that starts falling and have a good look through the programme. Although just a photocopy job, it's much chunkier than its Haringey counterpart, and is bursting with information: league tables, club histories, historical reports... There's a section called Traveller's Tales where a Brian Buck reports on matches he saw last season. From May 9th to May 12th he managed to fit in six matches, including three on one Saturday. Everything from a Spurs home game to Leeds City versus Featherstone Colliery. Apparently that took his yearly match tally to two hundred and ninety three. Possibly a very understanding wife, more likely a self-inflicted bachelor.

I also find out from the programme that the winners of these Extra Preliminary Round matches stand to earn five hundred pounds in prize fund payment. Fast forward fourteen rounds to the final where the winner pockets a cool million. Some quick maths on my phone's calculator function shows that the total prize fund that the FA will lob out this year is £9,652,500.

Meanwhile out on the pitch Jumo Mitchell is at it again. He's a tall, rangy, young left back with a neat touch who likes to get forward. On this occasion he works his way into space just inside the box and drills home a third for Wembley which totally seals the deal. The Wembley players know it, the Haringey Borough players know it, Club Secretary and Theo Paphitis know it too, and come and sit down near to me. If they had a towel they would have thrown it in to spare their players the final ten minutes.

The game drifts to its conclusion and at the final whistle there is little jubilation from the Wembley team who know they have merely produced the second half they owed from Saturday, while the Borough boys roll down their socks and pull out their shin pads, their Wembley dream, however unlikely, over for another year.

Wembley 3 (Mitchell 10, 83, Scott 53)
Haringey Borough 0

Attendance: 57
Money Spent So Far: £11
Miles Travelled So Far: 205
Winners Receive £500

1981

Spurned Villain

The closest that Haringey Borough have ever got to the FA Cup is probably their proximity to the other White Hart Lane team Tottenham Hotspur. One half of the famous north London footballing axis, Spurs have seen most of their recent domestic success in cup finals leading to the famous old saying that if a year had a one in it, then Spurs would win the cup. Admittedly that's going back a few decades now.

And two years after my first cup final adventure with Arsenal, I was back in the frame again in 1981, only this time with Tottenham. Of course I need to justify this statement as I am sure that the hackles of many football fans may be rising. I'd performed the ultimate act of treachery, moving from one side of a great sporting rivalry to the other. In fact there is no real justification except that as a nine-year-old boy, I was fairly ignorant of the gravity of my defection.

And in my defence, I was also involved in another rollercoaster of footballing upheaval that year. I'd started the season playing once again for Roma, but the arrival into the team of a boy called Gareth Gore (seriously) had led to me being dropped into the reserves. Gore was even taller than me and could kick the ball further and so had replaced me in the heart of the Roma defence. And although they made me captain of the 'B' team, I wasn't happy, so in the April I became part of a protracted transfer saga between Roma and Upminster Park Rovers, the team that my best friend at school Alan Maloney played for.

Maloney's father Rick, a gruff but kindly Irishman, was the new manager of UPR and the pair of them courted me with promises of a move up into centre midfield, which I thought infinitely more exotic than being stuck at the back. Rovers were only playing friendlies as the team had just been set up and at one point I was playing for them on a Saturday and Roma 'B' on the Sunday. Then came the crunch, a decision had to be made. My father says that this was one of the worst weeks of his life, to this day I'm still not sure if he is joking or not. First he had *me* changing my mind every five minutes, but to make it even worse he was getting regular phone calls from parents on both sides trying to keep me in the team or tempt me away, eventually though, the decision was made and I agreed to go over to the other side.

In a last ditch effort, Roma's management offered me the chance to play as a striker in my last game and I ended up bagging seven goals in a nine-nil gubbing of Rippleway Newham. Sitting in the car on the way home, proudly clutching my Man of the Match award, I told my Dad that I thought I would stay with Roma.

'No you fucking won't,' came his terse reply. I think it was the first time in my life that he actually swore at me. I've never seen him give me such a filthy look before or since. He went on to let me know in no uncertain terms that a late change of heart would not be happening as my decision had been made. Fortunately in my next game, this time as a fully-fledged Upminster Park Roverite, I bagged another seven goals in a thirteen-nil massacre of some mob called Aztec. So any thoughts of what could have been with Roma 'B' were put out of my mind and a new page was started in my father's exercise book.

Sandwiching this monumental stage of my fledgling career, were the small matters of the FA Cup semi finals and final of 1981. Growing up in the 1970s and early 1980s was an interesting time to be following football. English teams were dominating Europe and the FA Cup was as magical as ever. Yet I was still fairly naïve when it came to my awareness of the beautiful game. I was still more interested in playing than watching. Brian Moore still wasn't doing much for me on a Sunday afternoon and *Match Of The Day* was way past my bedtime, even on a Saturday night.

So I hadn't really been aware that Spurs were mounting the cup run which would see me get a third successive Wembley final in as many years. But Mark Gooding came up to me in the school playground one day and said that we had to get to a radio at lunchtime because the draw for the sixth round was being broadcast. We badgered the school office to let us listen to the radio, which they begrudgingly did, and we heard the draw announced. Spurs were to play Exeter City at home. I had no idea whether this was good or bad, but Gooding was ecstatic, apparently this was a home banker.

Tottenham went on to beat the Grecians two-nil and then drew two-all with Wolves in a Hillsborough semi-final, before a three-nil replay win secured a Wembley birth for the 1981 cup final against Manchester City. By now my attention had been well and truly caught and ahead of this final I could identify and name the Spurs team from one to eleven. And what a team it was – Ardiles, Villa, Perryman, Crooks, Archibald to name but a few. But there was one player who I held beyond esteem itself. Glenn Hoddle. Even today with all the baggage he has collected from his mediocre managerial career, his England aberrations, his faith-healing fanaticism, not to mention the Waddle-Hoddle pop debacle *Diamond Lights*, he's still one of the greatest players I have ever seen.

The ability to pinpoint any player in any position with one of his raking passes, silkier than a sultan's harem, and with an extraordinary ability to find the back of the net from open play or set pieces. The two defining Hoddle goals for me are the one he scores against Watford where he back heels it past the defender and then lobs the keeper from *inside* the box and then the breakaway scored in his last season at White Hart Lane, it may even have been in his last game at the Lane.

Ahead of this final, the one hundredth FA Cup Final, I needed no ritualistic talisman from *Roy Of The Rovers* because we had Glenn Hoddle. I pestered my mum to give me a white bed sheet so that I could paint a banner for the match stating: 'It's a doddle with Glen Hoddle,' but she pointed out that *a*: I wasn't going to the match so would have nowhere to wave it and *b*: if she caught me anywhere near her clean sheets with a tin of paint and a brush I was for the high jump.

But I took up the usual position in front of the TV wearing my Spurs shirt and waited for the magic to happen. I still didn't know where Manchester was, so there was precious little chance that any of my school friends did and therefore none of them were likely to be fans. Monday morning, come win or lose, held no fear. Added to that, the playgrounds had been ringing out *our* song this year, thanks to Chas and Dave taking the Spurs squad into the charts with the (hit) *Ossie's Dream*: 'Spurs are on their way to Wembley, Tottenham's gonna do it again…' Having lived through defeat the previous season, I felt I was better equipped emotionally to deal with a loss were she to raise her snake-like head again, but with a great song like that, how could we?

I knew little of the City lineup apart from the fact that they had some guy called Paul Power who had scored the winner for them in their semi-final against Ipswich. I wasn't worried about him. Power was a stupid name, even worse than that of my then P.E. teacher at school who was called Mr Strong. But there was only one player on the Manchester City team I needed to fear that day although he was to be both villain and hero. Tommy Hutchison, a £47,000 signing from Coventry, had me working on my juvenile swearing vocabulary when he opened the scoring for the Blues in the first half. I retreated outside at half time and offered some pretend goals to the back garden Football Gods in order to inspire Spurs to an equaliser. Unlike a year ago they were listening this time. With eleven minutes left, a Hoddle drive was deflected off Hutchison's right shoulder and spun off into the net past a wrong-footed Joe Corrigan.

The game played out to a one-all draw although the most memorable image of the day, and definitely in light of what happened in the replay, was that of an under-par Ricardo Villa who having been substituted, made the long, drawn out walk around the dog track to the tunnel, virtually in tears, while the match played on around him.

August 2007
Ware Are The Isthmians?

The Thursday night before the Preliminary Round weekend found me hunched over my laptop, surfing the internet and mugging up on the facts and form of Wembley and Ware. Since their comfortable replay win over Haringey Borough, the Lions had subsequently recorded a three-nil win over Epsom and Ewell in front of forty seven people. They had then drawn one-all away to Bedfont Green in front of seventy eight and now sat in eighth place in the league, four points off the top spot but with a game in hand on all of their rivals, and notably the only team in the league to remain unbeaten.

In the programme notes from the Haringey replay I'd read a comment from an unknown author who described the match as 'an additional fixture we could have well done without,' due to the team's focus on gaining promotion out of the Combined Counties league and up to step four of the Non-League Pyramid. So this weekend's cup fixture against Ware would be an interesting indicator of their ability to compete against a team from the higher level. I agreed with the programme editor. It *had* been an unwanted fixture. Now I faced another trip around the North Circular, a journey only slightly sweetened by the prospect of finding out which pest had made it to the Protex most-wanted poster that week.

So what of the opposition? Ware FC. How long would it take me to crack the lame gag about the whereabouts of Ware? Ah crap, just one sentence. Still with that out of the way, down to some business. I started with *Wikipedia* again, what did we ever do before it? I learned that Ware have been in existence since 1892 and originally played in Hertfordshire and north Essex leagues before joining the Herts County League in 1908 and winning the Eastern Division championship at the first crack.

When that league folded in the 1920s they joined the Spartan League, moved to the Delphian League, followed by the Athenian League and then the Isthmian League. Honestly, this was getting preposterous. Where did they get all these league names from? I know a lot of people moan about the fizzy-pop fuelled title of the

Coca-Cola Championship and that people of a certain age complain that League One should actually be Division Three, but honestly, Spartan, Athenian, Delphian? It conjures images of armour-clad warriors in leather skirts, swords and sandals, chasing a pig's bladder around a Grecian desert scrubland. The reality was probably a miserable December day with Woodbine-smoking, handlebar-moustached cloggers wearing ankle boots and heavy jerseys. Mind you the pig's bladder ball was probably right on the money. So the internet being the mine of all information, I disappeared off down a tangent to try to put some sense to the league titles. First I put the leagues into their historical order to see if that would help:

1863 Football Association formed
1885 Football League formed
1889 Football Alliance
1892 Southern Alliance
1894 Southern League
1905 Isthmian
1912 Athenian
1945 Corinthian
1951 Delphian

OK jump back up to 1905. Up until that point the league administrators had been quite happily going about their business calling their leagues by sensible if not very exotic names. Football Association, Football League, Southern Alliance. They do what they say on the tin. From Isthmian onwards they went all swords and sandals. So the Isthmian League must hold the key. I needed more data, so checked the word Isthmian in the dictionary. The closest response I got was 'Isthmus': '*An isthmus is a narrow strip of land that is bordered on two sides by water and connects two larger land masses. It is the inverse of a strait (which lies between two land masses and connects two larger bodies of water).*'

Hmmm. Not quite sure what that has to do with early twentieth century football. Time to press on. *Wikipedia* had a list of 'isthmi' and scanning down the list I spied that the first ever isthmus to bear the name was the Isthmus of Corinth and that an Isthmian is someone who lives at the aforementioned narrow land bridge which connects the Peloponnese peninsula with the mainland of Greece, near the city of Corinth. A light bulb appeared above my head. I'd sailed down the Corinth Canal in a murky old steamer on a school trip around the

Mediterranean when I was twelve, so I sort of knew where that was. Apparently the word 'isthmus' comes from the Ancient Greek for neck. But I didn't think that the Edwardian administrators were looking for a fancy way of calling their competition the Neck League.

'What does this have to do with football?' I shouted at the computer screen. I was lacking inspiration and doing that thing you do when you're surfing the web, where one eye's on the computer and the other is on a rerun of Inspector Morse, when suddenly I saw it. A link to the Isthmian Games...

'*The Isthmian Games or Isthmia were one of the Pan-Hellenic Games of Ancient Greece and were held at the Isthmus of Corinth every two years, at the second and fourth years of an Olympiad. If we are to accept the traditional date of the first Olympian Games (776 BC), we can say that the first Isthmian Games would have been held in 582 BC.*'

Pay dirt.

'*The games were reputed to have originated as funeral games for Melicertes. Theseus, legendary king of Athens, expanded Melicerte's funeral games from a closed nightly rite into a fully-fledged athletic-games event at a suitable level of advancement and popularity to rival those in Olympia. Theseus arranged with the Corinthians for any Athenian visitors to the Isthmian Games to be granted the privilege of front seats.*'

I loved the bit about the privileged seats. Corporate hospitality alive and kicking in Ancient Greece. So the Isthmian Games were held at the same time as the ancient Olympics and were obviously a big deal. A competition to rival the Olympics. Fast forward to the years around the turn of the twentieth century, when the Olympics had been revived in Europe, and the whole Ancient Greece thing would have been centre stage. The modern 'Olympics' were launched in Athens in 1896 just nine years before the Isthmian League took shape, so it seems fairly reasonable to surmise that our Edwardian league administrators, so taken by the success of the Olympics, would want to take a similar ancient name as their heraldic signpost. Hence the Isthmian League?

Of course this could all be a load of Ancient Bollocks. Chances are we will never know. Or at least I may never know. There may be some ancient Groundhopper out there who knows the truth, in fact let me rewrite that, there *will* be some ancient Groundhopper out there who knows the truth and no doubt he has a programme from the first Isthmian Games – or at least the team sheets copied out from the referee's changing rooms. Suffice it to say that I had a theory, I just needed some evidence to back it up. First I went to the Isthmian League entry on *Wikipedia* and was slightly irritated to read: '*The name presumably commemorates the ancient Isthmian Games, named after the Isthmus of Corinth.*'

Hmm, something told me I should have gone there first. Next stop – and let's face it, an even more obvious one – was the Isthmian League website itself, which had this to say about its history: '*Prior to the turn of the century, the only competitive games for amateur clubs in the South of England were various cup competitions. The Isthmian League was formed in 1905. The league's motto has always been 'honour sufficit'. Consequently no cup was awarded to the champions nor were there any medals for players. Honour was the only reward.*'

Honour above all. No rewards. A positively Olympic ideal. Very, dare I say it, *Isthmian*. I liked it. No cups, no medals, no signing-on fees, no contracts, no win bonuses, no Bosmans, just twenty two moustaches on a pitch playing for pride. Playing for the shirt. That's a concept that modern day football could learn some lessons from. Maybe not the moustaches.

And with the Isthmian League established as the pre-eminent amateur league in London and the south east, it follows that rival leagues would look to replicate that Ancient Greek ethos when they were setting themselves up, hence the naming of the Athenian, Delphian, Spartan and Corinthian Leagues in later years. Well that's my theory and I'm sticking to it.

Anyway, none of this had got me any closer to Ware, so I paid a visit to the Hertfordshire team's website which was a nicely organised, up to date affair featuring a club history, player profiles and news articles. A preview of the Wembley tie pointed out that both teams were unbeaten going into the game and that something would have to give. After finishing last season just three points off the play-off places in the Isthmian Division One North, they had started this year with two wins and two draws from their opening fixtures. They would offer a stiff challenge to the Lions from Vale Farm.

I was just checking how Ware had fared in last year's FA Cup when the study door swung open and Vanessa stalked in looking tired and fractious. She had returned from her French holiday at the weekend and had been frantically dashing around in the last week of the summer break getting school uniforms and equipment together ahead of the new term. I had decided to keep my latest obsession hush-hush for the time being.

'Can you have a word with your daughter please? She seems to think she doesn't have to go to bed.' She peered over my shoulder and looked at the computer screen as I swiftly shut down the Ware FC website window. 'What are you doing?'

'Nothing, just checking some emails from work,' I lied.

'Well can you stop that and sort out Eden please? I'm about ready to kill her and I've still got the ironing to do.'

'Of course,' I said conciliatorily, hurriedly getting up from the laptop.

'It would be nice just once to get some help around here', she said to my hastily departing back.

Ware would have to wait.

Saturday September 1st, 2007
Preliminary Round
Wembley V Ware

I wake up on Saturday and immediately think about the match, smiling with anticipation. Then I remember the impromptu party that ensued when our neighbour Sheryl turned up on Friday night for 'a quick drink,' which had gone into extra time and then penalties, and a creeping, insidious hangover kicks in. I creak my way out of bed and go downstairs in search of Paracetemol and water, my mouth feeling like the inside of one of Lee 'Team Bus' Pearce's Puma Kings.

I bumble around the house trying to rehydrate while keeping the signs of my discomfort away from Vanessa, remembering that she had warned me that I had drunk enough well before the Jack Daniels came out. At nine o'clock I have to take Evie and Jonathan for their swimming lessons. The greenhouse hot conditions of the local pool are not conducive to my recovery regime and I feel like shite. This is not the appropriate preparation for a big match and I make a mental note to myself not to let it happen again.

I get back from swimming and launch myself into a brittle frenzy of activity around the house to get a few weekend jobs out of the way and earn some Brownie points, cutting the grass and clearing up the nefarious presents left around the garden by our two Jack Russell dogs. Again I curse myself for my pre-match build up as the very act of moving has to be measured and delicate. All the time I am clock-watching, another habit that drives my wife insane when she knows that I am killing time before going out on one of my 'schemes'.

Finally the hands of the kitchen clock reach H-Hour and I give Vanessa a kiss and go and knock for Sheryl's teenage boy Tom, who I vaguely remember inviting when I told last night's party I was going to Wembley today. We set off at about quarter to one. Five minutes into the journey Tom asks me a question.

'So who's playing today?'

'Wembley versus Ware.'

'Wembley are playing at Wembley?'

'Of course,' I reply distractedly, concentrating on the M11 traffic, 'where else would they be playing?' He pauses, thinking.

'Wembley Stadium?' He asks, looking at me accusingly. My slow-moving brain screeches into focus.

'Err no. We aren't going to *the* Wembley. We're going to see Wembley FC play at *their* stadium. Well it's not so much a stadium… more of a… ground.'

'Not *the* Wembley?'

'Err no.' We drive on. He doesn't look impressed.

'You can see Wembley though,' I add hopefully, 'the proper one… on the way like.' We continue down the M11 in silence. Tom looking out of the window obviously feeling swindled, me driving, feeling like the swindler and again cursing the booze. However relations in the car begin to thaw as we pass Protex on the North Circular and gleefully note that this week's problem pest is the 'Feral Pigeon'. I let Tom take a picture with my ridiculously expensive camera and he is pleased with the outcome. Although the traffic on the North Circ is better than it was on a Tuesday night rush hour, it's still gloopy and we crawl along in places. I pray that Ware knock Wembley out so that I don't have to make this journey again. Well at least not until next April when the semi finals are played at *the* Wembley.

This time around I am relieved as I drive up the flyover out of Brent Cross. Tom *is* suitably impressed by the sight of the magnificent stadium, so my guilt at dragging him out into north London is assuaged. And this time around I'm also ready for the right turn off, so it takes just ten minutes from there to reach the Vale Farm Sports Centre. I pull out a tenner and we walk through the turnstiles of Checkpoint Charlie and into the ground. There are forty-five minutes until kick off so the ground is virtually deserted, no more than twenty people dotted around the terraces. I get a stroke of luck as I spy a man bent over a rickety table writing on some official-looking papers which I rightly guess are the team sheets. I ask if I can copy the names and numbers into my programme and he nods his agreement. I'm silently congratulating myself on this stroke of luck when it occurs to me that I have become just as obsessed by the minutiae of the matches as the Groundhoppers that I was smirking at two games earlier. Oh well.

Just then the corrugated shutters of the tea-bar rattle open and I suggest to Tom that we burger early, keen to avoid the problem of trying to take pictures while balancing cheeseburgers, chips and a cup of tea. Tom agrees stating that he hasn't had breakfast yet. I ruefully reminisce on the joys of a teenager's time schedule, where sleeping until mid-day is par for the course.

While Tom hunkers down on some grub I peruse the programme. Again it's the pink-covered photocopy job, but it's packed with good info all the same. Apparently this fixture features some nostalgia because Ware were Wembley's very first opponents in the FA Cup when the two teams met in an Extra Preliminary Round tie in September of 1949. That tie went to two replays. I pray that history is not repeated. The programme lists all of the Preliminary Round ties being played and I note that London APSA, the victors of the all-Asian tie are away to Tiptree. I also note that the form book is very much in favour of Ware, as the last time the two sides met in 2005/06, the Hertfordshire side won both of their Isthmian League Division Two encounters. Good.

The ground is slowly filling up. Well not so much filling up as becoming less-sparsely populated. Ware are of course a pyramid level higher than Wembley and with them comes a higher level in professionalism and organisation. The Ware Travelling Support, while numbering no more than ten, have taken station behind the Wembley goal and have draped some bedraggled Union Jacks across the back of the terrace with WARE FC plastered on them. Some of the Ware Travelling Support even have replica shirts. But more excitingly, Ware have brought some WAGs. As we wait for the teams to come out, two girls in their late teens or early twenties totter around the side of the ground on heels wholly unsuitable for the weed-strewn terraces and plonk themselves down in seats three rows away from Tom and me. If Posh Spice and Alex Curran are the Premiership of WAGs, then these two are definitely Ryman Isthmian League Division One North. Sponsored by Primark rather than Prada, but after a diet of pensioners, hobgoblins and Groundhoppers, I ain't choosy.

At five to three the two teams are led out onto the pitch by the officials, including a referee, Mr A Quelch, who looks as though he is eagerly awaiting the new school year when he will sit his GCSEs. Of course Ware are all completely new faces to me, but there's a comfortable familiarity about the Lions, led by player-manager Ian Bates who as Wembley's all time appearance record holder is making his 602nd start today.

After the toss, both teams go into a huddle to gather momentum but from the starting whistle the psychology of the situation is all too apparent. Ware are roaming the turf majestically, confident in the knowledge they are playing lower level opposition. Wembley play like frightened rabbits, the slick passing that carved swathes through Haringey Borough is now working in reverse as their constricted triangles head backward towards their own penalty area rather than forward into Ware's half. They are pressed by the organisation and authority of the visitors and when they lose possession it is Ware that show all the invention and penetration.

The first goal comes within two minutes. A series of one-twos orchestrated by Ware striker Paul Burton finds him on the edge of the Wembley penalty area and drilling a shot into the left hand corner. Wembley keeper Lee 'The Bus' Pearce dives in vain. Their worst possible start. Tom and I are automatically out of our seats clapping, we've discussed on the journey that our allegiances will be with Ware today. Wembley is a complete pain in the backside to get to and if Ware win, then I'm guaranteed to see another new ground.

For the next twenty minutes Ware are rampant. Fast, athletic, strong in the tackle and light of touch on the ball. Pearce takes the sting out of a fierce twenty five yarder from Ware striker Joe Stevens but the ball loops up into the air from his palm and then bounces onto the bar generating a magnificent 'Ooh' from the Ware Travelling Support. More pressure from the visitors and I hear the first football chant of my cup odyssey. The Ware Travelling Support – at least two of them – take up the strains of Joy Division's *Love Will Tear Us Apart* replacing the titular emotion with the surname of Ware skipper Danny Wolf:

'Wolf, Wolf will tear you apart, again.'

Again the Wembley bar is rattled this time by midfielder Sam Berry. Pearce drags himself up from his despairing dive and starts effing and blinding at his side: 'Come on, we haven't fucking turned up.' And it's at this point that I start to sense a subtle change in my emotions. Whether it's the underdog syndrome or familiarity, I'm not sure, but I start to feel myself rooting for Wembley. We've already come a long way together and I really dislike seeing them getting stuffed like this without putting up any sort of a fight. Of course this defies logic, because with a home draw in the next round I don't *want* them to win the match. I want to go to a different ground for the First Qualifying Round, not come back here. But my heart and my head are not in agreement. I look at Pearce frustrated in between the sticks, at Bates twisting and turning in central midfield trying desperately to find the time and space that he had against Haringey to knock cultured balls around, and at Jumo Mitchell who the Ware Travelling Support have already nicknamed 'Showboat'. Paul Shelton up front is a shadow of the striker from the earlier round and is getting caught offside with an annoying regularity. After three matches together, I *know* them now and I'm feeling sorry for them.

But then with about fifteen minutes to go a funny thing happens. Ware start to go all Goliath. Their confidence and authority gets replaced by cockiness and complacency. Things have gone so well for them in the first half hour that they, like Wembley before them, take their feet off the gas. Individually they probably don't realise it. They are still running, challenging and shouting brightly enough. But the team unit has definitely downshifted from its initial dominance. They give Wembley *just* enough breathing space to turn their passing triangles the right way around so that *they* are heading towards the Ware half of the pitch, rather than in reverse.

I'm watching the clock creep up towards the half time mark when Wembley break. It's three on three headed by Bates who plays a neat one-two with Shelton and then slips the ball through to striker Stephen Augustine, isolating two of the Ware defenders. Now Augustine just has Wolf to beat, and somehow he bundles it through the Ware skipper's legs to face the onrushing keeper, charging towards him narrowing the angle. Augustine jinks to his right but starts to lose balance. He sweeps out a foot and angles the ball goalward but without much pace. The ball rolls slowly to the line, too slowly, as a Ware defender is frantically overhauling it. On practically the goal line itself the Ware man scoops the ball clear for a corner and around the ground the Wembley followers slump as their best/only chance of the half goes begging. I groan audibly and Tom looks at me inquisitively.

'That was close,' he says. I'm nodding as the Wembley corner is taken, a deep one to the far post and rising majestically at the back post is Wembley defender Bradley Scott. He meets the corner with a powering header that thumps into the back of the Ware net.

'YES!' I'm out of my seat clapping. Then realise that Tom and the WAGs are staring at me curiously. Forty minutes ago I'd been cheering the Ware goal going in.

'They deserve that,' I say defensively to Tom, just as the referee Mr (Master) A Quelch blows the whistle for half time.

'Are you serious? But we don't want Wembley,' he replies.

'I know, I know, but I just thought they deserved that one,' I look away from his accusatory glare, 'fancy a cup of tea?'

'No,' he replies abruptly, then looks over to the pitch, 'what's happening here?'

I follow his pointed finger and see the Ware players trudging towards the side of the ground where we are sat, away from the changing rooms. I look along the terrace and spot a man in a Ware tracksuit leaning against the railings, steam emerging from his ears.

'I suspect that's the Ware manager about to dish out a roasting.'

The Ware players are looking sheepish as they ease down onto the grass around the touchline and start quaffing energy drinks. Wembley have gone back into the changing rooms, but Ware are getting a very public talking to. I take a couple of snaps. After five minutes a trainer starts handing out bibs and the Ware players are ordered to take part in a keep ball session for the remainder of half time. Tom and I walk back around the ground to get a position behind the Wembley goal for the second half. We walk past the Ware manager as he is making his way back to his vantage point in the stand. I'm wondering why he doesn't go and sit in the dugout with the rest of his support team when he barks at me.

'D'you want another effing picture of me*. You've been taking enough.' I'm not sure whether this is a joke or a threat, so I decide to smile awkwardly and change the subject.

'That reminded me of Sunday league football, seeing you do your team talk on the side of the pitch,' I say, 'what was that all about?'

'If I take them in there,' he points to the changing room, 'they just sit down and have a cup of tea. I want them to be working their bollocks off for forty five minutes, I can't expect them to do that if they're going to sleep at half time.' I nod encouragingly at him, hoping to portray a look on my face that I recognise I am in the presence of football management genius, then whip past him, mumbling something about the tea bar. At that point Wembley stroll out onto the pitch with amused looks on their faces as they watch their senior league opposition running around in bibs chasing a ball. The youthful Master A Quelch is also smiling as he calls a halt to the training session by peeping his whistle for the second half. The Ware trainers hurriedly pick up their cones and bibs and exit stage right.

Ware are puffing and perspiring somewhat from their half time exertions while Wembley look relaxed and refreshed. Perhaps too relaxed though, because after just four minutes Lee Pearce is picking the ball out of his net again. A great individual run from Danny Spendlove results in a fierce drive which Pearce can only parry and striker John Frendo is on hand to tap in from ten yards out. Their second worst possible start. I begin to wonder whether I *am* actually in the presence of footballing genius, as I can see the Ware manager glowing warmly to himself in the stand.

Just as in the Wembley-Haringey replay, the lower league team realise that the jig is up and they proceed to crumble in the second half. Ware have imposed themselves on the game and a third goal soon follows when Scott Neilson runs from an onside position through the Wembley defence to coolly slot past Pearce

---

* I later learned that Ware boss Glen Alzapiedi was at the time serving a touchline ban, and so presumably thought I was a Soho Square spy snapping pictures of him.

on a one-on-one. The Ware Travelling Support know that this is game over and start to enjoy themselves. The proximity of the snack bar and the waft from the sizzling meat therein, combined with the bulk of Pearce, encourages them to taunt him with barbed promises.

'Oy keeper. There's a burger here for you.'

'Come on, you know you want it.'

Pearce remains stoically engrossed in the game, refusing to rise to the bait. But the Ware Travelling Support have other plans. As Pearce strides purposefully up to hammer a goal kick down the pitch, the synchronised voices of the Ware faithful yell 'BURGER' at the top of their range and Pearce shanks a slice up and over the changing rooms with a rueful 'you wankers' stage whisper. Ware TS snicker gleefully at their success, truly a twelfth man, and Pearce gives them a wry smile. When you are an eighteen stone 'keeper with twelve jackals baying around your goal, there really is no place to hide.

The visitors' day completes with a fourth and final Ware goal from Neilson, his second on the day At this point my head has taken control over my heart again and I am preparing to say goodbye to Pearce, Bates and the Vale Farm Sports Centre. We have spent two hundred and seventy minutes (plus time added on for injuries) together. But now the cup odyssey is setting sail for Hertfordshire and a First Qualifying Round tie with the winners of Tilbury versus Great Wakering Rovers. Wembley and I have to bid each other farewell. When Master A Quelch blows his final whistle there is nothing remaining but to leg it for the car to try and get a head start on the North Circular traffic on the way home.

Wembley 1 (Scott 41)
Ware 4 (Burton 2, Frendo 49, Neilson 60, 65)

Attendance: 74
Money Spent So Far: £17
Miles Travelled So Far: 320
Winners Receive £1,000

1981
Spurred On

With Spurs and Manchester City closing out the 1981 final with a one-all draw we were treated to a replay which will go down in the record books as one of the most exciting and entertaining matches in cup history. It was all the more exciting for me because my team were in it, we got the right result, but more importantly I was allowed to stay up late on a school night to watch it live. Looking back on it now, I can honestly say that I remember absolutely nothing about the game bar that one magical moment which shines so brightly in my memory that everything else is cast into shade.

In fact come to think of it I remember very little about 1981. About being a nine-year-old boy and having a very normal childhood in a four bedroom, semi-detached suburban house. In some ways I envy those biographical authors whose early years are punctuated by defining events such as divorce, abuse, bullying or betrayal, as it gives them real meat to grind. I'd like to say that my father was an axe murderer and my mother a dope fiend, but they weren't, they were as normal as can be.

We didn't have bags of money, but then we never seemed to go short. Our family car was a Morris Marina that we traded in every two years for the latest model. Until of course they stopped making them and then we had to change to its successor the Ital. We went on the same summer holiday each year for a fortnight at Dawlish Warren in Devon. Always staying in the same small chalet just off the Exeter Road and every day trooping off together to sit on the beach with our buckets and spades, windbreaks and sandwiches, and fifty pence in two pence pieces to pump into the amusement arcade machines on the way home.

My school years had a regimented familiarity. New term in September meant moving up to a new teacher. Autumnal weeks collecting conkers from the giant horse chestnut trees in the back playground and dodging the Daddy Long Legs which congregated on the whitewashed buildings which bordered the front of the school. Interminable wet breaks in winter when we were locked up inside and where I would invariably end up drawing a Union Jack flag on A4 paper with a ruler and crayons, enjoying the symmetry and order of the design. Into spring and the religious festival of Easter, where attending a Catholic School as a Church of England pupil meant hours stuck in the back of the adjoining church while my classmates were indoctrinated in the ways of the cross. And then the summer, when the school ventured outside again for sports days and school fetes out on the big playing fields.

I still find it remarkable that they used to make those Catholic kids, aged nine, ten, eleven, actually attend Confession sessions with the priests. What could they possibly have to confess? The poor unfortunates would sit in the pews alongside the confessional booths and wait for the previous child to emerge. Then they would disappear across the threshold and a red light would shine out above the door. That was the cue for me and the other handful of heathens in the back of the church to start. We would launch into commentaries of imaginary horse races, the runners and riders jockeying for positions until whoever was leading the race when the green light came on was declared the winner. Well you had to do something to pass the time in that fuggy atmosphere, thick with incense and racked with guilt, and of course we didn't have Nintendos back then.

The child would emerge with their Catholic ASBO of having to say five *Hail Marys* and two *Our Fathers* and the process would be repeated until all the forty or so children in our year were cleansed... 'And now the 2.35 from Hornchurch featuring the two to one favourite Fat Bum, followed by Stink Pants with Tube Train on the rails...' Actually in light of some of my previous admissions and thinking back to the times I did get into trouble, perhaps it would have been better for me if I *had* been made to attend. But whether I can pinpoint any of these events to 1981 is debatable.

So what was happening in the world in that year? Or rather, what would have caught the attention of a nine-year-old who struggled to make it through the ten minutes of *John Craven's Newsround* without losing the will to live, let along *Nationwide* or God-forbid the *actual* news programmes. I recently took a look at a website showing the key events of 1981 and remember the Royal Wedding between Charles and Diana, Ronald Reagan becoming US president, the arrest of the Yorkshire Ripper, the first London Marathon and of course Bucks Fizz winning the Eurovision Song Contest. Naturally because of my Catholic surroundings I was *very* aware of the attempted assassination of Pope John Paul II, an event which left the teachers and nuns at St Mary's School in a very sombre disposition. But I'm disappointed to learn that I wasn't aware of the plight of

Worcestershire schoolgirl Donna Griffiths, who on January 13th began an uncontrollable series of sneezes which only ended after nine hundred and seventy eight days in September of 1983. I suppose it was still early on in that event, but how did I miss that?

Of course music is a great way of drawing a line in the sands of time and in the FA Cup month of May the charts contained Adam and The Ants (great), Shakin' Stevens (crap), Spandau Ballet (poncy), Tenpole Tudor (excellent playground marching fare) and of course the Tottenham Hotspur FA Cup Final Squad. Ozzie was on his way back to Wembley for a second time in six days when on the Thursday after the Saturday final the replay took place. Both teams went unchanged into the match. Tottenham went ahead after eight minutes through Ricky Villa, who joyfully pounced on a rebound to dispel the nightmares of the previous Saturday's substitution and subsequent walk of shame. But it took City just three minutes to respond with a sweetly-struck right-foot volley from Steve McKenzie. The game remained locked at one-all into the second half and then the blue touchpaper was lit. Shortly after the break City were awarded a penalty, only the fifth in a Wembley final, which was converted by Kevin Reeves to give them a precious one goal lead, but the last twenty minutes belonged to Spurs as they pressed hard, resulting in a messy Garth Crooks goal which levelled the game.

Now all of the above is just me paraphrasing a report that I have read about the final, because as I said earlier, I don't remember *anything* of the game apart from this.

I am sitting on the green, swirly-leaf patterned carpet cuddling up to a foot stool. The game is on a knife-edge but Spurs have the upper hand. My nine-year-old emotions have been put through the ringer by the rollercoaster of taking the lead, losing the lead, going behind and then equalising. For the first time in my life I have a partner in this turmoil. My dad is on the settee. After Derby County, Spurs are a team that he has a lot of time for. We are both totally engrossed. In a separate world from my mother and sister. When they speak to us we only hear background noise. When they walk past us they are as transparent as ghosts. All that exists is the television screen with its flowing images of greens, whites and light blues.

On the bottom left hand side of the screen, Tony Galvin passes the ball inside to the bearded Ricky Villa who sets off towards the City penalty box, where the blue shape of Tommy Caton is jockeying on the edge of the area. Villa shapes to go right and then goes left; My father and I are up on our feet. Villa, now heading towards the byline, nicks the ball past the challenge of Ray Ranson; 'Go on!' We urge together in unison. With blue shapes swirling around his white shirt he cuts back inside Caton again across the goal; Time starts to move in slow motion. The green jersey of goalkeeper Joe Corrigan desperately dashes from his line; We stop breathing. Villa drags his right leg across the ball and threads it into the back of the net; We leap into the air. As Villa stumbles across the prostrate body of Corrigan, my father and I are dancing around the room in delight.

We had never shared such an emotional moment before. Such an intense, concentrated, blinding moment of happiness. And I'm not sure that I can remember another occasion between us in thirty odd years where our hopes and desires have been realised at such a focal point again. Supporting Derby County from afar (another defection, I'll come to that) and England, the football successes have been few and far between and not necessarily shared. We've both followed the Rye House speedway team over the years, mainly travelling to meetings together, and while there have been exciting moments, a speedway match tends to build over a period of fifteen races and the winner-takes-all, last heat deciders are again few and far between. Plus you can't really compare a speedway meeting with the momentous occasion of an FA Cup Final.

To draw this to a conclusion I'd like to quote the journalist David Lacey who summed up the brilliance of this game in his report in the *Guardian* on the day after that memorable night: *'In the end the one hundredth FA Cup Final produced the game of the century. After a match which enthralled Wembley, with the lead changing hands three times, Tottenham Hotspur defeated Manchester City three-two in last night's replay and the winning goal, scored by Ricky Villa, will always belong to football history.*

'Before last night the 1948 final between Manchester United and Blackpool had been regarded as the outstanding example of attacking play to be seen at Wembley. Blackpool's four-three victory over Bolton in 1953, the Matthew's final, has always been regarded as the best dramatised match. Last night's borrowed something from the yellowing scripts of both these and put them into a modern setting with Latin American accompaniment. Where Saturday's one-all draw had been a tensely fought affair, a game of interest certainly but hardly the classic anticipated by some, last night's match surpassed the wildest expectations.'

September 2007
John Of The Rovers

In the week leading up to the First Qualifying Round tie between Ware and Great Wakering Rovers, the anticipation of another match increased with each passing day. I was developing a routine orchestrated by the fortnightly schedule. Research the match, watch the match, write about the match. In fact it was slightly irksome that I was having to wait a whole fourteen days for this game to arrive. Like all of my obsessions this project was burning fiercely, like a firework exploding from a milk bottle. Whether this one would have the longevity and climax to produce oohs and aahs at the end, or whether it would splutter and disappoint like a damp squib was yet to be seen. But most waking hours were spent considering the upcoming games and what had passed so far. Office hours spent in front of my laptop were routinely punctuated by diversions to the Ware, Great Wakering Rovers and FA websites in search of new nuggets of info.

But beyond Saturday's match I was entering into No Man's Land, because regardless of the result between Ware and Great Wakering, I knew nothing about where I would be going next. When I had started off on this journey, the draws for the first three rounds had already been published on the FA website. I knew who the winners of Haringey and Wembley would face and the range of teams that the subsequent victors had on the horizon. But from the Second Qualifying Round onwards, there was no information beyond the date of the round.

It was also apparent from the endless hours that I had spent studying the early draws that the competition was regionalised. Teams from certain areas of the country were being paired off locally, presumably to avoid the debilitating travel bills that could face small teams from opposite ends of the country were they drawn together. Questions needed to be answered, namely, when are the subsequent draws taking place and how is the competition structured in these early rounds? I *Googled* around for an answer, but finding nothing definitive, I decided to go direct to the source and so phoned the Football Association's Soho Square headquarters. After bouncing around the automated phone system, the

Customer Relations team and even an FA historian, I finally arrived at the end of a telephone line with Chris Darnell from the Competitions team and spent ten minutes quizzing him on the wheres and whys of FA Cup organisation. A very pleasant chap, he accommodated all my questions, despite having all the shenanigans of the First Round Proper on his plate.

It runs like this. The first three rounds are all drawn at the same time at the beginning of the season, but from that point on, the draws are not made until the Sunday or Monday *after* the Saturday games. The early draws get made at around 11am in the morning and after confirmation are published on the FA's website. The first draw which gets the full media glare is the First Round Proper which would be televised on Saturday October 27th after the Fourth Qualifying Round matches that day.

Chris also gave me the low down on the regionalisation: 'Once we know all of the clubs that have entered and been accepted, we start working on the exemptions, to see at which point of the competition the various clubs from the different parts of the football pyramid will enter. All the clubs that are in the first three rounds are then grouped into eight regions. The Second Qualifying Round has about five regional groups, then three, then two, with the competition finally going national in the First Round Proper.'

So it seemed that I would be staying in the south east of the country at least until November. But the good news from Chris was that there would be two highlights this weekend. First the match on Saturday and then at 1pm on the following Monday when the next round would be published on the FA website.

But who would make it through to the next phase? Time to study the form. Both teams had played Isthmian League Division One North matches the previous weekend with Ware losing their unbeaten record to top of the table Brentwood Town, while Great Wakering had recorded a morale-boosting first win of the season with a three-nil victory over Wingate & Finchley. It was still too early in the season for a pattern to be forming, but Ware looked the strongest with eight points from five games, compared to Rovers' four.

Just as I knew where Ware was without ever actually having been to it, the same could be said for Great Wakering, so I sniffed around for some more info. Situated six miles due east of Southend-on-Sea, it is apparently a picturesque village which gets a mention in the *Domesday Book*. It's dominated by the farming and brick industries and it has a low average rainfall of under twenty inches a year, due to its position in the rain shadow of the rest of Britain. And no, I don't know what a rain shadow is.

The Rovers were formed in 1919 by a group of men returning from the first world war who went to work in the farms and brickfields around the village once demobbed. And right up until 1989, punctuated only by the second world war, they played in Southend district leagues until making the decision to move up to intermediate football. A brief, successful, three-year tenure at that level and improvements to their ground then saw them move up to senior football, joining the Non-League Pyramid at the step five Essex Senior League. Their best performance in the FA Cup was in 1998/99 when they made it to the Second Qualifying Round losing at home in a replay to Welwyn Garden City. That same season they finished runners-up to Saffron Walden Town in the Essex Senior League, but as the latter failed to meet the ground grading requirements for a place in the Isthmian League, Great Wakering Rovers were promoted in their place where they have been ever since.

En route to the tie with Ware they had hammered Tilbury four-nil, scoring all of their goals before half time. While obviously I didn't see this match, I thoroughly enjoyed reading the report about it in the *Thurrock Gazette*. The stand-out sentence from *Gazette* scribe Neil Speight being thus: '*Tilbury had a golden opportunity to get back into the match on twenty eight minutes but Smith again wasted the chance, kicking his own leg and falling over the ball he was about to tap into an empty net after keeper Louis Green had already gone to ground.*'

Wish I'd seen *that* one.

Anyway the omens were boding well for a good match on Saturday. Both teams had scored four goals apiece in the previous round so their strikers were obviously in form. The weather forecast was sunny with highs of nineteen degrees and if the match went to a replay then I had the prospect of adding another ground to my burgeoning collection. It would be much easier to get from my Braintree home to Great Wakering's Burroughs Park, than it was travelling around north London to Wembley. So an additional fixture held no fear.

What *was* missing though was someone to support. I needed to get some skin in the game. To bet on red or black, to make the outcome a little more exciting. I hadn't spent enough time with Ware for them to feel like *my* team in the way that Wembley had begun to. They were still just a blur of team sheets and numbered shirts. Like an out of focus picture. And obviously Great Wakering were completely anonymous to me. I didn't know who would be at home in the next round so there was no point in rooting for the team that I hadn't visited yet. The Ware Travelling Support had injected some deliciously cruel humour into proceedings a fortnight ago, but I didn't feel like I was one of them yet.

So I tried to find a more scientific approach to my allegiance for this match. Football is all about supporting your local team right? So who was my nearest? Time to bring the Directions section of *Google Maps* to bear. I pumped in the Froms and Tos and hit Submit. Braintree to Great Wakering was thirty four miles while Braintree to Ware was thirty one miles. So Ware was my home town team. Ish. But Great Wakering is in Essex where I was born and raised and Ware is in Hertfordshire. County distinctions must count for something, surely?

OK forget the science. I tried to get a bit more touchy-feely. Great Wakering is close to Southend-on-Sea and Shoeburyness, two places that I have a soft spot for as they were the two closest seaside destinations from my childhood years in Romford and a trip to Southend with the bucket and spade in tow was always the highlight of any summer. But then Rovers play in green and white stripes, which is one of my least favourite kit combinations, especially when compared to Ware's blue and white stripes. And let's face it, these things count.

At this stage I was running out of reference points. There was just nothing left to decide on. I could flip a coin, but where was the fun in that? It would be just tossing a coin on the result. But if you can't decide any other way then you might as *well* toss a coin. I reached into my pocket. Heads I was going with Ware, tails it would be the Rovers. From the flotsam and jetsam in my trousers I pulled out a two pound coin. Heads turned up. That meant Ware. And that was the turning point for me. I wasn't happy with the result of the coin toss. Come on you Rovers!

Saturday September 15th, 2007:

First Qualifying Round
Ware v Great Wakering Rovers

Match day again. Last night it had been a Texas Hold 'Em poker session until two in the morning. Today it feels like another case of poor pre-match build up, but my morning is incident free and I am able to make a recovery at my own pace. I set off for football at 1.45pm, leaving me plenty of time to make the forty minute journey to Ware. It's a bright sunny day and the weather forecast of nineteen degrees is right on the money. It's going to be a hot one. I'm tingling with anticipation. Nobody wanted to come with me today so I have all the freedom I need. I'm thinking about the match and driving on auto-pilot. So much so that I'm in the wrong lane when I reach the junction with the M11 and I head off down the slip road towards London before I realise my mistake. I should have come off and taken the ring road around Bishops Stortford. This will add at least twenty minutes of time to the journey. Still I should be all right.

But when I hit Harlow, the Saturday afternoon shopping traffic in the town centre is crawling and I'm warily eyeing the clock as it ticks closer and closer to 3pm. I reach the outskirts of Ware with about fifteen minutes until kick off. Ware is a nice town, full of canals, renovated malting mills which are now apartments, and a pretty church. The high street is a winding affair bustling with people. I continue through the town centre and up a hill which takes me to the woody outskirts which are home to the Wodson Park Leisure Centre and Ware FC's home ground. I pass through the turnstiles at 2.55pm in a light sweat.

Both teams are already out on the pitch warming up and a portly gent with a microphone is standing on the turf with a cluster of others doing a presentation. Then to my joy he starts to announce the two line-ups for the day and I run a rule down the team sheets in the glossy programme, ticking here adding names and numbers there. I have just enough time to snarf a bacon and sausage roll from the snack bar served by two large fellows with greasy white vests and tattoos. Just as I am taking in the surroundings the referee blows his whistle for the captains.

Wodson Park is a fairly modern ground, clean and tidy with a large grandstand in front of the halfway line on the near side and a terrace stand running along the far side. A grey wooden fence runs around the perimeter with the trees behind boxing it in on two sides. Behind the right hand side of the pitch you can just make out an athletics track, while Perspex dugouts stand sentry duty on either side of the grandstand. Ware have gone into their pre-match huddle, psyching themselves up for the event, a writhing mass of blue and white. Great Wakering, wearing red shirts, are kicking out limbs and stretching nervously. Both teams are very quiet.

As the match kicks off more large people suddenly emerge from the main bar area like a school of released whales born free by a rip tide. Now I like a pie as much as the next man, but they seem to breed them big around here. The Ware Travelling Support have again taken station behind the opposition goal although of course today they are the Ware Home Support. If there is a Great Wakering Travelling Support then they are keeping themselves to themselves.

The match starts at a hundred miles an hour. Boots flying, studs up. Shoulder on shoulder, bodies smashing into each other. If there is a difference in playing style as the FA Cup bandwagon progresses up through the divisions then it is a substitution of the beautiful passing game for a Demolition Derby. The ball is bouncing around off the hard surface and even harder shins like a demented pinball. One particular set of goal mouth ricochets should come with a 'Tilt' warning.

I prowl around the touchline, camera in hand and consider what would be the best vantage point. While the early exchanges suggest that a goal is most likely to come at the Great Wakering end, the fierce, hot September sun is beating down into that end with a glare that would render my amateur photography useless. So I make my way right around the pitch to a point where the sun is on my back up near the Ware goal and to the right of the main grandstand. Another snapper has already taken up a similar position and we surreptitiously eyeball each other's equipment like two teenagers taking a shower after gym class. He is better endowed than me, photographically speaking.

'Are you from the *Mercury*? They're not coming today.' I ponder a suitable reply to his question. Yes I am the man from the *Mercury* who isn't coming or no I'm not the man from the *Mercury* who has come. For that matter what's the *Mercury*? I keep my answer simple.

'Nah.'

We both spend a couple of minutes fiddling with our zoom in the absence of conversation. I line up a picture of the Ware Travelling Support.

'Christ, you don't want to take a picture of them,' says Lensman, 'they're all on ASBOs.' Just then a trio of Ware substitutes come hustling up the line for their first warm-up session of the afternoon. One likely lad in his early twenties hitches a leg up onto the railing and winks at me.

'Are you ready to take my picture yet? Let me know when you are.' I smile a 'Riiight' back at him and refocus on the game.

'I tell you what, wait until I've got me training top off, when I'm just about to go on, then take the picture.' Again I smile awkwardly.

'Of course that's if I do get on. I've only had sixteen fucking minutes this season.' Out on the pitch the teams are continuing to crash into each other like two violent weather fronts. Accurate passing is at a premium because the players have so little time on the ball, but when there are glimpses of sunlight breaking through the storm clouds, it is shining in Ware's direction. Their midfield flair players – Sam Berry, Scott Neilsen and Danny Spendlove – are winning the battle in the middle of the park, while strikers John Frendo and in particular Joe Stevens are looking tasty up front.

The Great Wakering bench is getting edgy, they can see that today is going to be an uphill struggle and as such, their language is getting fruitier than a Christmas cake. In fact the other noticeable point about the rise in level this week is the general increase in moaning and swearing throughout. Every decision by the referee is challenged by both teams and both benches regardless of which way it goes.

'You must be fucking joking ref / About fucking time ref'.

A short, middle-aged man in the Rovers dugout wearing a blue shirt and beige chinos is Wakering's chief profanity artist. He grumbles about *every* Ware challenge.

'Did you fucking see that?' He waves his arms like a pint-sized windmill. 'He's a fucking animal. Dartford warned us about these dirty bastards on Tuesday night.'

With limited goalmouth action the game is in danger of getting ugly. Tempers are flaring under the beating sun. Ten minutes before half time, Great Wakering's flair player Joel Etienne-Clark, picks up the ball and starts a mazy run down the left wing. Ware midfielder Berry bears down on him and forces him out of play. As an added extra he gives him a final shove to the ground, unfortunately this is right beside the Ware dugout and Etienne-Clark slams into the Perspex with a sickening thud.

Both teams pile over to the scene of the crime and it looks as though it is going to kick right off. But there is more concern for Etienne-Clark than for full-on fisticuffs so physical contact is reduced to some shoving, a bit of dragging and that strange head wrestling where forehead to forehead they try and force each other backward, like a pair of rutting stags. Once the referee has calmed things down, Berry receives a yellow card, which for a minute I think might be a red, while the unfortunate Etienne-Clark departs on a stretcher carried down the tunnel by the Ware subs.

The game kicks off again, theoretically calmed down. But the anonymous assassins in both red and blue shirts have marked each other's cards and are now just waiting for their chance. They don't have to wait long. Rovers full back Mark Cartlidge is chasing a ball back toward his own goal at full speed when his heels are clipped by Scott Neilson. Both players go down tumbling and come back up wrestling. As Harry Hill would say, there's only one way to sort this out... FIGHT!

Both benches clear as twenty two players steam into each other in and around the wrestling protagonists. To my delight it is unfolding right in front of me, and my camera's shutter is clicking away merrily. A horde of small boys wearing Ware FC polo shirts – presumably one of the club's junior teams – also come gleefully up to the railings to grab front row seats for the whole mess. An impossible job for the referee and his assistant to sort out and strangely one of the names to go into the book is Ware captain Danny Wolf who legitimately had appeared to be in a peacemaker role amongst the warring factions. When the game finally restarts, Chino Man in the Great Wakering dugout is apoplectic. Muttering to himself about the warnings that Dartford had given them earlier in the week.

'We're in danger of getting bullied out of this game,' he exclaims to no one in particular apart from those in the crowd. 'Dartford warned us about these bastards.'

With a minute to go before half time, Wakering skipper Kevin Cole decides to redress the balance with a spot of vigilante action, committing himself one hundred per cent to a challenge he has a thirty per cent chance of winning and ending up in the book.

'Did Dartford warn you about that?' A Ware fan screams at Chino Man who slinks into his Perspex pillbox to take cover. A collective sigh of relief is expelled around the ground when the referee finally blows his whistle for half time after forty five minutes which lasts just short of an hour. Nil-all. I retire to the grandstand for the break to catch my breath, make some notes and take cover for the second half. Yet another fat Ware supporter edges his way up the stairs beside me with a two-month old baby balanced precariously over one shoulder and a pint of lager in his other hand. The Ware Juniors are in good voice with a nice chant:

'Who are we?'

'What are we?'

'*Ware* are we.'

The Ware Home Support have not been in good voice though, they know that their team has wasted various good chances in the first forty five minutes, and that the fireworks that closed the half will be put to good use by the Rovers manager in his team talk, to try and develop a siege mentality from the visitors. Indeed Wakering are first back onto the pitch and looking fired up.

As the second half begins to take shape it is clear that Rovers are committed to some resolute defending while conceding possession in the middle of the park. Come on you bastards, break us down if you can. Ware continue to waste the few chances they get. Stevens, who is my player of the match, is guilty of trying to burst the net at the end of a jinking run through the Wakering defence, and instead he blazes wide. Frendo, bundled to the ground in the box, grabs the ball in his hands and rather than get a penalty, gets a handball charge against him. And then from a Ware corner Danny Wolf towers up at the far post to thunder home a match winner only to see it crash against the underside of the bar and somehow stay out. With every Ware attack I know I want Rovers to win, but my head says the home team must get a goal.

Then as the two teams begin to tire the game starts to go end to end. Wakering are inspired by a left-sided attacking midfielder called Steve Butterworth, nicknamed 'Scouse' by the odds and ends of Rovers fans dotted around the ground. Scouse has a touch of class about his game. But even Scouse can't manufacture an elusive away goal. Rovers are also channeling in a livewire substitute Dean Pearson who has tricks in his locker and a sense of comedic timing which is demonstrated on a mazy run when he tries to run faster than his legs can manage and nearly ends up on his nose.

Then as the game moves into the phase where the next goal wins it, Scouse is tripped on the edge of the Ware box and the referee blows for a free kick. This is it. The home support inwardly groan. This happens so often in football, especially cup football. The old smash and grab raid. Defend for eighty nine minutes and attack for one, just make that one count.

To my astonishment, the player lining up to take the crucial kick for Great Wakering is their right back Danny Pitts. He has stood out for me today as the player least likely to make a positive impact on the game. I won't say he's terrible, because I couldn't do any better, but there have been numerous occasions where his misplaced passes or poor decisions on the ball have left his team at full stretch. Then I realise it. He must be the dead ball specialist. The sniper in the church tower. The guy that is called upon to find the back of the net with devastating accuracy. He's in the team for *just* this occasion. It's a *fait accompli*.

The Ware fans around me are in agreement with my prognosis. They are moaning and groaning as Pitts sets his sights to bend one into the top corner. The referee marches the wall back the required distance and then backward sprints to his station on the far side of the box. Pitts is already starting his run up as Mr Michael Downey blows his whistle on this pivotal moment. The sniper lines up his sights and pulls the trigger, unleashing a complete daisy-cutter which bounces tamely off the boot of a Ware sentry in the wall. Pathetic.

It's a pivotal moment all right. I start to pack up my reportage kit. This one's going to a replay. By the time I have stowed my bits in my bag and walked down to the turnstiles at the end of the ground, the remaining minutes are played out and Mr Downey calls an end to this dubious spectacle. We are all going to Great Wakering on Tuesday night.

Ware 0
Great Wakering Rovers 0

Attendance: 125
Money Spent So Far: £24.50
Miles Travelled So Far: 381

1982
An Unlucky Break

The year of 1982 saw me cheering on a team for a fourth cup final in a row. Little did I know at the time that this would be the last occasion when I would be actively supporting one of the teams contesting the Wembley showpiece. At ten-years-old you just don't consider things like that. And in fact to my shame I think I was probably starting to take the May occasion for granted. You see my biggest regret about this final is that apart from knowing that QPR were led out by Terry Venables, that they featured a young Clive Allen among their number and that the match ended in a Tottenham victory, I can't remember a single thing about the game. Not the line-ups, not the build-up, not the scorers. Not even the score.

The thing about writing a book like this, as you may have noticed, is that the structure has a familiar ring to it. Dipping back into the mists of my memory for a historical review of cup matches that have influenced me, previewing the teams that are playing in my strand of this year's competition and then reporting on my experiences of attending the different matches which take place. Repeat to glorious denouement. But by far the hardest sections to write are the historical ones. Trying to dredge through the memory banks for the things which held my attention or caught my fascination as a young boy. But what happens when your memory lets you down?

The easy answer to this is of course to cheat. Or rather to consult some historical signposts to point the memory back in the right direction. Reading a match report on the game, looking back on what was happening in the world, what was playing on the radio. The vast resources of the internet make this a relatively quick and simple task. But even if I don't remember the minutiae of those matches, I have so far been able to recall unaided what *happened* in the cup finals of my childhood. Alan Sunderland's last-gasp winner. Brooking's heart-breaking, headed goal. Ricky Villa's stunning solo effort. Take these as pencil drawings of the time and use the internet and other resources to help with the shading in. 1982 is different. For 1982 there is nothing.

I've also pointed out how these big events can actually make it harder to remember the *other* things that happened in the final. For instance I can clearly remember every detail of what was happening on the pitch, and in our house, when Villa struck his winner but I have no recollection of his opener. But I do have one very vibrant memory of 1982 and it came one month after the FA Cup Final when I badly broke my leg. It was a summer day and we were playing in a five-a-side tournament at the St Mary's School fete. I was playing for the third year juniors' team – the Third Year Tornados. There were a handful of other teams but the favourites, naturally, were the fourth years or year sixes to translate them to modern times, who made up St Mary's 'A'.

The summer fete was the usual combination of coconut shies, lucky dips, lollipops in the sand and jumble. I remember pumping most of my allocated pocket money into the crockery smash, which to a ten-year-old boy seemed a highly appropriate use of cups, saucers and plates. Every twenty minutes or so we would be hailed over by the tannoy to return to the hastily-constructed five-a-side pitches to compete in a ten minute game. We had won two matches already and it was clear that the Round Robin tournament would be a showdown between my third years and the fourth years. There was an added spice for me, because I had actually spent some of my early schooling in with the fourth years and I knew many of them as very good friends. The star player for them was a boy called Mark Houseago, built like an eleven-year-old brick outhouse but with a competent touch on the ball and some tricks up his sleeve. He and I had been very good friends when we shared classes and I had been to his house on a number of occasions.

When our PE teacher Mr Stong called our showdown to order it was a predictably tight affair. Like any one of the thousands of playground matches that we had already played together, only this time with goalposts for jumpers and a proper referee. Into the second half with the scores level, and close to the centre circle, the ball broke free equidistant between Houseago and me and we both sallied forth for a full-on fifty-fifty challenge. He was wearing shin pads and I wasn't, having thought them unnecessary for a five-a-side tournament. The hustle and bustle of the summer fete was brought to a standstill by a sickening crack and a high-pitched scream.

I have never felt pain like it in my life. Houseago's leg had cleanly fractured my tibia, although of course at the time I had no idea that I even had a tibia. My head swam with the pain. I lay on the floor and the pale faces of Mr Strong, Houseago, my father and Rick Maloney, my Sunday morning club manager, appeared above me asking how I was. I remember feeling embarrassed at saying 'I want to puke' in front of them. I wasn't crying, because it hurt too much even for tears.

I was carried shoulder high off the pitch by Rick and my father, out past the whitened faces of the parents and children attending the fete, straight through to the car park where they gingerly laid me on the back seat of our car. I was driven directly to Oldchurch Hospital in Romford where I waited in turn for an X-Ray, and where the fracture was confirmed. Then to an ante-room where a nurse cast a plaster on my right leg from hip to toe. Then back into the car and the fifteen minute drive to our house where we were met at the door by my mother who promptly burst into tears.

I guess it is no surprise then that the trauma and shock of that event dominates my memory of that time. But the circumstances of my rehabilitation led to a strong memory of one aspect of the 1982 final and that is the inclusion of Clive Allen in the QPR line up. As I've mentioned before, we had a tenuous association with the Allen family. Father Les, a member of Tottenham's double-winning side in 1960-61, had trained my former team Roma and brother Bradley had played up front. In the build-up to the cup final on the morning of the match, *Grandstand* had run a feature on the Allen family, probably because of Les Allen's long-time association with the team that Clive would be competing against.

We had just taken delivery of a brand new video recorder. One of those early machines where pressing the eject button would see the cassette compartment rise slowly from the top of the device with a whir of gearing and servos that resembled Thunderbird Two emerging from the cliff face of Tracey Island. In our excitement to record *anything* remotely interesting, we had recorded the feature on young Clive and QPR.

There was a section where the BBC cameras had filmed Clive's twenty first birthday celebrations at the gloriously-named Orsett Cock pub in Essex, Clive opening a present from his then fiancée (Lisa, I think). An interview with Les where he wishes his son all the best while sticking to his Tottenham roots, and an interview with young Bradley taken in the changing rooms of a Roma match, with my former team mates all sitting around looking wet and muddy, and grinning delightedly at being caught by association on camera.

This was at the beginning of the tape and on the afternoon of my leg break, my sister had added *Batman the Movie* to its contents. So lying immobile on the living room sofa, with my leg propped up on a pillow, and in the days before remote controls, that tape became imprinted on my brain. The video recorder would play the tape through, rewind, and then play again, rewind, play again, rewind…

So while I have no memory of the 1982 final between Spurs and QPR. I do know that Spurs won, I know that Terry Venables led QPR out and I know that Clive Allen was given an executive-style briefcase by his girlfriend for his twenty first birthday.

I'm going to leave it that way.

September 2007
Bore Draw

So *two* names were going into the hat. Ware *and* Great Wakering. Deadlocked at Wodson Park, we were to find out who they would be playing in the next round before we found out who would survive the tie. The draw for the Second Qualifying Round was on the Monday and the First Qualifying Round replay on the Tuesday. I'd imagined that the draws would be significant moments for me in my cup odyssey. But on this occasion the reality was far from the truth.

Throughout Monday morning I regularly checked the FA website waiting for the draw to be announced. Chris Darnell of the FA had told me to look in around 1pm, but my curiosity had the better of me and I was continually frustrated when the FA home page reported no news. Finally I had to attend a couple of work meetings in the West End and so was unable to log on, so I missed the moment when the website was updated.

Sat on a Central Line tube train travelling back out of town at around 4pm on Monday afternoon, I remembered that the draw must have taken place and so tried to get onto the FA website using the internet browser on my mobile phone. I had to wait until Leyton when the Central Line finally emerges from under the ground before getting a connection. A few clicks later and the news was there. A home tie against Thurrock of the Conference South. Staring at the eight characters on the small screen I was washed with a sense of complete anti-climax.

After all an FA Cup draw should be all about the drama of velvet pouches, numbered balls clacking away and whispered commentaries. Former FA Secretary Ted Croker and old soccer legends winking knowingly at the camera as they drew favourite against favourite, or killerwhale versus minnow. Sat on the Central Line, staring at a tiny phone screen, and finding out that I was heading back to a place I would have visited already, against a team from one of the arse-ends of Essex, did not quite manifest the magic. I made a mental note. Until the Football Association and their production counterparts at the television companies made the draw more exciting for me, I would have to generate the drama and tension myself.

Tuesday September 18th, 2007:
First Qualifying Round Replay
Great Wakering Rovers v Ware

The home of Great Wakering Rovers is my favourite ground so far. I realise this the minute I arrive at Burroughs Park, forty five minutes before kick off. Walking through the turnstiles I'm the only person in the ground. The sun has just sunk below the far end and the wide-open skies of the Thames Estuary are awash with all the colours of a fabulous sunset. I stand at the near end of the ground and take in my surroundings. The pitch is flat, lush and green like a billiard table. Freshly mown and with stripes running from side to side. To my left is a short terrace behind the dugouts, while to my right is a small grandstand with about one hundred and fifty seats. The ground, somewhat ambitiously, has three separate turnstile entrances, one behind the goal where I entered and two more in the corners. Allotments back onto the terrace side, reminiscent of Haringey Borough, while beyond the far end is parkland.

A white-haired gentleman emerges from the low single-storey clubhouse in one corner and limps purposefully to the far end of the ground. He disappears into a wooden structure and the noise of a generator roars into life, followed by the smell of diesel fumes, and then one by one the floodlights flicker on. As I walk around the ground the two teams emerge from the clubhouse to begin their warm-ups, and spectators start to dot themselves around the terraces, led by the commander in chief of the Ware Travelling Support. It occurs to me that I did not see the Wise Monkeys from ZigZag Productions at Saturday's game. If Ware is too far for them, then Great Wakering should be the back of beyond.

The waft of chips and vinegar from the snack bar reaches my position on the halfway line as the two teams complete their calisthenics and trudge back off the pitch leaving just the subs on the park for a spot of crossbar challenge. A half moon is covered by wispy clouds and the first autumnal chill of the year is in the air. Perfect football weather. The atmospherics invoked by a floodlit game simply cannot be matched.

Eventually the ground has over one hundred people inside as the two teams are led out from the clubhouse by the referee and his assistants. Both teams have changed strips. Ware are now in their away colours of amber and black, while Rovers are in their favoured green and white striped shirts and white shorts. Once the toss has been made, Ware revert to the now customary team huddle and I look around the crowd, recognising Lensman standing by the tea bar and certain faces from the Ware Travelling Support. Then with a flourish the referee blows his whistle to light the touchpaper on an incendiary football match.

Two minutes in. Rovers striker Martin Tuohy is upended, edge of the box. Sniper Danny Pitts steps up. The first chance for the dead ball specialist. A chance to atone for Saturday. A chance he drills into the wall again. The ball breaks loose and Ware are on it. Fluid, fast, the passing game. The ball skimming off the billiard table pitch, every bounce true. The grass moist and forgiving thanks to the chill conditions. Rovers spend five minutes chasing amber shadows in their own half. Scouse relieves the pressure, grabs the ball and takes flight. Past one, shoulder dips, past two, lets fly from twenty five yards but the ball sails over the bar. The home fans 'Ooh' with frustration, the Ware fans 'Aah' with derision.

Then on nine minutes Ware break through. Frendo snags the ball, control close turning tightly. He slips in an overlapping Spendlove who bears down on goal, Rovers backpedaling desperately. Spendo lets fly but the shot is palmed away, into the path of Joe Stevens who side foots home, finally collecting the goal that on Saturday he put a deposit down on. Ware are ecstatic, relieved. Rovers regroup, dejected. The worst possible start.

Ellerbeck replaces Spendlove, injured by some Wakering studs. Scott Neilson goes in late. Scott Neilson goes in the book. Ware are dominating, rampant. Ellerbeck is fleet of foot. He gives chase to a through ball. Tangles with Rovers keeper Louis Green. They both fall down. Ellerbeck bounces up, spies Stevens, edge of the box. Pulls it back. Stevens lines up and drives low into the corner, wrong footing Green. Two-nil. It's twenty seven minutes in and game over. But no let up from the visitors. The Ware Travelling Support are gleeful. Their team hustle, tackle, pass, chest down, lay off. Rovers are *still* chasing amber shadows. Sam Berry drops a Ware corner onto the head of Danny Wolf. Three-nil. This game is *over*.

Then Ware let up. They sit back and admire. Rovers take over. Rovers hustle, tackle, pass. Striker Martin Tuohy, lean, lithe and pale as a wraith. Collects on thirty two minutes from a poor back header. Turns, shoots, scores. Bottom corner. Three-one. Rovers are inspired, Rovers glimpse belief. Skipper Sam Clarke tries from distance. James White tries from distance. Down–shifted Ware are stunned, slow–

footed. Scouse carries the Rovers class and he slips in Neil Richmond in the penalty area. Richmond jinks past Wolf, Ware goal at his mercy. Richmond needs no bidding. Three-two. This game is *not* over.

The Ware support, management and players are dazed, and willing half time to arrive. Wounds need licking. But just before the whistle they get a chance. Free kick on the left side from a Pitts foul. The ball is lofted in from a corner, tantalisingly. The Rovers keeper should come and collect but doesn't. Kai Ramshaw nuts it against the bar. The crowd 'Ooh', Ellerbeck reacts. A flying bicycle kick in the six yard box. Back of the net. Four-two. Ecstatic Ware bundle Ellerbeck into the back of the net to celebrate. Relief is palpable. Ware think this game is over again. Actually it's just the first half. On Saturday we struggled for one goal. On Tuesday we have six in the first forty five minutes.

The two teams disappear into the bungalow changing rooms, the fans mill around the snack bar. Emotions ranging from disbelief, through despair and delight. Everyone is catching their breath. I spy Wise Monkey from ZigZag Productions. I sulk. He has all the footage he needs after that display. The evening grows chiller and the moon raises higher, a focal point above the floodlights, powered still by the softly humming generator at the corner of the ground.

The teams re-emerge, Ware cocksure, Rovers equal parts chivvied and crestfallen. It still seems an improbable task. Two minutes in it becomes impossible. Ellerbeck has the ball some twenty five yards outside the Rovers goal with no support but time at his feet. He dips a speculative drive low across the turf and into the right hand corner of the Rovers net. Five-two. Rovers shoulders sag, fans look away groaning. It's the worst possible start, again. The referee may as well call it now. This game *is* over.

Any remnant Ware nerves are dispelled. A three-goal cushion with forty minutes to go. It's more than comfortable. They pass neatly while Rovers chase floodlit amber shadows. Ware always look a man extra. Always have an outlet. Always win the challenge. Wolf and Hammonds in the heart of the Ware defence are composed. The team is functioning as a unit. I feel sorry for Rovers. This is too easy for Ware.

Then the final turning point. Frendo is upended outside the Rovers box and decides on a little retaliation of his own, butting into the Rovers defender like a stag. Saturday's aggression bubbles up to the surface and again the twenty two players come together in a tango of pushes, shoves and clinches. The referee wastes no time in showing Frendo the red card and Ware's extra man on the pitch is suddenly gone. Rovers glimpse light at the end of the three-goal tunnel. Rovers pick up the pace. Rovers hustle, tackle, pass. Ware take both their lead and their numerical disadvantage for granted. A ball is lifted over the Ware defence towards Sam Clarke, twenty yards out. He tracks the ball like a hawk as it arrives over his shoulder, pirouettes on cue and flails out a leg as it sweeps passed him. An immaculate connection between ball and boot. The ball volleys up over the head of Luke Woods, rooted to the spot in the Ware goal, and nestles into the far corner. A wonder goal. Five-three. *Is* this game over?

The magnificence of the strike and their numerical superiority galvanise Rovers. The crowd find voice again: 'Green Army, Green Army.'

Ware Travelling Support respond: 'Come on, Ware Boys.'

'Green Army, Green Army.'

'Come on, Ware Boys.'

'Green Army, Green Army.'

Rovers still need a miracle, they settle for Martin Tuohy. Another high ball is lofted toward the edge of the Ware box. Tuohy rises and meets it with the back of his head, sending it on its way toward goal. Keeper Woods is stranded again. The ball sails over his head and into its familiar nestling place. Five-four! This game is *not* over!

The home fans urge the Rovers on with a roar. Twenty three minutes of the half remain. More than a quarter of the game. Rovers have a man over, Rovers are at home. But can they find the back of the net? Ware know what they have to do. They have to defend, defend, defend. Their strikers dominated the first half, the defence has to stand up in the second. Now it's Ware chasing the floodlit shadows as Rovers spray the ball around. Woods in the Ware goal reacts to a point-blank header, Ramshaw clears off the line, Hammonds clears off the line. The tension is unbearable. But Ware defend, defend, defend.

Rovers huff, Rovers puff, but Ware are solid. The clock ticks down. The chances dry up. The equaliser remains elusive. Finally, unbearably, time runs out on the Rovers and the final whistle blows mournfully out over the allotments. I'm gutted and stalk back to my car with the hump.

Great Wakering Rovers 4 (Tuohy 32, 67, Richmond 35, Clarke 62) Ware 5 (Stevens 9, 27, Wolf 31, Ellerbeck 43, 47)

Attendance: 121
Money Spent So Far: £33.00
Miles Travelled So Far: 450
Winners Receive £2,250

1983
Lifting The Cup

I was fortunate that the fractured tibia occurred during the *summer* fete as it gave me the whole of the six-week holidays for rehabilitation, and by the following September I was back playing football. It was a memorable season for Upminster Park Rovers. We won our division of the Echo League having played twenty four, won eighteen, drawn five and lost one. But more importantly we put together a cup run of our own. Victories over Farm Athletic (three–nil), and league title rivals Sabadell (one–nil) saw us set for a glorious cup final day of our own. Unfortunately I think Wembley Stadium was booked that day, Sunday April 10th 1983, so we had to settle for a visit to Rainham Town's Deri Park. And the opposition? Well of course there's only one team it could have been right? My old club Roma.

Throughout the weekend of *our* cup final, planks of wood at local builders' merchants had been in short supply and animals had been assembling themselves into pairs. It had rained so hard that by the time we arrived at the ground on that Sunday morning, Deri Park was a complete quagmire. Under normal circumstances I doubt that the game would have been played, but of course we had a limited window of opportunity to utilise the stadium and so we kicked off.

We still have a very grainy, ancient video of the match and every now and then I will force the children to sit through it. The only patches of green on the entire pitch were the corner flags and all the usual spectacles of a waterlogged football match were present. These included sliding tackles which started in one penalty box and finally came to a graceful conclusion at the other end, and opposing small boys chasing after a rolling ball which abruptly halted in a deep puddle as they went flying past. It's a training video for how *not* to stage a game of football.

But in the end it was the conditions which saved us. A tight, if somewhat comical, first half had remained goalless and deep into the second half, one of the Roma players found himself in space in our penalty box, with goalkeeper Jason Abbs racing from his line to close him down. The striker, whose name was Ian something, neatly sidestepped the Abbs lunge and rolled the ball towards the empty net. The deadlock broken surely and too late for UPR to respond. However the ball's momentum was arrested by the tacky mud of the goalmouth. The goal line, if there ever was one, was just an unclear morass of squelchy puddles. Full back John Wallace came racing across the box and hammered the ball out of the goal, and with no Russian linesman to bail them out, the Roma players' delight turned to instant despair as the referee bellowed 'Play on!' The goal that never was. It still brings a smile to my face.

Into extra time and with penalties looming, UPR got a chance at the other end which was coolly converted by our slow-moving, slightly tubby striker Lee Hales. For the remainder of the game you can hear on the video the croaking, Irish lilt of manager Rick Maloney yelling at us to 'get back' to see out the match, which we did, to secure a league and cup double. I have a highly-cherished memory of lifting the cup as UPR skipper before my team in front of the dilapidated Deri Park grandstand, although it is juxtaposed by the embarrassment of me as an eleven-year-old not wanting to join in the naked, prepubescent, post-match celebrations in the big team bath in the changing rooms.

As part of the research for *The Road From Wembley*, my father bought me a book called *History of Non-League Football Grounds*, by Kerry Miller and from it I learned the fate of the ground which had seen my earliest triumph. The grandstand had been constructed from asbestos and concrete and its position between a number of neighbouring houses meant it was unsuitable for development. Added to that, there were methane emissions wafting up from underground and both Deri Park and Rainham Town Football Club collapsed through a lack of finances.

Mr Miller writes: *'Deri Park died as a football ground some three years before Rainham Town FC conceded defeat in 1994. It succumbed to the worst elements and is now a dreadfully vandalised, overgrown bomb site, where what cannot be stolen has been destroyed and what cannot be ripped apart has been set alight.'*

However going into May, my footballing fervour would have been in fine fettle but that season's FA Cup was something of a let down. Holders Tottenham, who were still being underpinned by my most loyal support, had survived clashes with Southampton and West Brom before falling at the Fifth Round hurdle to Everton. Defeat to the Toffees brought a seventeen match unbeaten run of cup games to an end. It also left me with something of a void on the big Saturday out.

The two teams competing the grand affair at Wembley in 1983 were Manchester United and Brighton & Hove Albion. I sat down in front of the game on cup final Saturday and tried to pick a team to support, but my heart wasn't in it. Things weren't right. *Roy Of The Rovers* magazine had printed out the teams rather than let you write them in. The only player I liked among the two sides was Steve Foster of Brighton, because he wore a white headband, but he was suspended for the final. Even the green, swirly-leaf patterned carpet at home had been recently pulled up for a newer model. Things just weren't the same.

Very shortly into the game I realised that for the first time in my FA Cup Final watching career I really could not care what the result was. It was just another game competed between two other teams. By half time I had given up and was outside in the back garden hammering my ball up against the wall of the house. The realisation that I did not have a divine right to have a vested interest in the cup final was tinged with an irrational anger directed at Keith Burkinshaw's Tottenham for having let me down.

1983 was also my final season at St Mary's Primary School, and that too was a parting of ways. The friends I had made over the last eight years were all heading off to their grant-maintained Catholic senior schools, while I was destined for an Upminster comprehensive. For most children the transition from junior school to senior school is one which is made in the company of friends, but for the few jokers who find themselves dealt into different packs, you are taken from an environment where everyone is familiar to being a lone figure among thousands. I was marginally better off than those poor unfortunates. I knew one person in a thousand. A boy who played alongside me for Upminster Park Rovers called Jonathan Folwell. My Sunday morning football would act as the link between the comfortable surroundings of St Mary's and the unknown world of the seniors at Hall Mead School in Upminster.

2007
Ware Are The Underdogs?

After my initial funk at seeing Great Wakering fail I had to admit to myself that Ware were the better side. Over the course of the two games, if you measured it on the quality of the teams alone, then they deserved to go through. Their invention and endeavour overwhelmed Rovers for most of both games, it was just the Frendo sending off and two classy, if somewhat lucky, goals which kept Great Wakering in the tie. But if either of the two were equipped to take on a Step Two team from two divisions above them, it was Ware.

Now that I had some closure on the outcome of the First Qualifying Round it was time to turn my attention to the challenge of Conference South outfit Thurrock. Anyone who has ever crossed through the Dartford Tunnel from Kent to Essex will have seen Thurrock's ground although unless you were in the know, you probably would not have realised it. As you emerge from the tunnel and continue around the M25, you approach a flyover which towers above a roundabout connecting the motorway to the A13. Below to your left is a large building, the Thurrock Hotel, and backing directly onto that is Ship Lane, the Thurrock ground, its floodlights just visible behind the hotel structure. For anyone who doesn't know the area, remember the funeral bit in *Four Weddings and a Funeral* – a picturesque church dwarfed by massive, smoky industry – a Procter and Gamble factory I think. That's Thurrock.

I've described the area as the arse-end of Essex and indeed the entire corridor of land between the A13 and the Thames, from London to Southend, is a fairly grim vista. Modern equivalents of the dark, Satanic mills. Motoring down the A13 from London, you first pass the ageing sky rises of West Ham and Newham on your left, then the toxic Beckton Alp on your right. If the tide is out and the sun up, your car can become filled with the noxious whiff of Barking Creek, before you then pass directly through the giant Ford plant at Dagenham, slaloming through two huge wind generators, then past rows of parked cars and a towering, perpendicular mountain of stacked lorry containers. From your high vantage point it looks like Matchbox cars on one side and Lego bricks on the other.

Escaping this industrial heartland you then wind through the barren, wind-lashed marshes of Rainham, a place now solely inhabited by protected species of wildlife – no doubt needing protection due to the previous occupants, a Ministry of Defence firing range. Finally you hit the first of a series of petro-chemical plants, sitting like verrucas along the northern coastline of the Thames, ending in the giant gas cylinders at Canvey Island. As a boy footballer, I was terrified of away matches on Canvey Island – frightened that at any moment the place would go up in flames. The plant at Coryton, with its giant chimneys billowing mixtures of smoke and flame up into the sky are like a scene from a *Mad Max* film. Thurrock's claim to fame is arguably the Lakeside shopping centre. I can remember the area from my childhood when it was just a dirty, great gravel pit. I think it was probably more appealing then.

All right so I'm painting a fairly bleak picture, but there's nothing wrong with this. If you've never done the journey, or seen anything similar, I would heartily recommend it, because it is a truly magnificent example of man's ability to build stuff. I *like Mad Max II.*

But why anyone would want to stay at the Thurrock Hotel is beyond me, however a hotel there indeed is and a football club is undoubtedly behind it. Naturally the two have strong connections. The club is actually just a young upstart in the grand scheme of footballing history. Only founded in 1985 and initially competing under the name of Purfleet, the club started in junior football when the dressing rooms were part of the hotel itself. Senior status was achieved when a self-contained set of changing rooms were built and the club started in the Essex Senior League, earning quick promotion into the Isthmian. In 1994 they finished runners-up to Bishops Stortford and gained promotion to the Premier Division. To quote the Thurrock website: '*In just nine seasons the club had gone from junior level playing on a roped off pitch to the premier division of one of the country's leading Non-League competitions.*'

But the advancements didn't end there, the club changed its name from Purfleet to Thurrock to attract a wider audience (*Eh? – Ed*), and then advanced to the Conference South. The team also managed to reach the First Round Proper of the FA Cup attracting the BBC TV cameras for a tie against second division Luton Town. A one-all draw at home was followed by a three-one defeat at Kenilworth Road. A year later and again into the First Round Proper the TV johnnies again pulled Thurrock out of their own velvet bag to broadcast a one-nil defeat at the hands of Oldham Athletic.

But wholesale changes of management and players in recent seasons had seen Thurrock fall onto harder times, and the tide which had swept them so high up the leagues had begun to recede. They narrowly escaped the clutches of relegation in 2006/07 and were doddering around at the bottom of the Conference South in the early exchanges of 2007/08. Ware would go into the match as the underdogs, but also with the confident swagger of a Biblical David walking out, trailing his slingshot to face the giant Philistine warrior Goliath.

I read somewhere that the origin of the word 'underdog' comes from the world of shipbuilding, when the planks of wood were sawn for ship construction. The planks were placed over a pit on wooden trestles known as 'dogs'. The senior saws man, the 'Top Dog' would stand above the pit, while the 'Under Dog' stood down below in the pit and hence got covered in all the sawdust. And while you find underdogs in all walks of life, social and political, for instance, it is the sporting reference which seems to garner the most sympathy. The rank outsider, the fortunate no-hoper. There's something about a plucky minnow that stirs the sympathetic heart strings. I'd already witnessed it on the FA Cup trail when Wembley had been totally dominated, and then when Great Wakering were being out–classed by Ware, but I'd yet to see the Hertfordshire team when the roles were reversed. This would be interesting.

Saturday September 29th, 2007:
Second Qualifying Round
Ware v Thurrock

For the first time in three matches I get the preparation right. A nice early night on Friday, a leisurely build up during Saturday morning, and come quarter to two I'm ready for my second expedition to Ware's Wodson Park. This time I have company, expert company. My dad. He's *always* paid attention to Non-League football. He knows his Isthmian from his Spartan, his United Counties from his South West Peninsula. He tells me that not only does he buy the Non League Paper every week, but that one of the paper's columnists, Stuart Hammonds, is the same Stuart Hammonds who plays in defence for Ware. I know none of this.

Dad is tagging along as he and my mother are visiting us this weekend. We drive along the A120 toward Stansted and make chit-chat. I say that I fancy Ware to win. He says it's unlikely because although Thurrock have started the season poorly, they have had a slight up turn of late with a five-nil win away to St Albans City. The chit-chat dies off as I make the correct turn this time off the M11 and we head around Bishops Stortford and go across country to Ware.

I start thinking about my relationship with my parents. Two years ago they moved from Essex down to Dorset to live a life of retirement on the south coast and explore a part of the country that they knew little about. But if the truth be told our separation started long before that. In fact you can trace it back to my decision to leave the family home in 1992. I've never been particularly giving when it comes to social interaction. Not just with them, but with anyone. And as such I've never really been proactive in keeping them up to date with what's going on in my life. Of course the big events – births, marriages, relegation, they've been among the first to know. But the incidentals of life less so. Even though we lived just twenty miles apart, contact was limited to the occasional phone call or a monthly visit. It wasn't a considered separation, it was more my apathy. I'm the polar opposite of my sister whose phone bill must make a call centre's finance manager wince.

When I first left home I moved to South Woodford in east London, still only half an hour or so away from Mum and Dad's, but it was the beginning of the end for the regular interaction between us. We never passed on the stairs anymore and we rarely shared the same dinner table. I got out of the habit of talking to them about things. This is all polarised in the car journey as both my father and I have little to talk about outside of the football, but we are comfortable enough in each other's company not to need to fill the silence.

We arrive with half an hour or so in the bag. The familiar surroundings now of Wodson Park are strangely reassuring. Both teams are on the pitch and I can point out names and faces from the Ware team. This is the fourth time I have seen them now. And for the first time they are underdogs. For the first time I know I want them to win, uncategorically. We hassle the snack bar for a cheeseburger, bacon roll and two cups of tea and then disappear into the clubhouse to check on the progress of Man City versus Newcastle.

'Do they read out the team line-ups here?' Asks my father, the veteran.

'Yes.'

'Better make sure we are outside for it then.' I nod in agreement and continue on the cheeseburger. On completion I whip off to the loo and then head outside just as the announcer starts to run through the teams. I flap around my pockets but find I've forgotten my pen. I scan around frantically, but my father is there, head cocked to one side like a hawk, pen floating over his programme, ticking here, adding a name there. I smile and walk over to him.

'Where do you want to stand?' I ask. He looks around with authority.

'Over there, by the away dugout. Let's see what they have to say.' We make our way in front of the main stand just as the protective cage from the tunnel to the pitch is dragged into place and the two teams are led out by the officials. Thurrock seem to be playing in a mismatched collection of white shirts which looks like two kits combined into one. Hardly the mark of a higher league outfit, more Sunday morning on Hackney Marshes. Ware are in the familiar blue and white striped tops and blue shorts. They disappear off to the far end of the ground and engage their group hug huddle. Thurrock look over at them and with a snigger call themselves into a replica. Is this huddling gamesmanship?

We find ourselves by the away dugout and standing again next to Lensman. He of the well-endowed Nikon. Today he has a companion with a similar sized appendage. No doubt the person from the *Mercury* who's come this time.

'You've come back for some more then,' he says.

'Couldn't stay away after the Great Wakering replay,' I replied.

'Oh yes that. I nearly tore all of my hair out.' Just then the referee, Mr Ian

Gosling, calls the two teams to order and they take their positions. This time it is Ware looking nervous as they stretch and kick out, limbering up. Thurrock look assured despite the dodgy shirts. Mr Gosling gets us underway bang on the stroke of 3pm. It takes Thurrock just three minutes to break down the Ware defence when danger man Leon McKenzie tries a volley which flashes just wide. As the Ware keeper goes to retrieve the ball I realise that their usual custodian Luke Woods is not in goal, instead it is first team coach Matt Allen. A scan through the programme reveals there is a mini-injury crisis going on at Ware at the moment – this does not bode well.

Neither does the way that Ware are playing. The team is decidedly edgy in playing higher league opposition. The swagger and sweeping passes have been replaced by raw challenges and hoofing clearances. They are defending with eleven players, but this means that whenever the ball is cleared, the Thurrock defence are able to collect, turn and start another wave of attacks. McKenzie is causing havoc in the Ware defence, fleet of foot on the ball and winning challenges in the air. When the home side get a goal kick, Allen has to step aside for right back Dave Blower to take it, another scene reminiscent of Sunday morning kids' football. The first fifteen minutes are all Thurrock.

But then one of the goal–scoring heroes from the Great Wakering replay, Chris Ellerbeck, picks up a through ball from Joe Stevens as the Ware boys make a rare foray into the Thurrock half. Ellerbeck sidesteps it around Thurrock goalkeeper David Blackmore and as the two go down the ball bounces off the knee of Thurrock defender Rob Swaine and heads goalward, slowly, slowly, slowly…

The Ware Home Support behind the goal are virtually sucking the ball into the back of the net as it trickles across the six yard box, finally making it over the line. One-nil Ware. Totally against the run of play. A roar ripples out of the tight little grandstand and from the noted suckers behind the Thurrock goal. I find myself punching the air with delight, amazed at how I could go from resenting a team one week, to such delight the next.

'We'll see how long that lasts,' says Lensman, unconvinced. Thurrock's players look offended and petulant, like teenagers shown up in front of their mates by a younger brother. But their assurance is still there and if anything when the game restarts they up the ante. It takes them just twelve minutes to respond. A spate of threatening chances lead to a corner and as the two teams mass around the Ware box I marvel at the size differences between the sides. Thurrock are much more athletic-looking than the home side. The corner is swung in and met at the far post by striker David Bryant who crashes the ball goalward towards stand-in keeper Allen who makes a half decent save at point blank range. But Bryant is following in and on hand to bundle the rebound into the back of the net. The teenager has his revenge and now it is younger brother Ware looking upset, ready to tell Thurrock that they are going to go and tell mum.

Thurrock are piling on the pressure now and Allen makes an amazing save to keep out a back header from McKenzie that was bound for the top corner. Then with about five minutes to go until half time, disaster for the home side. The ball is floated into the box and as Bryant rises to meet it he is pushed in the back by defender Michael Bardle. The referee takes no hesitation in pointing to the spot. I make no hesitation in dashing down the touchline in front of the Ware grandstand, camera flailing, to get a good position for the penalty.

But in the time it takes me to run the fifty yards, the referee has noticed the flag held aloft by his linesman signifying an offside infringement. A brief consultation between the two and Ware are reprieved by the timing of the offences. Offside given, penalty denied, and I receive a good jeering from the home support in the grandstand as I stalk back past them, camera back in its holster.

Another flurry of Thurrock corners amount to nothing as Ware ride their defensive luck and it comes as some relief to the home side when Mr Gosling blows for half time. At least here are fifteen minutes when Thurrock can't score.

'There are more goals in this game,' Dad says, as we walk around the ground towards the tea bar.

'For Thurrock,' I add as we grab a hot drink each and check on the Derby score. One-all against Bolton. A game that Derby can ill-afford to lose. We both know it, but neither say it. There is a consolation we can share. West Ham are losing one-nil at home to Arsenal. We decide to walk around to the far side for the second half and stand near to the Ware goal. After all that's where the goals are going to come from. A passing distraction occurs as we walk behind the near-end goal as an errant warm-up shot from the substitutes ricochets off the fence and just misses my dad's ducking head. His quick reactions garner a cheer from the Ware Home Support. They really are easily pleased. Just as we reach our chosen position alongside a gaggle of away fans the two teams re-emerge for the second half.

Whatever Ware manager Glen Alzapiedi said to his team at half time seems to have worked. You may remember that Alzapiedi was the man who made his team warm up through the second half at Wembley. He's obviously a man-management scholar because he's instilled a modicum of belief into his charges. For the first time in the game Ware are trying to pass their way out of trouble. And as I've seen from the earlier rounds, Ware are *definitely* a passing team. Perhaps the game is merely getting stretched as legs began to tire, but Ware are starting to *use* the midfield rather than by-pass it.

Thurrock are still a threat but Ware are playing with more belief. John Frendo has fought a tireless battle as a lone striker against a six foot five defender and in the sixty third minute he loses his marker for a second, allowing him to pick up the ball and turn. He sets off towards the heart of the Thurrock defence, jinking left and right, avoiding the tackles and digs from his pursuers. The closer he gets to the penalty box the more reluctant they are to get a foot in, but as he crosses the line and bears down on goal the threat overcomes any caution and Thurrock's Rob Swaine hurls in a challenge which misses the ball and upends Frendo. Penalty to Ware. No question and no reprieve from the line-o's flag this time.

As Joe Stevens steps up to take it, I dash down the touchline (again) to snap it. I line up my lens as Stevens lines up his sights. He shoots, I snap. His shot is saved, my snap shows keeper Blackmore diving to his right. Stevens reacts quickest of the three of us and blasts the rebound into the empty net. I end up with a second picture of a net. Again the stadium erupts with the sound of one hundred jubilant voices. Again Thurrock react like irritated teenagers. Now they have to score twice. It's so unfair.

But Ware are buoyant. The pep talk at half time put a spring in their step. The goal brings them on in leaps and bounds. The passing triangles emerge. Frendo in particular has the measure of his man-marker. His strategy in the first half had been to compete physically in the challenge. Now as the ball approaches he gives his marker a slight nudge before bouncing off him and towards the ball, creating a split second gap that is all he needs to collect and turn. As Thurrock are licking their wounds, this strategy pays off again and Frendo squirms his way to the byline before rifling the ball across the face of the goal straight into the path of substitute Kai Ramshaw who clatters it home from five yards. The grandstand ripple is now an eruption. In six minutes Ware have taken a two-goal lead. The upset is on.

Dad and I are applauding with gusto. We just catch our breath to talk about the amazing turn of events when Thurrock force a corner which is lofted over right onto the head of defender Rob Paine who thumps it home to pull one back. The jubilation turns to trepidation. In the space of two minutes the game has been turned on its head *again*. There are twenty two minutes of regulation time left. The momentum is back with Thurrock and as the ball is returned to the centre spot for the restart, you can almost see the siege engines being wheeled out of the Thurrock team coach, while Ware dig hasty fortifications around their goal.

Countdown to a giant killing. No point in worrying about injury time yet. Let's just get to the end of ninety minutes. Reinforcements are made on both sides. Thurrock substitute their attackers for attackers. Ware change their attackers for midfielders. Now is the time for Ware skipper Danny Wolf to stamp his mark on the game. Up to this point he has been fairly anonymous. Did nothing wrong, but nothing spectacularly right. Now he is barking out orders around the barricades. Putting the boot in wherever possible. Finding an extra couple of inches as he leaps to clear the ball. Feature writer Stuart Hammonds must swap his pen for his sword. Clear the lines and organise. First team coach Matt Allen, an unlikely figure between the sticks, must protect the precious one–goal lead and not put an oversized glove wrong.

Thurrock press and press. But the arrogance of the first half has been replaced by jittery nerves. The wholesale changes to the front line has left them without any sort of attacking fluency. And yet despite themselves they still pour the attacks onto the Ware goal. As each chance and half chance goes begging the home support breath sighs of relief and look at their watches. The ball ping pongs around the Ware penalty box and Hammonds sticks a head in where the boots are flying to gain a free kick and a few moments of relief.

With five minutes to go Bryant pulls the ball back to Thurrock striker Matt Bodkin but he shanks the ball wide and with that chance evaporating so too goes Thurrock's belief that they can get the equaliser. The ninety minute mark passes. We all stare at the referee imploring him to look at his watch and reach for his whistle and yet the injury time minutes pile up. Three, four, five, six. Blow man, blow. Finally after seven minutes of stoppage time he does just that, the whistle ringing out around Wodson Park to spark scenes of jubilation from the home fans and players, and signal agony and despair for the visitors. Ware have played over four hours of FA Cup football to get to this point. Thurrock have played just over an hour and a half. But despite the disparity in playing time, the agony and ecstasy is all too apparent for both teams. Because this is the magical FA Cup. And only the magical FA Cup can make people feel like this.

Ware 3 (Ellerbeck 18, Stevens 60, Ramshaw 66)
Thurrock 2 (Bryant 30, Paine 68)

Attendance: 172
Money Spent So Far: £40.50
Miles Travelled So Far: 511
Winners Receive £3,750

1986
Stonemen United

Prior to the Ware versus Thurrock match, the only time that my father and I had attended an FA Cup game together was in 1986, when the team he supported as a boy, Woodford Town, made it through the qualifying rounds to the First Round Proper and a mouth-watering clash against the nearby league side Orient.

My father was born in Leytonstone, but grew up in Woodford Green, with my grandfather, an accounts clerk at Smithfield meat market in London, and my grandmother, who raised her two children while also working as a cook in a nearby school. As a boy my father would go on a Saturday to Woodford Town's ground at Snakes Lane East as well as cycling to away matches all over east London. He says it is this early schooling in Non League football which has kept his interest in it for so many years.

My family, at least the Stoneman side of it, can trace its roots back to a small Devon village called North Molton on the edges of Exmoor near to Barnstaple. But in the late nineteenth century and for reasons I have yet to discover, my branch of the family moved up to east London, opening a butchers shop in Hackney. My grandfather was born in 1900 above the family shop in Terrace Road, which still stands today, although it is now an Asian-run convenience store. Grandad's name was Albert Robert Stoneman but he was known to everyone as Joe, again for reasons I have never been able to unearth.

He narrowly avoided call up to the first world war. His eighteenth birthday coming seventeen days after the armistice was signed at Compiègne in France. And in 1936 he married my grandmother Hilda Margaret Harris, at Holy Trinity Church in Wanstead. They settled in together at Twelve Lilian Gardens, in Woodford Green, a typical 1930s semi-detached family house with a porched entrance and bay windows.

I spent a lot of time there as a boy. Family visits at weekends and every Christmas Day. Solo visits in the school holidays when my sister and I would take it in turns to spend a week being waited on by our doting grandparents. They also looked after me when I was unexpectedly suspended from school for a fortnight as a fourteen-year-old for a firework-related offence. Actually it wasn't the letting off of the firework which saw me suspended, but the bare-faced denials I had made stating categorically that I had nothing to do with it. All was going well with my resolute defence until the box of Swan Vesta matches, which I had hastily chucked out of a classroom window as my fellow gunpowder plotters were being rounded up, was placed by the headmaster onto his desk with the flourish of a courtroom maestro. Exhibit A! Got me bang to rights.

It was always tremendous fun staying at Lilian Gardens. They had an open fire in the back room and a gas fire in the front which my Gran would toast bread on for afternoon tea. In the mornings when she was cooking the dinner and listening to the phone-ins on LBC Radio, I would sit in the back room with Grandad reading the ageing Biggles books from their bookcase while he plodded through his favourite large-print westerns from South Woodford Library. Or we would play endless games of draughts.

In the afternoon it was Granny's turn with the cards teaching me rummy and cribbage while she sat on the floor, knees doubled under her, smoking a moderately steady stream of cigarettes, the smoke from which had flecked her grey hair with a browny-yellow quif. The television would be on delivering a visual diet of the sport programmes that she loved, afternoon quiz shows, *Crown Court* and *The Sullivans*. She would always prop a folded sheet of newspaper at a right angle on the top corner of the set, held in place by a wooden ruler, to protect the screen from the glare of the afternoon sunlight which came through the net curtains of the front window. The noise from the TV was accompanied by a scratchy, old, electric clock which took pride of place on the mantelpiece above the fire, chiming out every hour and half hour mark with a strident bonging. The house always had a rich variety of smells – of roast potatoes done in lard, cakes baking, fruit stewing, cigarettes smouldering and the coal-fire burning.

Meal times had a very colonial ring about them. At eight o'clock in the morning, Granny would be delivered a cup of tea in bed by Grandad Joe along with the Daily Express, which she would read from the back to the front – a habit which I have picked up to this day. Up until the age of about ten, it was always our custom when staying over to climb up into the giant double bed and cuddle up beside her in the crisp, white sheets. Breakfast would then be taken downstairs in the kitchen. Giant crusts of bread, toasted, heavily-buttered and cut into soldiers alongside a steaming mug of tea. Grandad would be peeling the vegetables for dinner which was delivered into the back room at noon sharp. Then at four o'clock it was tea, cakes and more toast in the front room, transported from the kitchen on a giant wooden tea trolley. 'Tipple time' came at 7pm when Granny drank her customary single bottle of Guinness, each and every day, while I would delight on cream soda and a Mars bar cut into chunks. There is something about older people where they seem to spend their entire time eating – life revolving around meal times in a way that latter generations seem to find far too constrictive.

On shopping excursions to Debden or Epping we would always keep an eye out for the circular snake-like forms of the underground trains whose tracks criss-cross the area. On walks to South Woodford we would stand on the bridge across the line and wait for a train to pass, waving furiously until the driver peeped his horn. I now travel on those same train lines every day to and from work and smile when I hear the horn going as we pass that spot. Although I can't see them from within the carriage, I know that there is another happy customer up on that bridge.

The whole house was from a different era, cut adrift from the one I knew and grew up in by the great divide of the 1960s. Granny's house was pre divide, our family house in Harold Wood was post. Granny's house had a coal bunker, we had central heating. At home we slept under duvets – or continental quilts as they were known then – at Granny's you had sheets, blankets and hot water bottles placed in the bed half an hour before you went to sleep. We used toothpaste, Granny had tooth powder. Whenever a new electrical appliance was brought into Granny's, the plug had to be removed and replaced with one of the old style with three round pins. Even then you couldn't buy replacements for those plugs in the shops, so Granny's electrical appliance count was always limited to a certain ceiling dictated by plug availability.

Grandad Joe would sometimes take me to football matches when I stayed with them, either to Woodford Town or to the Orient. If it was Snakes Lane East then we would walk together at his elderly snail-like gait. If it was Brisbane Road, the home of Orient, we would go in his Austin 1100 car, at a similarly slow pace which would see scores of cars tailed-back behind us. As I grew more mature, less naive, the furious faces of the stream of overtaking motorists would see me squirming in the back with embarrassment.

Woodford Town were another (relatively) famous east London team with a long-standing history which dated back to their formation in 1884. Among their famous alumni were Fulham favourite Johnny Haynes, who played for them as a boy, and Spurs and England legend Jimmy Greaves, who finally retired from the game after a spell at the club. In 1986 Town had begun their cup run with home

Haringey Borough v Wembley... Watched by just 62 people

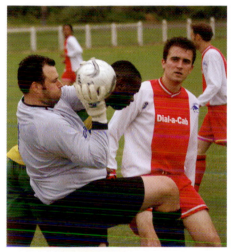

Wembley's Lee Pearce

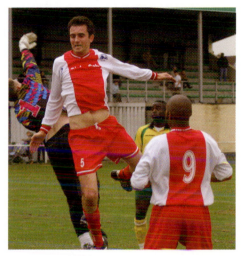

Wembley's Andrew Walker

Paul Shelton (obscured) rifled home the first goal of my Cup Odyssey

Wembley v Ware...Wembley Stadium seen from the Vale Farm terrace

Lee Pearce in control

Paul Buton opened the scoring

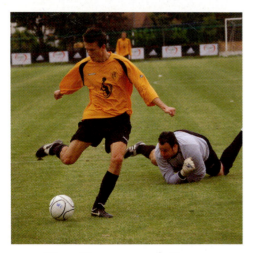

Steve Horsey rounds Pearce

All over for another year

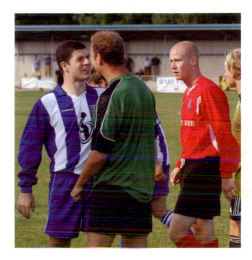

Ware v Great Wakering…There's only one way to sort this out…FIGHT!

Hythe Town v Ware… Crowds are on the up at the unique Reachfields

Tin hats for ball boys

Goalscorer Joe Stevens

Hythe Town goalkeeper Paul Hyde sees yellow late in the game

Ware v Tonbridge... Heads up Stuart Hammonds; Sam Berry misses from the spot

Chris Ellerbeck holds off an Angel and is mobbed by his team mates after scoring

Delight for the Ware players as they secure a place in the First Round Proper

Ware v Kidderminster...Wodson Park was packed to the gunnels

The Ware boys had a commemorative strip with their names on their backs

Kidderminster showed their class with a guard of honour at the end of the match

wins over Isthmian League sides Hertford Town from Division Two North and Grays Athletic from Division One. Victories on the road against Harwich & Parkeston and then King's Lynn saw them into the First Round Proper for the first and only time in their history. I doubt if anyone at the time would have believed it when the draw pitted them against Orient, a team from the Fourth Division of the Football League and only five miles away as the crow flies.

It was an occasion which my father simply could not ignore and when he invited me to go with him to the FA Cup match at Snakes Lane East it was through invoking memories of those visits with Grandad Joe that I agreed to take a day's holiday from my Saturday job in a clothes shop in Romford and tag along. Despite being thirteen days short of his eighty sixth birthday, it was an occasion that Grandad Joe was also determined to attend.

I remember that we sat in a giant temporary stand that had been erected on the far side of the pitch facing the main grandstand. We got there early to ensure a good seat and waited in the cold November air for the two teams to emerge. Both sides were well supported among a crowd two thousand eight hundred strong. It was one of those typical FA Cup matches between David and Goliath with Woodford defending in numbers and trying to catch their league opposition on the break. The solitary goal came in the eighty eighth minute and at the wrong end as far as we were concerned. A killer blow. Just as the home fans were beginning to savour the prospect of a replay at Brisbane Road, Orient defender Colin Foster – who would go on to play for West Ham and Nottingham Forest – came up for a corner and nodded home to break the Woodford Town hearts.

At the final whistle, we left the ground and walked (embarrassingly) slowly back up the hill to Twelve Lilian Gardens, three generations of Stonemans united together by the lure of this magical trophy.

October 2007
Drawn Together

After the sensational Saturday at Wodson Park it was time to find out who the wonders from Ware would be playing in the Third Qualifying Round. This meant following the draw on the Monday again and this time I would not make the same mistake as before. If the FA and the BBC were not going to provide me with any televisual tension then I would create my own.

I'd been working from home all day so had ample time to prepare. Vanessa and my parents had driven off in the morning to visit one of Dad's old clients up in Harwich and then go on for lunch. They would not be back before 5pm. The kids would be home at about half three. That gave me a clear ninety minutes. Plenty of time. I picked up Evie and Jonathan from their junior school and waited for Eden to arrive back from the seniors. This was her first year at big school and every time she walked through the door in her grown-up blazer and trousers it amazed me at how old she looked and how the years had flown by since she came into the world as our first born. She came through the front door to find me sat on a row of chairs in the hallway with Jonathan beside me and Evie grinning co-conspiratorially.

'What's going on?' She asked accusingly, her mother's daughter.

'Don't ask questions. Just go into the study with Evie. On the computer you will see the FA Cup section of the FA website. There is a link which says Third Qualifying Round Draw. Click on it. You will see the Draw for the Third Qualifying Round of the FA Cup. It will be two lists of teams. Print out two copies. One for you, one for Evie. Once you have done that come back in here and read out the fixtures. You read the home team and Evie reads the away team. Read them out slooow-ly. If I go 'Ooh', then wink knowingly at me like an old footballer.'

'What do I get to do?' Asked five-year-old Jonathan.

'*We* are audience. If I go Ooh, you go Aah.'

'Dad, this is completely stupid,' said Eden, 'where's Mum?'

'Your mother is not here right now. I am in charge. Please proceed as advised.'

'Yeah come on Eden,' added Evie, 'this is going to be fun.' The two girls disappeared into the study. Jonathan sat fidgeting next to me.

'Why don't I get to read anything?' He asked grumpily.

'Being the audience is more fun than doing the reading,' I replied. He grimaced at me showing his displeasure at my response.

'No it isn't.'

'Shh, they're coming back.' The chattering of the printer had finished and the two girls returned into the hallway.

'You stand there and you there,' I said. 'Now say the draw for the Third Qualifying Round of the Football Association Cup is as follows.'

'The draw for the Third Qualifying Round of the Football Association Cup is as follows,' they echoed in unison.

'OK Eden, read one out.'

'Harrogate Railway versus Matlock Town.'

'No, you have to read out the first name and then Evie reads out the second.'

'Dad, this is completely ridic…'

'Eden, please. You're always saying we don't do enough cool things together, well this is one of them.'

'Oh is that right?' Eden, folding her arms. Eleven-years-old and already mastered in the art of scorn. I blame the TV. And the parents.

'Just read the names out,' I growled, 'or I'll get Jonathan to do it.' Eden scowled again and continued begrudgingly.

'Harrogate Railway versus…'

'Matlock Town,' chimed in Evie, like a pint-sized game show host.

'Harrogate Town versus…' Eden, warming up a bit now.

'Clit-heroe,' said Evie with embarrassing emphasis. Who put the clit in Clitheroe?

'Barrow versus…'

'Fleetwood Town.'

'Ooh,' burst out Jonathan.

'That wasn't an Ooh,' I said, turning to him. 'We're in the northern part of the draw at the moment. We don't care about these ones. And you don't say Ooh, you say Aah and only when I say Ooh.' Jonathan grimaced at me again, then folded his arms and flumped back in his chair.

'West Auckland Town versus…'

'Bamber Bridge.' And so we continued. Traversing our way down the page of forty matches and around the country. I was just starting to lose their cartoon-length attention spans when we arrived in the south.

'Wealdstone versus…'

'Bishop's Stortford.'

'Aah,' I said with disappointment. Stortford was just ten minutes away from home and not much further from Ware. If those two had been paired off it would have been a cracking local derby.

'You don't say Aah you say Ooh,' growled Jonathan.

'Sorry.'

'Brentwood Town versus…' Yes, yes, that would be a good one.

'Staines Town.'

'Ooh.'

'Aah,' Jonathan pleased. This was more like it. The tension was building nicely. I knew that Ware were going to come out soon. But who would it be? Would they be at home or away?

'AFC Hornchurch versus…'

Yes, yes, that would be a good one too. I played at Hornchurch's ground in a cup final when I was an Under Twelve.

'Dulwich Hamlet.'

'Ooh.'

'Aah.'

'Eastbourne Borough versus…'

'Welling Town.' Hang on a minute. We seemed to have gone a bit *too* far south now. Had they missed them.

'Where's Ware?'

'Where?' The girls trilled together, laughing.

'Oh never mind that now,' I growled, 'have you missed Ware?' Evie replied by winking furiously and cocking her head at the paper.

'All right, I see,' I said, adding an Ooh for effect and getting an Aah echoed back from the boy.

'Hyyy-the Town versus…' Now Eden was the game show host.

'Ware!' Evie flung her arms up in the air excitedly.

'Ooh.'

'Aah.'

'Where's Ware,' chuckled Jonathan. A delayed reaction as he finally got the joke. It generally took him a while.

'Where's Hythe?' said Eden. Good point.

I tidied up the chairs and sent the kids off upstairs to watch the endless reruns of *The Simpsons* on Sky before slipping back into the study and logging onto the internet. I had the routine down now. First stop *Wikipedia*. It turns out that this Hythe is in Kent, right on the coast. They play at the Reachfields Stadium and are nicknamed the Reds. That should be OK then against the Blues from Ware. Hythe Town FC was formed in 1911 and until the 1970s was playing in junior football. Remember, that's not kids, but adults who aren't playing at intermediate or senior level. However in the 1980s they got a sugar daddy by the name of Tony Walton, a property developer with ambitions of bringing league football to the coastal town. He pumped in his cash and the club prospered, racing up the divisions into the Southern League. At that time the team also progressed to the semi final of the FA Vase, a game which had they won, would have seen *them* on a day out at Wembley. Unfortunately for them they didn't. Two years later, the property developer decided to resign. Starved of finance, the club freefalled into junior football and took three seasons to make it back to senior status. They now plied their trade in the Kent League (Step Five), but on the way to the clash with Ware, they had scalped local rivals Dover Athletic of the Isthmian Division One South (Step Four) in front of a huge crowd of 1,109, the third highest attendance of the round.

I then visited the Hythe website and was amazed to see that they had video highlights of this season's matches, including the game against Dover. Like I said earlier some of these websites are unbelievably good and a credit to the efforts of the dedicated bunch of webmasters who piece them together. There I was sat in the comfort of my own home in Essex, watching an obscure cup match from the south coast, and from what I saw, Hythe seemed to go about the business of taking apart their near neighbours in relatively comfortable fashion. But of all the teams that Ware could have drawn at this stage, this was definitely one of the easier options.

I fancied their chances.

Saturday October 13th, 2007:

Third Qualifying Round
Hythe Town V Ware

Waking up on match day I'm grinning with expectation from the moment my eyes open. The fortnight wait between matches adds to the anticipation and it's a relief when Saturday comes. The routine is observed. Evie and Jonathan are taken to swimming lessons. Saturday morning chores are completed. Then at mid-day it's time to pack my camera, notebook, pen and watch into my rucksack and head off. The sun is shining, England's footballers are set to play Estonia in a Euro 2008 qualifier at Wembley and the rugby boys are preparing to face France in the semi-final of the World Cup. I'm driving to a small, no doubt dilapidated stadium on the Kent coast and wouldn't swap it for any of the above.

This is the first proper away day of my travels so far. It's just under a two hundred mile round trip to the seaside in Hythe. On the M25 I see a broken-down minibus with Edgware Town written down the side and a gaggle of track-suited footballers spilling out onto the hard shoulder. My new Non-League education is such that I can pinpoint Edgware Town to the Isthmian Division One North, the same league as Ware. This may be a bad portent but nothing can spoil my good mood. Further along the M20 the Eurostar flashes past on the way to Paris adding to the exotic flavour of the day. All right so I'm easily pleased. And anyway it could have been going to Brussels.

The journey is motorway heavy. M11, M25, M20 and then finally a twiddly A-road bit into Hythe. I approach the outskirts of the town by dropping down a long, winding hill and then sat-nav my way to Fort Road and the Reachfields Stadium. As I enter the complex, a track-suited steward is directing cars into neat rows on the gravel car park. He takes one look at my Land Rover and sticks me away from the others into some long bumpy grass. Cheers mate. I exit the car, shoulder my backpack and make my way to the entrance.

Reachfields Stadium from the outside is unassuming. A concrete wall affair with four sets of skeletal floodlights poking over the top and the ubiquitous mobile phone radio mast. I enter through the turnstile and emerge into the arena behind one of the goals. Reachfields from the inside is still unassuming. Both teams are warming up on the pitch, which while green and lush, has some undulating ripples which could be testing of a true bounce. On two sides of the ground run terraces of concrete and corrugated iron. The rust discolouration merging with Hythe Town's red paint scheme. Behind the far goal is a row of fir trees and on the right-hand flank of the ground is a red two-tier grandstand. If you can call it a grandstand mind. There are precious few seats on the lower level while the top tier is a row of balconied boxes overlooking the pitch. Along the touchline towards me is the obligatory burger bar and a set of toilets. I take advantage of both.

I buy a cheeseburger and a Coke and take a seat in the lower level of the grandstand to scoff and scan the Hythe Town programme. Nice layout, printed in two colours, but with only a few interesting articles. The Manager's and Chairman's Notes both praise the victory over Dover Athletic in the previous round and bemoan a five-nil gubbing they received at the hands of Arundel in their following league match. An FA Cup hangover if ever I heard one. At that moment the clatter of heavy-calibre gunfire ricochets around the ground making me almost drop my Coke. What the hell was that? I stare around the stadium at the low number of people who are milling about. No one seems in the least surprised by the gang, gang, gang, gang, gang noise which continues with another volley, apparently coming from the far side of the ground. I get up and decide to investigate, walking around the top end of the pitch.

On the far terrace opposite the grandstand there is a door, presumably left open to allow Row Z-style defensive clearances to be retrieved. Through the door is a sign – *Warning: Ministry of Defence Firing Range*. Beyond the portal I can see a large military complex although any sign of the range itself is obscured by some tall warehouse-like buildings. Gang, gang, gang, gang, gang, clatter the big guns again, the reports echoing off the grandstand. I half expect to see ballboys wearing steel helmets and flak jackets.

Turning back towards the pitch I can see a housing estate beyond the stadium and further still the hills in the distance which the main road into Hythe runs down. It would be rather picturesque were it not for the well-weathered state of the stadium, and rather tranquil were it not for the constant rattle of gunfire. Still in an age of cookie-cutter professional stadiums (Southampton, Derby, Leicester…), it's certainly a unique setting for ninety minutes of FA Cup action. A flock of seagulls cawing above the pitch reinforce the seaside feel, as they wheel about in the bluest of blue skies, not a cloud in sight.

With half an hour still to go before kick off I decide to investigate the inside of the grandstand, as I can see people starting to peer out of the upper deck. As I walk around the ground again, the other way this time to complete a full circuit, I watch Ware go through their warm ups. It is funny how different they look from a fortnight ago. Before the Thurrock match they were edgy and anxious, acknowledging their status as the significant underdog. Today they are once again playing the part of Goliath and it sits lightly on their shoulders. They know they *should* and probably *will* win. They go through their preparations with a laugh and a joke, an inherent confidence.

Passing the tea bar I approach the grandstand and walk up a flight of iron steps which are tacked onto one end taking me to the top level. Through the door and into a clubhouse which features a bar, dartboard, pool table and *Sky Sports* blaring out of a TV. On the wall beside the door is a notice board pinned with newspaper reports of Hythe's recent successes including the win over Dover Athletic. From reading the reports it is obvious that Hythe's danger man is a certain Buster Smissen with eleven goals already this season. I'm pondering how parents could give someone a name like Buster when a voice hails me.

'Ahh, it's the lunatic photographer from Braintree.' I turn and peer into the bustling bar and spot Lensman sitting with some of the other Ware officials. I nod an acknowledgement and walk over.

'Hello, how's it going?' I ask.

'Good thanks.'

'You must fancy a win today.'

'Yes we should do.' The Ware officials are all looking up at me expectantly and I cast around my head for something else to say.

'Did you hear those gunshots out there?' I ask, pretending not to know. 'What's that?'

'It's a firing range, apparently they don't normally shoot up this end, but today they are.' I nod sagely and try and think of something else to say. The Ware officials are getting bored and starting to talk among themselves. Lensman is giving me a polite smile. It's a strange encounter. We've gone from being strangers to almost good friends purely because of the emotional journey that Ware's cup run has taken us on, and the fact that we both like taking pictures from the same part of the ground. Are we friends though? It's something strange – but it *is* a relationship, of sorts. The first date at Wodson Park against Great Wakering, a second at the rollercoaster replay and then things blossoming in the heart-stopping Thurrock slaying. But actually we are still complete strangers with little to say to each other beyond this cup run. I don't even know his name. When he talks about Ware's other matches I fob him off with a nod as I haven't seen, heard or read anything about the team in the days between our cup dates. I give him a 'see you later' and edge awkwardly away, deciding to depart from the clubhouse to avoid any further exchanges. I walk past the Ware Travelling Support who are on hand sporting their club colours and pints of lager. As usual we eye each other cautiously. I can see them thinking that my face looks familiar, but they don't quite know if I'm one of them or not. I don't think I am. Yet.

Back outside I head towards the goal beside the entrance and take up a place sitting on the terrace as the minutes count down. The announcer crackles onto the loudspeaker and gives out the teams. Of course Hythe are completely new to me, the only name registering is Buster the Danger Man, but I appraise the Ware line up and make note of the changes that manager Glen Alzapiedi has made.

There's no place for the hero of the last round John Frendo because of the suspension he received from being sent off against Great Wakering and for some reason Danny Spendlove, a marauding pirate of a player with long, flowing blond hair held off his face by a headband, is only on the bench. His replacement in the side is Danny Gudgeon. Just then the two teams emerge from the clubhouse and make their way out onto the pitch led by the referee Mr C Brook and his two assistants. The Ware players clap to the Ware Travelling Support as they ring out a 'Come on, Ware Boys' and then group up in their pre-match huddle. Mr C Brook whistles for the captains and we get ready to go.

The two teams change ends and the Ware Travelling Support hastily move from the halfway line to the terrace behind the Hythe goal in order to pour their own brand of poison into the ear of the home keeper Paul Hyde. He looks like a very easy target for them with rugged looks and long, bleached, blond hair, straight out of an eighties rock super group. There's a slight delay when for some reason a corner flag falls down and Ware keeper Luke Woods has to run over to pick it up, and then we are underway – again.

If you look back at my transient allegiances throughout this FA Cup campaign it has been fairly heavily-biased towards the underdogs. Today this would be Hythe, but today I have no such emotion. I want a Ware win. The more clinical then all the better. I get the feeling that Hythe upped their game against Dover because of the eleven hundred crowd and the south coast bragging rights, but now they must be dismissed as a footnote in the cup journey. Forty three seconds in and a booking for Joe Stevens for tangling with goalkeeper Hyde and you wonder if this is going to be so.

The first ten minutes unfold. Different to anything I've seen so far. Both teams are contesting in all parts of the pitch, but Ware look as though they have slightly the upper hand. But they can't convert this slight dominance into any sort of attractive, attacking play. The Ware passing triangles have not been brought on the team coach today, possibly because of the absence of Frendo as the furthest forward point of the triangle. In fact it is Hythe who go closest in this period with a Simon Rainbow header which sails over the bar three minutes in. Then after a quarter of an hour, Joe Stevens lines up to take a free kick with his left foot from the right hand side of the pitch. One of the Ware officials close by, resplendent in his Ware tie and blazer, urges him on from behind the barrier.

'Go on Joe, you can stick it in from there.' Stevens is obviously ear wigging. Rather than loft in a cross, he curls one. Fast and with a bemusing last minute dip, it evades the despairing hand of Hyde and nestles into the far corner. Absolute cracker. Unfortunately I had my camera trained on the melee of players in the box. Stevens' shot had also caught me out.

'Did you get it?' Enquires Ware Official of me, grinning broadly.

'No.'

'Did you hear me though? I told him to do that.' Ware Official is taking as much pride in the free kick as Colin Montgomery's caddie would after a nine-iron out of the rough and onto the green. I'm watching Hythe's reaction to the goal. It's not good. They too believe in the inevitable outcome of this match. They know they will have to huff, they know they will have to puff, but ultimately the Ware house will not blow down and the first foundation has just been cemented in. Shoulders are already slumping dejectedly. They slump further still after twenty minutes when a slide rule pass from striker Chris Ellerbeck frees left back-cum-midfielder Michael Bardle, who deftly rounds a flailing advance from Hyde and then slots home from the left hand side of the box. Two-nil Ware without *really* breaking a sweat.

Generally it's about now when I start feeling sorry for the team on the receiving end and I start to feel my allegiance wavering. But today it is rock solid and I realise as the first half progresses that I have become brainwashed into the Ware cause. I've left the no man's land of impartiality and jumped into the Ware trench. And now whether it is a cakewalk or a bloody last stand I'm with the boys in blue and white stripes. I even consider going and standing with the Ware Travelling Support, but the low autumnal sun means the light's wrong down that end for a good snap. I do echo the sentiment of the WTS however, with a good barracking jeer when Hythe striker Roy Godden goes in the book for dissent two minutes later. I'm also royally pissed off when completely against the run of play, Luke Woods spills a Hythe free kick from the right into the path of that man Smissen, who makes no mistake in reaching Buster's dozen with a drilled shot from five yards. Two-one. From a half which offered the spoils of dominance without playing outside themselves, Ware have contrived to let the home team make a game of it.

Mr C Brook blows up for half time and I trudge with mixed feelings around to the tea bar for a reviving brew. Standing in the queue my thoughts drift towards the possible outcome. This is Ware's game to lose not Hythe's to win, but what about a replay on Tuesday night? That would be an extra game to slip in. Extending the adventure. However to get to a replay would mean the scores would need to be level (obviously) and that could lead to a sticky last ten minutes if the home team get their dander up. And what if they actually got a winner? No, return to the original game plan. A clinical win by the sea and then bugger off home never to return. I suspect that at this point in time the Ware Manager Glen Alzapiedi is probably saying exactly the same thing to his troops in the changing room, although no doubt he hasn't had to queue up for his tea, nor has it cost him fifty pence.

Fifteen minutes later as the teams trot back out I'm *still* waiting for my cup of tea and wondering how the elite Hythe catering crew managed when all those Dover Athletic fans descended on Reachfields a fortnight ago. The referee gets us underway and I have to spend the first five minutes of the half twisting around my fellow queue-mates to get a gawk at the game. I'm delighted to see that Spendlove the Pirate has come on for Steve Horsey, no doubt because the latter missed an open goal just before half time. And I'm also delighted a). to finally get my tea, and b). when Stevens is upended in the Hythe box and Mr C Brook points without hesitation to the penalty spot.

I'm in the wrong position to get a good picture and carrying by now what has become a sacred brew, so there is no frantic dashing for camera position and I sit back to watch Stevens step up, dust himself down, and restore the two-goal lead. But Joe hits a powder puff penalty to the keeper's left and Hyde is going that way. Straight into his arms. Penalty saved. That's the third penalty save I've seen in nine matches. I'm not sure whether that stat is interesting or not, but there you go, interpret it as you will. Needless to say that like the WTS who are now standing in the lee of the fir trees I'm not best pleased. It's things like this that turn matches. The open goal missed, the gifted penalty wasted. The next thing you know the opposition will regain heart and that's not part of the clinical win by the sea and then bugger off home strategy.

I start to walk back around the ground to see if my presence at the Hythe end of the pitch will inspire a Ware goal and just as I reach the far end, it's déjà vu all over again when Ellerbeck this time is upended in the Hythe box and Mr C Brook has no hesitation. Joe Stevens hesitates however and (my) man of the match Sam Berry quickly picks up the ball and the penalty-taking duties and shapes up for the spot kick. Meanwhile Ellerbeck and Hyde have both gone into the book for some post penalty infringement handbags. Hyde is looking furious as he faces down Berry the penalty taker, but Sam has his eyes on the netting and his right-footed drive into the corner sets it rippling. Three-one.

It looks like game over to me so I pack away camera and notebook and saunter slowly to the far end of the ground. Close to the exit ready for the quick dart. Hythe captain Ian Ross picks up a second yellow card and first red for a clumsy challenge as the game drifts into injury time and finally Mr C Brook brings things to a close. A clinical win by the sea, now time to bugger off home.

Hythe Town 1 (Smissen 34)
Ware 3 (Stevens 15, Bardle 20, Berry (pen) 79)

Attendance: 236
Money Spent So Far: £50.50
Miles Travelled So Far: 693
Winners Receive £5,000

1987
Twin Obsessions

The following chapter comes with a parental warning. If you're my parents then you may want to skip to the next section because this part contains scenes of a sexual nature. You may cringe reading it, I may cringe knowing you've read it. But by 1987, the year when Spurs would once again pay a visit to Wembley for an FA Cup Final, I'd discovered the other of man's twin obsessions. Football and girls.

The reader may be forgiven for thinking that a Tottenham visit to Wembley would find me in bullish mood but unfortunately by then Spurs had become just another team to me. I had already made my third and final (so far) football team defection. At some point in the mid eighties I had rather bizarrely found myself following my father into the family profession of being a Derby County supporter. It's another one of those irrational footballing idiosyncrasies. I'd never *been* to Derby, we weren't *from* Derby, but somehow the plight of a fallen giant of Midlands football had lured me away from the glitz and glamour of White Hart Lane. Here's the rationale behind it.

The first ever league match that I had been to see was on the 19th of January 1980 when Dad had taken my sister Sarah and me, at our request, to Highbury to watch Liam Brady and Arsenal play. Back when we were staunch Gunnerites. The opposition? Well naturally it was a certain club from the midlands. The result? A two-nil win for the home side which was topped off for me by Liam Brady getting the match ball stuck behind one of the AFC crests on top of the stand behind the goal.

My second league match attended came in May of that same year. Dad and I travelled to Norwich's Carrow Road to watch his beloved Rams as they struggled with the threat of relegation. This time I had no loyalties towards the home side, so I commiserated with him as Derby slipped to a four-two defeat and the Rams supporters' chants of 'We'll be back in Eighty One' echoed around the ground. Only they never did come back in 1981. Or 1982 for that matter. In fact things went from bad to worse. Being a Derby supporter had become a miserable existence, something that a young boy from Essex would never countenance, especially with my magical run of consecutive cup finals. It never even *occurred* to me to be a Derby fan.

But then I moved into my 'wilderness years' as far as watching live league football was concerned. My next game attended was not until August of 1984 when I travelled to Roots Hall to watch Southend play Crystal Palace. And I only went then because my Sunday morning team had been invited to be ball boys. For historical accuracy I got my one and only touch of the match ball in the eighty second minute thanks to Southend's woeful finishing.

But then two things happened. The first was the 1984 launch of the film *Ghostbusters*. A movie which touched me immensely. You can keep your Oscar winners, your art house classics, give me Bill Murray and some dubious CGI graphics any day of the week. The second momentous occasion was a slow and steady galvanisation of Derby County under the stewardship of the great Arthur Cox, who took the Rams from the third to the first division in consecutive seasons.

I slowly became aware that my pessimistic father was getting increasingly optimistic as the Division Two title race hotted up at the end of the 1986/87 season. He would sit studiously in front of the teleprinter on a Saturday afternoon at a quarter to five, before emitting a 'Yeah-Hess' as the Rams posted another victory. It was incredibly compelling and before long I was sat alongside him, waiting for that one single moment of release as the letters jabbered up on the screen and Derby banked another three points.

And when *Ghostbusters* and Derby County's promotion converged before me, there was no turning back. After the Second Division Championship was clinched, BBC2 released a documentary called *'The Rams Are Back'* charting the team's glory days under Brian Clough and Dave Mackay, the implosion following boardroom disputes and near financial bankruptcy and the recent meteoric rise of Cox's side, which in the words of the programme's narrator, *'were laying the ghosts of the past to rest'*. This was a cue for Ray Parker Junior's titular movie theme as a backing track for a montage of free-scoring Derby highlights with Phil Gee and Bobby Davison hammering home goal after goal. The combined propaganda had an incredibly profound effect on me, but then again as anyone who knows me will vouch, I am an incredibly shallow individual. Glenn Hoddle's shirt was consigned to the back of the wardrobe, a Derby shirt was procured and I followed Cox's 'Pippins' into the first division. This meant that my *next* league game attended, on October 3rd 1987, was West Ham versus Derby at Upton Park. So if you eliminate the Southend match, where I was effectively attending as a member of ground staff, then my live football-watching history has always been with Derby County. I rest my case.

So that's one obsession dealt with now on to the other. I can pinpoint the occasion when having a 'girlfriend' became more than just playground slander. It was early in the second year seniors, when we were travelling on a coach from Upminster to London for a school visit to the Science Museum. Our class had commandeered the rear seats and very quickly, once the coach was in motion, we switched from a boy-boy, girl-girl arrangement, to boy-girl, boy-girl. My transition from naivety to maturity happened at a set of traffic lights on the A127 near Ardleigh Green.

The lights went red and the coach stopped.

'Go on,' crowed one scholar, 'I dare you to give her a kiss.'

'All right,' I said, looking at the girl beside me for implicit permission. We leaned together, my lips puckered but firmly closed, eyes shut anticipating a peck and then retreat. Before I knew what was happening, her tongue had slipped between my lips. I recoiled in shock.

'Oh blimey, I didn't know we were having a Frenchy session,' the words blurted out of my mouth before I had a chance to realise their social impact. The back of the coach peeled off into hearty guffaws of mocking laughter. I quickly realised the only defence for my immature *faux-pas* would be attack and lunged at my companion again, eager to silence the jackals around me. Our lips came together, no holds barred this time.

The lights went green and the coach pulled away.

The rest of that journey to Kensington was a series of frenzied embraces. Quite what the teachers were doing at the front of the coach I'm not sure, as I was engulfed in the unchartered sensations and smells. I spent four, frustrated hours at the Science Museum frantically killing time before the coach journey home again with its promise of hitherto forbidden pleasures. It wouldn't be fair to name the girl who suffered my Octopus-like maulings, but suffice it to say she holds a special place in my heart for giving me that green light.

Lesson Two came in the promiscuity of the annual school discos. In the build up to these events, different couples began to pair off through a series of secret assignations. Love-letters would be discreetly dispatched or teenage Cyrano de Bergerac go-betweens engaged. The code of practice was to ask a girl if you could take them to the disco. A negative reply meant that either some other young buck had got in first, or that you were plug ugly. A 'yes' was the green light. Of course you didn't *actually* take them to the disco, we were all brought and picked up in cars by our parents, but when the first bars of *Zoom* by Fat Larry's Band, or *True* by Spandau Ballet stole out of the loudspeakers, it was on.

But opportunities to improve one's techniques at the school disco were limited by the interference of the headmaster's secret police, the form tutors, who would rove the perimeter of the dance floor yanking juvenile couples out from under the piano and from behind the curtains. Depending on the teacher in question you were either looking at a stern talking to, a clip round the ear, or a visit to the headmaster's study, the latter particularly if either of the protagonists' necks looked as though they'd suffered a nasty dose of bubonic plague.

Between 1986 and 1989, during his term as Secretary of State for Education, the Right Honourable Kenneth Baker introduced a series of in-service training days for teachers which became known as 'Baker Days'. And through these non-pupil school days the Conservative politician should be applauded for improving levels of sexual education amongst an entire generation. Baker Days became Lesson Three. Given a parentless week day when we did not have to attend school, a group would assemble at the house of some child whose mother and father were at work. We would crowd around in a circle on the floor and play the familiar parlour game of Spin The Bottle, only one with an adult theme where the forfeit would be either a kissing dare or to remove an item of clothing.

These teenage kicks all helped to break the natural barriers between the boys and girls in our year until the stage when more serious, semi-permanent relationships began to emerge. My own 'first love' was with a girl in my year who sent a dispatcher to summon me after home economics with the magical mantra: '*I know someone who fancies you.*' Negotiations continued through the lunch period and geography, so that by the time the school bell rang at the end of double maths, I found myself walking her home.

A doorstep kiss and a hallway clinch later and we had agreed to meet on Saturday at the Odeon Cinema in Romford for the matinee viewing of *Top Gun*. My sister Sarah, by then eighteen and four years older than me, took great delight in driving me to my first official date. At last her irritating, younger brother was starting to provide some interest. When I accepted a cigarette from her in the car she almost gagged with excitement.

The first date was declared a success and was followed by further excursions to the pictures. I discovered that *Night of the Living Dead II* and other such horrors were particularly powerful at invoking a desire to cuddle up close together and so we worked our way through the Wes Craven back catalogue on video.

The relationship ebbed and flowed as these things are wont to do when you are that age. But by and large we stuck together to present ourselves as something of an item.

Our relationship was serious enough that it would have caused quite a stir if she had ever found out what I got up to during the 1987 FA Cup Final between Tottenham and Coventry. On the big day in May of that year I had travelled with my parents to a family wedding down in Devon, held in a small village called Poltimore close to the M5 as it approaches Exeter. While my father's descendents all come from north Devon, my mother was born in Sidmouth on the south Devon coast and the small towns and villages around the Exeter area are riddled with relatives.

I forget which two were tying the knot, but I do remember most of the men attending were grumbling because of the scheduling snafu which had left them in best suits on a cup final day. The ceremony took place in the morning with the reception set for the early afternoon and then a disco in the evening. I was dressed to kill in a sharp, nearly-new suit that my mum had bargained from a charity shop and a pair of authentic Ray Ban sunglasses, either going for the Tom Cruise in *Risky Business* look, or more likely Dan Aykroyd in *The Blues Brothers*. The black of the glasses beautifully juxtaposed against my Modern Romance-style, flicked, blond hair. Babe magnet.

However *amour* was far from my mind as I perched on a pew watching two vaguely-recollected relatives being brought together in front of God. But when I sat down to lunch at the reception, I clocked a young waitress who could be no more than a year older than me and who had clocked me clocking her and was clocking me right back.

Sat beside me, my meddling sister's antennae were sizzling as I got an extra large portion of butter and the pick of the bread rolls. Unbeknownst to me she made some discreet enquiries through one of my cousins and proceeded to adopt the role of Cilla Black on *Blind Date*. Dinner came and went, speeches were made, telegrams read, and the knowing winks were flowing as freely as the toasting champagne. Eventually there was a lull in the proceedings, as the women went to attend the bride and the men went in search of a TV to watch Spurs take on Coventry.

For a brief instant the ghosts of Hoddle, Ardiles and Villa flickered before me. I was in two minds. Clive Allen was by then playing for Tottenham and was close to scoring fifty goals in a single season. But the lure of a different kind of away victory was too much for me, and with an appropriate shove in the right direction from Cilla, I snuck out of the reception to the yard behind the village hall where the empty beer kegs and soda bottles were stacked in high, maze-like columns. Waiting for me down one keg alley was my waitress.

That should have been enough. But no. Fifteen minutes of activity later, I was like the cat who had the cream and arrogantly, *naively*, paraded back into the reception with my new friend on my arm. The disco was by now in full flow, my sister and our harpy cousins squealing with delight at my chosen course of action. Fat Larry's Band came on and I was history. I don't know if you've ever *got off* with someone on a dance floor as a fifteen-year-old, in front of your parents, uncles, aunts, cousins, second cousins, unknown cousins… I don't recommend it. I have *never* been able to live it down. Still today I sometimes wake up bathed in sweat, having just dreamt that on my death bed, my ageing sister walks into my room to pay me some last respects and then says: 'Do you remember that time you snogged that girl in front of Mum and Dad?'

For the record Spurs lost. I blame myself. The timing of the decisive Gary Mabbutt own goal correlates directly with the introduction of *Zoom* into the DJ's set.

October 2007
An Afternoon In The Drawing Room

Another result for Ware meant another draw. This time the Third Qualifying Round and this time I had the whole family on board. Vanessa was slowly, patiently coming around to the fact that this was becoming one of my more hardy obsessions. She has had twelve years of married life to deal with both them and me. I was concerned that the crunch would come later on when the distances and prices became more significant, but in the mean time I was making hay.

When I'd returned from Hythe on the Saturday night, my three children had swarmed around me clamouring to know both what the result had been and also when the next draw was taking place. Even Doubting Eden had been interested. It had been impossible to hide their enthusiasm from Vanessa and so the story of the mocked-up draw from the previous round had come to her attention. As Evie spilled out the details I had watched her bemused face take in what had happened before she turned her attention on me and said simply, 'You're mad.'

Nevertheless, when the chairs were arranged in the hallway for the second time, on the Monday after the Hythe match, we had a surprise new Master of Ceremonies. Jonathan and I were sat down waiting for the girls to come out of the study with their printouts. But to my astonishment they were lead out by their mother keeping the straightest of faces, determined to play along. She looked like a referee flanked by two juvenile linesmen. Before I could step in to organise she held up her hand to shush me.

'The draw for the Fourth Round of the FA Cup is as follows…'

'Fourth *Qualifying* Round,' I interjected, to the briefest of glares.

'The Fourth Qualifying Round of the FA Cup is as follows…'

'The *draw* for the Fourth Qualifying Round…' again I interrupted with an apologetic grimace. I was treading a fine line between the appropriate protocol and a whack round the chops. She gave me one of those looks which said, 'I'm throwing you a bone here so pipe down.' The kids were stifling giggles as their mother stumbled on the correct words.

'The *draw* for the Fourth *Qualifying* Round of the FA Cup is as follows…'

Up stepped her two linesmen, Eden and Evie.

'Evesham United versus…'

'Halifax Town.'

'Ooh.'

'Daddy, that's not an Ooh,' growled Jonathan. The boy was right. He'll go far.

'Corby Town versus…'

'Droylsden!' Evie hopping gleefully around again.

'Workington versus…'

'Boston United!' Blimey, that was a bullet dodged. The last thing I wanted to do was to have to go to Cumbria. No offence to my Cumbrian-based reader intended of course.

'Ooh.'

'Aah,' Jonathan responded giving me his big moon eyes. Vanessa looking on benignly at father and son. The love of her life, and me.

'Harrogate Railway versus…'

'Harrogate Town.'

'Aah.'

'Daddy you Ooh not Aah,' said Jonathan crossly.

'Oh come on that's a complete fix. Harrogate Railway versus Harrogate Town? Out of *all* the teams that could have come out?' I looked up at Vanessa for support but she was shaking her head at me with a puzzled look on her face. I could read her thoughts. I could see she was asking herself the question just *how* did she got involved in all this? But the kids were enjoying themselves as they rattled confidently through the fixtures. Everyone was smiling and laughing. Jonathan and I were Ooh-ing and Aah-ing. It was going perfectly. Vanessa looked back at me and for the first time she gave me a look of acceptance.

'This is actually quite good,' she said to me.

'Sssh!' Hissed Evie. 'It's coming…'

'Ware versus…'

'Tonbridge Angels.'

'Who?'

'Aah.'

★

So... Tonbridge Angels. Never heard of them. Didn't even know if they were better or worse than Ware. Bit of a silly name though, almost but not *quite* as bad as those weird Welsh teams like NEWI Cefn Druids. I paid another visit to Sir Tony of Kempster, patron saint of the Non-League, to find out the gen. Between him and *Wikipedia* I mugged up. Tonbridge played in the Isthmian League Premier, so they were a division higher than Ware, but their season was not bearing much fruit and there were only fifteen positions between the two teams. Ware were at home, Ware had momentum, while Tonbridge would be away and shackled with the pressure of being the favourite.

But and this is a big but, Tonbridge had a not-so-secret weapon. And his name was John Main. The Tonbridge website was full of praise for their deadly striker so I decided to look him up on *Wikipedia* and discovered that he was '*a Benedictine monk and priest born in 1926 who presented a way of Christian meditation which utilised the practice of a prayer-phrase or mantra*'. At this point I figured I may have the wrong man, so checked my case of mistaken identity and found a crucial spelling mistake. The lad I was after was Jon Main, no 'h' in Jon.

The appropriate Main was born in Erith in Kent and played for a number of junior teams in the area before joining VCD Athletic and then Cray Wanderers, where he helped them win promotion from the Kent League. In 2005 he scored sixteen goals in under twenty games before signing for the Angels. A second season with Tonbridge saw him bag forty four goals in all competitions leading to trials with Wolves, Swindon Town and M.K. Dons, although amazingly all of these amounted to nothing and he re-signed for Tonbridge this year.

Main's position as chief goal scorer was a notable one. Particularly when considering the illustrious boots that he was filling. Because among the ranks of former Angels was no less than Geordie net-finding legend Malcolm Macdonald. They could also claim Aston Villa maestro Ron Saunders as an old boy. The team was originally formed in 1947 as just plain old Tonbridge FC, but they played their home games at a stadium known as the Angel Ground, a former cricket ground named after a nearby pub. You could see where this one was going and it was one of the things that I had grown to love about the whole Non-League scene. Every ground, every goalpost, every penalty spot was steeped in its own unique history. The hopes and dreams of chairmen, boards, managers and players from every layer of the sport, be they Saturdays, Sundays or mid-week five-a-sides. Every club was underpinned by a basic devotion common to all. It was fundamental to our lives. Football was the national sport, despite the Premiership, despite the England national team, despite 1966 and all that, but because we lived, played and dreamt about twenty two men hammering a ball around a pitch at every level you could imagine.

The history of the Angels was no different to a number of clubs that I had researched for this piece. Kicked off by a bunch of enthusiasts. Yo-yoing between leagues, in this case the Southern and Kent Leagues, before being elbowed sideways by re-organisation of the pyramid system into the Isthmian. Sometimes success, sometimes failure. Disputes over grounds, eviction from grounds (this time the Angel Ground falling foul to property developers) and then negotiations with the local authority to find a piece of land to call home, in Tonbridge's case the Longmead Stadium.

Not that I ever intended to visit Longmead Stadium. Why would I need to? The draw had actually been quite kind to Ware and I fully expected the Wodson Aces to clip the Angels' wings and book their historic place in the First Round Proper. Main man Main or not.

Saturday October 27th, 2007:
Fourth Qualifying Round
Ware V Tonbridge Angels

'You're in a good mood this morning.' I've just brought Vanessa breakfast in bed and been humming my way around the bedroom getting dressed.

'Yep,' I reply, without giving her a reason. Resisting the urge to scream 'BECAUSE IT'S THE FOURTH QUALIFYING ROUND TODAY...' and then marching around the room shouting 'O-LAY, O-LAY, O-LAY, O-LAY, WARE BOYS, WARE BOYS...' But every quiet minute I have to myself I am thinking about the match. What will happen? Can we win it? If we win, will we get the dream ticket of Leeds or Forest in the next round? In equal measure comes the doubts. What will it be like if we lose? What happens if Tonbridge gets that dream tie? I realise that without a shadow of a doubt I have become a Ware fan. It's an amazing transformation. It has snuck up on me. I had no real intention of developing any major allegiance with any team on my journey to Wembley, not to *this* level anyway. Not the kind of support where it *hurts* to think of what will happen if the team lose. And three matches ago, in the Great Wakering replay, I was actually rooting in the second half for a Rovers equaliser not a Ware win. But something has happened over the last month and I am definitely now a blue.

Or am I?

I haven't been to any other Ware matches apart from the FA Cup ones, I haven't really been following their other fixtures or results that closely. The Ware Travelling Support would no doubt consider me a fair-weather fan who only turns up for the 'glamour' FA Cup games. They would mock me for missing the five-one drubbing suffered at Bury Town in September, or the two-one Isthmian League Cup defeat at Walton Casuals in midweek. There is only one way to be a true fan of a team it seems and that is to attend every match in their history, including the ones which took place before you were born, or at least to have a doctor's note excusing your absence.

So I guess that puts me down for the Ware (FA Cup) level of membership rather than a full platinum member. But whichever way you stack it up, my stomach is churning with a powerful combination of nerves and excitement as I set off for Wodson Park at half past one.

No wrong turns, no diversions, the car is on auto-pilot now heading to my spiritual (FA Cup) home. The sky is heavy with thick grey clouds and a light drizzle is every now and then drifting across the windscreen. This is the first day match which will be played in proper football conditions. The smell of turning leaves and liniment. Turf which takes a stud nicely and delivers a true to soggy bounce. A crisp chill which leaves you blowing in your hands at half time as you line up for a pie and Bovril. The Indian Summer which resided over the first seven matches of the cup run has left the reservation for good.

On arrival at the ground I am preparing to swing left into my usual (FA Cup) parking space when I'm confronted by an orange-jacketed marshal. Another first for the cup run. Proper car parkers. He directs me off towards a section of the car park which is well away from the ground. Surely there can't be *that* many people coming? But indeed even when I drive to the furthest section of the leafy car park there are already legions of cars lined up and I struggle to find a space. I reflect ruefully that this is probably the first of many transport problems that I will face from here on in. The days of turning up with fifteen minutes to go and finding a parking space by the stadium entrance have also left the reservation.

If attendances are on the up then so too are admission prices. It appears that the Fourth Qualifying Round has a two pound surcharge on top of previous visits to Wodson Park. I hand over my eight pound entry, buy the one pound fifty programme and decline a strip of one pound raffle tickets. Through the turnstile and Wodson Park is bubbling with bodies. I've not yet seen a ground so busy. People are already queuing twenty deep for the tea bar, the main bar is stacked with people and the smell of beer. They've even opened up the extension to the bar for the first time. Lots of small boys are running around in football kits and boots, possibly some pre-match or half time entertainment.

I decide not to join the snack bar queue but quickly read through the programme paying closest attention to the team sheets. There is no Joe Stevens for Ware for some reason. I decide to seek out Lensman to find out why. As I walk past the main grandstand I see a trio of people in the press box with headphones and mics and climb up the steps to investigate.

'Hello who are you with?' I ask boldly.

'BBC Radio Kent,' comes the reply, just as one of the group is thrust a sheet of paper by another man who climbed the steps behind me.

'Is that the team sheets?' I ask, 'mind if I have a look?' I get a nod and hastily compare the line ups to those in the programme. It's confirmed then that Joe Stevens is out. That's a blow. I descend out of the stand and walk around the pitch watching the two teams warm up. Tonbridge look athletic, all bar their main threat. I recognise the prolific Jon Main from his picture on the Tonbridge web site. Main is whippet thin and turns to salute the Tonbridge Travelling Support who have been calling out his name.

I'm feeling *really* nervous now. It's the feeling that I get before big sporting occasions where I have skin in the game, like a Derby County play-off final or an important match that I have played in. It's the same feeling that I used to get when I was a teenager and getting ready to go out on a first date. Or the feeling I had when my first romance came to a juddering, unrequited end. After twelve years of marriage to Vanessa, that feeling has had few opportunities to bubble up, only after some monumental cock up in the relationship, usually generated by me. It's a strange combination between desire and trepidation. A desperation for things to go *my* way. Just this once. It's the same sensation I had when Arsenal were beaten by West Ham in 1980. Please, please can the Footballing Gods smile on Ware and me today.

I still have twenty minutes to go before kick off and so find a space on the far terracing to sit down and write out the team line ups in my notebook. Just for something to do to fill the time. Halfway through scribbling out the names it occurs to me that I have subconsciously resurrected the old *Roy Of The Rovers* wall chart ritual from the FA Cup Final days of my boyhood. I envy the players who have their warm-up routines as a way to kill these last, desperate minutes before the match kicks off and we can get down to the real rollercoaster ride.

'Come on lads,' bellow the Ware coaches orchestrating these routines, 'let's get switched on.' That's right, I echo under my breath. Get switched on. Win this bloody thing. Start fast and play hard. I cannot *believe* how involved I feel. The pessimist in me immediately flips that around and starts complaining that I may not feel *this* involved again on this cup odyssey. I can't see myself getting this excited if the final itself is played out between Chelsea and Manchester United. I hate both of them in equal measure. Better make the most of this then.

The ground is *really* filling up. All of the seats in the grandstand are taken and they are two deep around the far goal. There is also a hive of activity outside the main bar. I'm not going to have the freedom of the ground that I experienced in previous games. But I can't sit still and *have* to keep walking around the terraces, counting off the minutes until the two teams come out. I visit the loo for a second time and emerge just as the players are cheered onto the pitch by both sets of support.

Tonbridge are looking confident but so are Ware and with justifiable reason after their recent run of FA Cup and FA Trophy wins against higher level opposition. Referee Mr Sean Feerick whistles for the skippers and Ware retreat into that pre-match huddle. The two captains, Danny Wolf and Scott Gooding, exchange handshakes before the coin toss and then Mr Feerick calls the game to order. The crowd bellows out more encouragement and then with a flourish the man in black gets us underway.

The opening exchanges give me a chance to measure up Tonbridge. They play neat football across the back four but as the ball moves upfield, Ware are more than a match for them, shackling main man Main and his strike partner Hamid Barr. A Tonbridge fan behind the Ware goal produces a human fly exhibition, climbing up the wire fence to hang two Angels flags, but out on the surface it is Ware who are buzzing around their opposition with more purpose.

Fifteen minutes in and the ball is lost by Tonbridge just inside their own area and a Ware through ball finds John Frendo with his back to goal in the penalty area. Frendo allows the ball to bounce across his body and starts to turn, waiting for the inevitable challenge from Tonbridge defender John Beales. One touch from the tall centre half on Frendo's back and the Ware man goes down like the proverbial sack of spuds. Mr Feerick has no hesitation and points to the spot with a curious hop and skip motion.

'Yesss!' The word is out of my mouth before I realise I've uttered it. A penalty to Ware, the perfect start. Midfielder Sam Berry picks up the ball, but before he can spot it, play is held up by an injury to the Tonbridge player who lost the ball back on the centre circle. The delay gives me time to scurry down the far touchline, looking for a gap in the crowd where I can get a better vantage place for a picture of the penalty. The delay also gives Sam Berry time to think of what is about to happen. In the next few minutes he has a glittering chance to put Ware ahead. A chance, albeit early, to propel Ware towards the First Round Proper. A chance to set up a dream away day to the likes of Leeds or Forest.

Anyone who has ever taken a pressure penalty will know this feeling. I've taken a few in my time but never one of this importance. I watch Berry and can sense the thoughts racing through his head as he stalks around with the ball under his arm well away from the Tonbridge penalty box. I get edgy. Berry looks edgy. Mr Feerick is finally satisfied that the injury has been dealt with and turns his attention to the penalty. I turn my camera's attention to the penalty spot as Berry places the ball and steps back to wait for the whistle.

He strides up. Milliseconds prior to the point of contact I click the shutter, my attention focused down the camera's viewfinder on the strike. The ball disappears off to the left of the viewfinder. It takes under a second to leave the spot and reach the goal line, but I wait for what seems like minutes to hear the crowd's reaction. The cheers of jubilation erupt, but from the far end of the ground, and the ball whistles past my peripheral vision around the camera. Tonbridge keeper Matt Reed has dived to his right and saved Berry's spot kick. Three sides of the ground are flattening like a slowly deflating balloon. The psychological war between Berry and the Tonbridge trainer has ended in victory for the away team. I stalk back disconsolately to my previous viewing position by the halfway line. I pass Lensman on the way. We look at each other with dejection.

'Hello,' I say, 'what's the matter with Joe Stevens this week?'

'Suspended, five cautions.' I nod and walk on. Neither of us brave or willing enough to discuss the glorious, spurned chance. The game continues. Ten more minutes of nip and tuck and then a speculative through ball sees the danger man Main bearing down on goal with Ware keeper Luke Woods rushing from his line like an out-of-control train. Whippet Main wins the race and nudges the ball past Woods as the Ware Express comes clattering through, collecting the Tonbridge striker in his cowcatcher. Mr Feerick's whistle is straight to his lips. A hop, a skip and he points to the spot. Tonbridge penalty. I groan. Three sides of the ground groan. The Angels fans war dance ecstatically on the far terrace offering tribal chants of 'Off, Off, Off.' Woods survives with a yellow card and stalks back to his line to face Main who has dusted himself down and composed himself with an eye on extending this season's goal tally. Main's demeanour is the polar opposite of Berry. This is going to script. Main was expected to score today. Main knows he *will* now score today. On Mr Feerick's whistle he approaches the ball with the swagger of a player who scored forty four goals in all competitions last season. It's a total mismatch. Woods dives the wrong way and the ball nestles itself in the corner of the home net. Nil–one.

It's at this point in the proceedings that I start sulking. I'm a good sulker, although I can't sustain it for long periods. I'm more of a sprint sulker than a marathon man. But I know I will cover the remaining minutes to half time with some top-class sulking. I swear silently at the fickle Footballing Gods who have lured me into supporting Ware, just to desert me at a key moment. It's everything I know and have come to expect from being a fan, not just an impartial observer. Supporting football teams is misery. Hopes and dreams are regularly dashed. Why do we even bother?

I decide to take solace in food so walk around the ground to the tea bar to get a greasy cheeseburger to numb the pain. It means running the gauntlet of the drum-beating, flag-waving Angels fans. Coming from common old Tonbridge, rather than its wealthier, more illustrious neighbour Royal Tunbridge Wells they do look like Angels with dirty faces, or maybe that's just me being catty. I am after all in mid sulk.

I join the end of the still twenty-deep queue for the snack bar when it happens. Chris Ellerbeck, whose first appearance to me was as a cheeky substitute asking to have his picture taken a month ago, breaks clear on the left hand side and darts towards the Tonbridge goal. Ellerbeck has that rare ability of making it look as though he has held on to the ball for too long just before delivering a killer pass. On this occasion it is a whipped cross to the near post where marauding pirate Danny Spendlove glances it with his head to the left of Tonbridge keeper Reed. One side of the ground falls silent. For the rest of us it is delirium. One-all, and completely deserved considering the performance that Ware have produced so far. I put my sulking mode on hold.

Just as I arrive at the front of the queue the referee blows up for half time. Frankly it's a blessed relief. For the next fifteen minutes, Ware can't go behind again. I end up going for a sausage in French bread and chew valiantly through the doughy concoction, but as soon as it hits my stomach with its *pot pourri* of churning muscles and stomach acid, the sausage has no chance and my digestive system puts on the brake lights. This occasion has even knobbled my digestion. How can this be a pleasurable experience? Is it the same for everyone or is it just me? After forty five minutes of a fairly low grade global event, I've lost the ability to scarf a hotdog.

I shoot into the loo for yet another slash and the match has kicked off again by the time I return to the touchline barriers. This time I go down to the end that Ware is attacking. If Tonbridge score then I don't want to see it.

I have just seven minutes to wait for the pivotal moment of the game. I've waxed lyrically in the past about Ware's passing triangles but it sums up their approach to attacking. Fluid one-touch passing which is practically impossible to defend against. On this occasion a series of short, sharp passes down the right hand side sees the ball at the feet of Michael Bardle who feeds Frendo marauding into the box. The Ware striker lets fly and Tonbridge keeper Reed can only palm the ball across the face of his goal into the path of Ellerbeck who slots it home. It is without question the best piece of play I have seen so far in over twelve hours of cup football.

The grandstand erupts. The touchlines around me erupt. Ware have a precious lead. But Tonbridge still have over half an hour of the game to go, so it is impossible to get too carried away, although apart from the penalty the Angels have threatened little throughout. The glances at my watch become increasingly frequent as the second half unfolds. The clock hands tick around agonisingly slowly as Ware defend, harry and frustrate the opposition. Their tactics become increasingly focused on a big boot down the field, playing for territory like the England rugby team. Every free kick awarded to them is a chance to regroup and take a breather. Every stop in play is welcomed by the home fans as a chance to creep ever closer to the dream of a place in the First Round Proper draw.

Tonbridge's support behind the home goal is thinning minute by minute. The visitors become more desperate, chasing every loose ball and reverting to long punts into the Ware box which Wolf, Woods and Stuart Hammonds happily deal with.

Then in the eighty second minute, substitute Scott Neilsen finds himself in a wide position deep in enemy territory. He flicks the ball over a defender's head to the tireless Frendo who lashes a shot goalbound, his effort blocked by a desperate Tonbridge lunge. The ball ricochets out to Sam Berry on the edge of the box who angles his body over the ball and drives for goal. Reed palms it away and there is Ellerbeck, chasing in again. Almost in slow motion he thumps home the decisive goal. The relief is palpable. There is no way back for Tonbridge now. Their players know it, their fans know it and the seven hundred strong Ware faithful know it too. The entire team race to meet the goal scorer. The dream is a reality. Ware are marching on.

The final minutes are played out in a party atmosphere. Tonbridge have one chance of note but striker Fraser Logan lashes a volley over the bar and their fate is sealed as the ball disappears into the wire-mesh fence. Mr Feerick signals the conclusion with his trademark hoppity, skippity flourish and cues the Ware celebration. The fallen Angels disappear rapidly down the tunnel as the home bench clears to join a huge scrum of players on the halfway line, flinging themselves on top of each other. Ware may never go all the way to Wembley, but they are going to their own FA Cup Final – ten grand in the bank and a coveted place in the First Round Proper.

Ware 3 (Spendlove 36, Ellerbeck 57, 82)
Tonbridge Angels 1 (Main 25)

Attendance: 816
Money Spent So Far: £60.00
Miles Travelled So Far: 754
Winners Receive £10,000

1990
Glad All Over

When I was in the Sixth Form at Hall Mead School around the time of my eighteenth birthday I was tapped up by a football club. Sadly it wasn't a scout for Arsenal, Spurs or even Derby County who came calling, it was my P.E. teacher Mr Morgan. He told me that he played for a team in the Mid–Essex League called Braintree & Bocking United and asked what I was doing that Saturday as they were a few players short. I agreed to turn out and was told I would be picked up from my Harold Wood home by my English teacher Mr Smith. He duly arrived at 1pm driving a battered old Vauxhall Chevette and drove me to the ground, where I was astonished to see another two P.E. teachers Mr Harvey and Mr Hall, plus a motley selection of Hall Mead old boys from years above mine, Kenny Lingwood, Tony Clary and Steve Drury. It's the closest I've ever come to joining a coven. Spared a gruesome induction ritual, unless you count seeing your English teacher wearing a jock strap, I found myself playing up front as part of a striking duo with Mr Morgan. It took me a while to stop calling 'Sir' whenever I wanted the ball, but I was delighted to find the back of the net on my debut against a team from Chelmsford called Galleywood Social.

And so for the rest of my final year at Hall Mead, I led something of a double life, tugging my forelock on a school day to the same people that I would prop up a bar with on a Saturday afternoon after a match. It was made slightly easier, firstly when my best friend James Lovett was drafted in to fill a vacant left back position and secondly when I passed my driving test. Having my own banana yellow Ford Escort meant I no longer had to make small talk with the P.E. teachers on the way to and from the games.

Braintree & Bocking United played in the Premier Division of the Mid–Essex League, which if we remember our football pyramid lesson from previous chapters, is the highest level of junior football before the intermediate standard of the aptly-named Essex Intermediate League. It's the lowest level of Saturday afternoon football you can get before heading off to the hangover-strewn world of Sunday morning football. And while the standard is pretty low in the grand scheme of things, it did give me my greatest playing memory. Because Braintree & Bocking went on a cup run.

By 1990 I had repaid the earlier debt to my parents of being suspended from school by getting elected as Head Boy. Candidates had been voted for by our sixth form peers and then a group of eight had attended interviews with the headmaster and governors. I got the job after ace-ing my session. It's strange, but appearing good in interviews is something I have always been able to do. I just seem to have the ability to say exactly what people want to hear in these things. It's something which has followed me through life and probably why I've ended up doing a job in sales.

However I was a *lousy* Head Boy. I was forever getting into scrapes which my position did not condone. I was caught by the head of the Governors clambering commando-style around the roof of the Sixth Form Block with a water pistol during a study period and organised a Sixth Form Fancy Dress Disco which ended in a drunken riot. These may have been minor misdemeanours, but I knew that the top brass at the school realised that they'd been conned in the interview by my rose-tinted manifesto promises. Unfortunately I was just more interested in the social side of sixth form life rather than academic achievements, hence the reason why I topped the Common Room Subbuteo League in both lower and upper sixth, while others were achieving the three 'A' grade exam passes required for university.

And yet for some reason I was never implicated in a major drugs scandal which rocked the sixth form during my tour of duty. The first I got wind of it was when I saw James Lovett standing in line outside of the headmaster's study one break time.

'What are *you* doing here?' I asked. James was one of the people who *would* be going to university. He liked his fun, but he also had a dedicated core.

'They think that I've been smoking grass.'

'But you don't even smoke.'

'Tell *them* that.'

The great diplomat Stoneman gathered his gravitas and went off in search of the Head of Year, Mr Butters. I found him in the Science Block in one of the Physics Labs and demanded an interview, invoking my rights as student representative. The allegations were laid out.

'But he doesn't even smoke, Sir.'

'I appreciate your loyalty Stoneman, but allegations have been made and an investigation is under way.' It transpired that a group of about six pupils were under suspicion of drug-related offences, focused around a party we had all attended at the house of a friend of a friend of a friend, two weekends previous. The only reason that *I* wasn't on the suspect list was because they knew (how?) that I had been the designated driver on that occasion. It was bizarre. This hadn't even happened on school property, or in school time.

But this was apparently just the tip of the narcotic iceberg. James lived in a house which was a two-minute walk from the school gates, so naturally we would all pile around there at lunch time to have a sausage sandwich and see if Scott and Charlene were getting it on in *Neighbours*. These excursions were woven into the misguided case for the prosecution to the extent that Seventy Seven Ingrebourne Gardens was condemned by the teaching top brass as a suburban crack house, where sixth formers chased dragons through lunch period before sitting down to quadratic equations in the afternoon.

Ultimately it was this line of enquiry which undermined their case. Lovett's mum Jackie got wind of it and was up the school office in a gunshot. As the purveyor of the sausage sandwiches she gave us all a cast-iron alibi and demanded full and frank apologies from all of the senior staff. Of course the irony was that if the teachers had stuck to the original allegations of a couple of puffs of blow at a party, they might have had a case.

Naturally these events were the talk of the scholastic dressing room at Braintree & Bocking on a Saturday as we made our way through the league cup rounds. A three-two win in September against Margaretting was followed by a one-nil victory over Danbury Trafford in November. Listening to the P.E. teachers laughing at the inadequacies of their litigious peers gave an interesting insight into the office politics of our school. They thought it hilarious that the senior brass had been embarrassed in such a way.

The league cup semi final in March against Sandon Sports proved a formality as we trotted out six-nil winners to book a place in the cup final, which would be held at the famous Non-League ground of New Writtle Street, then home to Chelmsford City. Unfortunately our opposition was Galleywood Social, the same team against which I had made my debut and the same team which had given us a ten-nil thrashing in a league match back in October. Our omens weren't improved when the match was scheduled for Good Friday, which that year fell on April 13th. However on the Sunday before the match we received hope from an unexpected source.

In that season's FA Cup, Crystal Palace had shown that when it comes to a one-off cup match, the form book can be thrown out of the window. The Eagles had entered the competition in the Third Round with a two-one win over Portsmouth, then beaten Huddersfield Town four-nil, before victories over Rochdale and Cambridge United propelled them into a semi final clash with league title favourites Liverpool. The Reds' line up read like an international select XI: Hansen, Whelan, Beardsley, Houghton, Rush, Barnes.

Steve Coppell's Palace had one eye on a relegation dogfight and had infamously been gubbed nine-nil at Anfield earlier in the season, coincidentally this was right around the time when we received our own hiding at the hands of Galleywood.

I was rooting for Palace partly because they were the underdog, partly because of my dislike for the dominant Anfield footballing dynasty, but mainly because of the uniquely endearing song that the Eagles' fans had adopted as their own. For some reason a Palace match would always resonate to the tune of 'Glad All Over' by The Dave Clark Five. But nobody was under any illusions that Palace could actually win this match. A point underlined when the deadly Ian Rush grabbed a soft opener before the quarter hour mark. The Reds enjoyed almost complete domination of possession in the first half but failed to add to their tally. This gave Palace a sniff and the Eagles came screaming out in the second half. An equaliser from Mark Bright boosted their confidence and led to an attacking onslaught which was finally rewarded when Gary O'Reilly bundled home a second.

The mighty Liverpool knew then that they were in a game and desperately tried to respond, finding their own equaliser with eight minutes to go through a ferocious drive from midfielder Steve McMahon. This was the cue for a Palace panic attack and a minute later John Pemberton snagged Steve Staunton in the penalty area and the referee pointed to the spot. It looked all over for the Eagles when England winger John Barnes converted the penalty.

Palace then had five minutes to salvage the tie. In fact they nearly won it there and then. All through the second half they had been bombarding the Liverpool penalty area from set pieces and again they loaded the box with players. The Reds repelled two waves of attack but finally conceded another equaliser when Andy Gray stood up at the far post to head home. In the dying seconds defender Andy Thorn hit the bar with another header which would have undoubtedly been the winner had it gone in.

I had been sat at home watching this thrilling match unfold, experiencing the highs and lows by myself. Mum and Dad had gone out for Sunday lunch with some friends and Sarah had moved out a year before. It had been one of those games which you were desperate to talk about. But with no one around and in an era before the ubiquity of mobile phone communication, I had to prowl around the front room jabbering madly to myself. What a game. And what a battling performance by the Eagles.

The sobriety of extra time again left me under no illusions. Palace had battled well, but they had seen their best chance to win the game disappear with the Thorn header. The Red juggernaut would wash over them as they had so many other teams in league and cup matches throughout the eighties and nineties. I'd seen it all before.

But somebody hadn't told Palace. They continued to hold their own throughout the extra thirty minutes and still looked more likely to score from their set pieces. This held true when Thorn flicked on a Gray corner with ten minutes to go and Alan Pardew arrived at the back stick to nod home the winner.

It was the greatest FA Cup semi final I had ever seen and I was practically exhausted from just watching the TV. Incidentally the match was immediately followed by the second semi final between Manchester United and Oldham. Another apparent mismatch. Gathering breath while waiting for that one to start, you sensed it would be a complete anti-climax after the previous game. No such thing. That one ended in a three-three draw. What a draining day of viewing that was.

And so five days later when we arrived at Chelmsford City's ground on Good Friday we had an air of optimism. All right so Galleywood had thumped us in the league, but anything can happen in a cup final.

What did happen was that it rained. The pitch was soggy, the weather overcast, the wind freezing and the match dour. A crowd of maybe fifty people in the stands, mostly family and friends, saw ninety minutes free of incident or excitement. Even thirty minutes of extra time could not generate a goal. I was playing up front with Mr Morgan and I don't recall getting more than the briefest sniff of a chance. Galleywood dominated possession but could not unlock our resolute defence. Like Tottenham and Man City in 1981 we would have to do it all again, only the next visit to New Writtle Street would be a night game under the floodlights.

October/November 2007:
I've Got A Golden Ticket

There was a depressing footnote to the Tonbridge Angels match. Earlier that Saturday, before I had even left for the stadium, my father had phoned to tip me off on the draw for the next round.

'They're having the draw live at 5pm,' he said, 'I just heard it on the radio. Are you on your way to Ware?' I half-smiled. After his initial comments that this was a thorough waste of time and resources, it seemed like the old man was getting a real kick out of what I was doing.

'Not yet,' I replied, 'I think I remember the man from the FA telling me that this draw would be on after the matches. I'll make sure I tune in.' I'd then gone and checked the programming information on Sky Plus but could see nothing about the draw being on either Sky or the BBC. On the way to the match I had tuned in to BBC Radio to see if they were going to report anything about the programming of the station for 5pm and whether it would feature the live draw. I heard nothing. So I figured that perhaps we had both been mistaken. But while I was at the stadium, just minutes after the joyful conclusion as Ware were propelled into the first round hat, I heard a fan speaking to his young boy.

'Come on let's get back to the car and hear who they get on the radio.' Perfect I thought and made my way out of the ground to the car to make sure I had my radio tuned in. This was even better than a mock-up with my kids in the hallway, this was the real thing. A live draw. The excitement of the balls. The blind fumblings in the Perspex bucket. Top stuff. But to my disappointment there was nothing. BBC Radio was focusing on the Premiership games that had taken place as usual that day, with not even a sniff of the FA Cup draw. I flicked up the dial to TalkSport and almost immediately heard DJ Adrian Durham say that they had the draw for the FA Cup coming up. Excellent.

I waited. And waited. And somewhere towards Bishops Stortford I finally got what I wanted. Only it wasn't the live draw at all. It was just Durham reading out the list of ties. My heart skipped briefly as each name came out. One of the glamour ties quickly went as Leeds drew Hereford and then Forest were pulled out. The two big guns gone and nothing from the Wodson Aces. Just as I was beginning to think that he was reading out the wrong list. He spoke the four letter word.

'Ware versus Kidderminster Harriers. That's Ware in Hertfordshire, not Ware where.' Grrr. The bugger had nicked my 'where's Ware' gag. Then his words sunk in. A home draw against Kidderminster...

Kidderminster Harriers. Kidderminster *Bleeding* Harriers. I was gutted. We'd had the opportunity of seeing Ware, my Ware boys, travel to a great stadium, even just a *good* stadium and have the day out of their lives. Now we were all heading back to Wodson Park for a match against a Conference team which were probably too good for Ware to overcome. It would be Ware's FA Cup Final, but it would not be the big day out they deserved in the fancy stadium in front of tens of thousands. It would be a home defeat in front of three thousand tops. The one and only time in the club's entire history that they had got this far in the FA Cup before they had drawn Luton away. That was more like it. But Kidderminster Harriers at home...

I felt like the kid in the old milk advert.

'Kidderminster Harriers? Who are they?'

'Eggsactly.'

From Bishops Stortford to home I tried to talk myself out of it. Kidderminster weren't *that* lowly. They may not be league opposition but it's still an achievement for Ware to get to the First Round Proper. And frankly speaking, I shouldn't be worrying about this. I'm supposed to be the impartial observer who's following the route from Haringey Borough to the National Stadium, not some diehard Ware-ite. But I was lying to myself. Somehow on the way I'd been bitten by the Ware bug. And while I knew they were not going to the FA Cup Final itself, if they were going to be knocked out by someone, I wanted it to be a big club. Not Kidderminster *Bleeding* Harriers. And not at home.

There was only one thing to do. Power sulk.

After all, twenty minutes earlier, I had been summoning the Footballing Gods. Praying for them to allow Ware the right to progress into the hat for the next round. I had been delirious when they had achieved it. I had left the ground with a beaming smile and a happy heart. But the Footballing Gods are fickle bastards and they always get their pound of flesh. Kidderminster *Bleeding* Harriers. Thanks for nothing.

And yet the misery was not over.

On my arrival at home I went through the pleasantries with Vanessa. I waited patiently for her to ask me about the game. I gave her the good news of the Ware success and the bad news of the first round draw and then I went over to the computer in the study to log on to the Ware website and read on the bulletin board what people thought about the draw.

The first comment I read had me snarling with frustration. I won't name the person who posted the message, or quote the comment, but the basic jist of it was how excited this person had been to have stood in the club bar at Ware, alongside the players, manager and fans, and to witness the draw for the First Round Proper live on TV with Ware in the hat for the first time in thirty nine years.

So it *had* been on TV. And I'd missed it. A live draw on TV. A live draw on TV in company with the very players who were being drawn. Joining in with the 'Oohs' and the 'Aahs' for real. With the very players and fans that I had stood with on the terraces and endured every minute of their FA Cup journey so far. And worse than that. We'd drawn Kidderminster *Bleeding* Harriers at home.

★

But life moves on. Football moves on. You curse the Footballing Gods for dishing you up another dose of misery and then start planning for the next match. At least I do. And I'm sure that most football fans do. I can but wonder what it is like to support a team which is regularly good. Who are always in with a sniff of any competition they enter whether it's the Champions League or the Amsterdam Tournament. Do these people who *expect* to win each week take failure or disappointment any worse than we mere mortals? The poor suffering individuals who have become accustomed to a life of footballing misery? Where a bleak nil–nil draw away to Hartlepool in the League Cup is actually something to be cherished? I remember working for a boss who was a big Arsenal fan. Right around the time when the Gunners were starting to kick serious Gallic arse under the wily stewardship of Arsene Wenger. The Bergkamp years. Racking up trophies for fun. One season they had just signed Christopher Wreh on a Bosman and I recall my boss coming in spouting the delights of his season ticket Highbury afternoon with a fellow office Gooner.

'It's funny,' he said that Monday morning, 'how you start to accept a new player into the team. When he first joined we referred to him as *Wreh*, but now he has started to score a couple of goals, we are calling him *Chris*.' It was a reasonable comment. Probably well observed and well made. But for some reason I couldn't help thinking you smug bastard. Just because Arsenal have turned over another team, you're now pontificating about the pleasantries of fandom at the highest level. Try gagging on the misery of relegation and then see what you call the eleven lunatics who pull on your team's beloved shirt. It won't be their first name *or* their second name, and it definitely won't be printable. This whole football thing is a curse. But hey, like I said, life moves on.

Fast forward a couple of days from the double depression of missing the live draw and then getting Kidderminster *Bleeding* Harriers and I started to think about the logistics. Kidderminster are a reasonable side in the Conference, they are going to have some travelling support. Ware have gone from a home attendance in the Second Qualifying Round against Thurrock of 172 to a Fourth Qualifying Round turnout of 816. The last time at Wodson Park I had been marshalled into a car parking space. I could have a problem here with getting in. This could well be a case of the dreaded 'All Ticket'.

I had known that ticketing would rear its ugly head at some point. Or rather I'd been consciously ignoring the possible problems of obtaining tickets for some of the later rounds, particularly the semi finals and final. But I had *not* thought that the problem would emerge this early in the competition. However if only three thousand can get into Wodson Park and if a large chunk of away fans would be coming, then this was surely going to be an all ticket game.

I regularly visited the Ware website for an update and after two days it was clear. An article stated that yes there would be segregation and yes this would be ticket only. The tickets would go on sale the following Sunday from 10am until 2pm, from the turnstiles at Wodson Park. I would need to make *another* trip to Ware to secure entry.

Saturday came and went. A barren football-less day for me. Brownie points were secured from a family perspective by not buggering off to a game. I checked the Ware website and the boys in blue had secured a win in the league against Great Wakering Rovers, they of the earlier cup clashes. How different this may all have been if Rovers had grabbed a late equaliser in that replay.

On Sunday morning I awoke late. Scanning the clock I saw that it was already gone nine and that the tickets would be going on sale in under an hour. I leapt out of bed and starting pulling on my clothes from the night before. Vanessa's tousled head emerged from under the covers.

'Where are you going?'

'Yes.'

'What?'

'Ware.'

'What?' Then recognition. 'Oh you idiot. Why are you going there?'

'I need to get tickets for next week. They're going on sale in an hour and there will be loads of people trying to get them.'

'Did you tidy up downstairs last night?'

'Yes,' I lied, slipping on my shoes.

'Well I won't be up when you get back.'

'OK see you later.' I stole out of the room, I'd tidy up when I got back or face the ramifications of her rising early and finding the remains of last night's Guy Fawkes party still littering the kitchen surfaces. Right now there was serious business to attend to.

I jumped in the car and quickly followed the now well-worn route. A120, Bishops Stortford. Through the little villages and onto the A10, dropping into the northern end of Ware and Wodson Park just as the digital clock on the dashboard flipped over to 10:00. The car park was packed. A combination of ticket hunters and Sunday morning football entourages preparing to play on Wodson's junior pitches or saddle up a convoy for an away trip. I parked on the far side of the car park and hurried through the crisp, autumnal morning air to the stadium. Already a long queue of about one hundred people was winding its way from the turnstiles into the car park. I got on the end and waited for things to move. Ahead of me people were lighting up cigarettes and flicking through their *News Of The Worlds*. I calculated that I would need each person in front of me to buy thirty tickets for me to miss out. Unlikely. My heart rate slowed as confidence began to emerge. There would be no ticket disaster *this* round.

When I finally reached the turnstile I noticed that prices had been hiked by another four quid to now stand at twelve pounds for adults. We'd now doubled the entry fee from that first match at Haringey. I handed over my cash and the man behind the turnstile handed back my Willy Wonka Golden Ticket. I then stepped through the barrier and into Wodson Park. The man who had been standing in front of me reading the Sunday paper suddenly turned and yelled, waving his ticket furiously.

'Yes, we've got them!' I nodded edgily. I assumed the fellow was joking but it was hard to tell. Because it was quite a surreal feeling buying a ticket and entering the stadium a full one hundred and twenty five hours too early. Everyone was walking around with grins on their faces. Equally delighted to have secured entry to this predicted historical moment. I imagine this is what the TV and newspaper reporters mean when they say there is a 'feel good' factor running around a small town ahead of big David and Goliath cup fixtures. Despite the potential timebomb of not returning home to clear up the kitchen before Vanessa woke up, I didn't want to leave. Not just yet. Not straight away.

I walked up to the main bar and headed in. The place was packed. People were chatting to one another while sipping teas and coffees. All the buzz was of the upcoming fixture. Lensman was standing by the bar.

'Hello again,' he smiled amiably, 'got your ticket then.'

'Yes,' I replied, 'how many do you think you will shift?'

'Hopefully all of them.'

'So what did you think of the draw?'

'Reasonably happy. If we weren't going to get a league team away, I'd rather have a Non-League team at home.' I nodded unconvinced and looked around me as the barman brought me a foul looking cup of coffee in a paper cup. Lensman nodded a goodbye and walked off towards the changing rooms. I took my coffee outside and had a look around the familiar surroundings. It didn't feel right. The place was so busy and yet the pitch was empty of activity. Swallowing the dregs of my coffee I three-pointed it into a nearby bin and then made my way out of the main club exit. The queue to the turnstile had evaporated now that the first tidal wave of hardcore fans had been dealt with.

As I passed through the car park I noticed a copy of the Hertfordshire Mercury on the floor with a big feature on Ware's giant-killing act. I picked it up and made my way to the car reading ruefully the report about the fans, players and management watching the draw live on the main bar's big-screen TV. Manager Glen Alzapiedi was quoted on the front page: '...I'm reasonably happy. If we weren't going to get a league team away, I'd rather have a Non-League team at home...' This was obviously the company line. I bet they were all thinking the same as me. Kidderminster *Bleeding* Harriers.

★

So what of Kidderminster *Bleeding* Harriers then?

They are probably best known for some FA Cup giant-killing heroics of their own. They were the last Non-League side to reach the competition's fifth round, when in 1994 they battled their way past Preston North End and Birmingham City before a narrow one-nil defeat to West Ham. And pertinent to my cup odyssey, they played in the first competitive game to be staged at the new National Stadium when they lost three-two to Stevenage Borough in the 2007

FA Trophy Final. In fact they have been to Wembley four times as Trophy finalists, with one victory and a hat-trick of defeats notched on their belts.

The club traces its roots back to 1886 when it was formed from an existing athletics and rugby union club. They pottered around in the Birmingham and District League for the first half of the 20th Century, finally completing a full season in the Southern League after the second world war. Their real head of steam emerged in the 1990s. Having risen to the top tier of Non-League football they were controversially refused promotion into the Football League despite ending the 1994 season as champions, because a wooden stand at their Aggborough Stadium was not considered suitable enough. This was completely unfair as there were plenty of Premier League grounds like The Dell or Goodison Park with similar arrangements at the time. The appointment of former Liverpool star Jan Molby as manager in 1999 gave the team another platform for success and he took the Harriers into the Football League at the first attempt. But they managed only a five-year tenure before dropping back into the Conference. This season they sat in tenth position in the league having won eight, drawn three and lost seven.

The branch of the cup that they had entered for the first time in the Fourth Qualifying Round had started off up north at Pontefract Collieries and Washington, hovered around the Leeds area at Selby Town before shooting up to Gateshead, dropping back down to Guiseley and then arriving at Aggborough. Their visitors were Vauxhall Motors, a Conference North team from the Ellesmere Port area of Merseyside. According to reports the *Bleeding* Harriers were unconvincing in the match and trailed Motors one-nil at half time, but the introduction of substitute Michael McGrath saw them motor past Vauxhall with three goals in the second period.

Ware on the other hand were now one of the three lowest ranked teams left in the competition, all of them coming from Step Four but all three from different leagues. Harrogate Railway of the Northern League Division One North, Chasetown of the Southern League Division One Midlands and of course the Hertfordshire boys from the Isthmian Division One North. Ware were fast becoming mini celebrities. Local news camera crews were lining up to shadow three of the players in their 'daily' life outside of the Wodson Park theatre of dreams and Sky TV's *Soccer AM* had been down to the stadium to get the players to perform the Crossbar Challenge feature which would be shown on the Saturday morning ahead of the game.

By Wednesday, announcements were made on the website that not only would parking at the stadium be restricted to permit holders only, but also that there were only a handful of tickets left for the game. A sell-out looked on the cards. The *Bleeding* Harriers had been given a couple of hundred tickets so there would be over two thousand Ware fans, or hangers-on as I liked to call them, cheering on the side. The total attendance figure would be pushing the three thousand capacity. All this a far cry from the seventy four people who attended Ware's first outing in the cup at Wembley FC back in September. Ware sat sixty seven places below the *Bleeding* Harriers in the English football pyramid. They couldn't possibly go any further. Could they?

Saturday November 11th, 2007

First Round Proper
Ware V Kidderminster Harriers

As ever on match day I wake up and instantly think of football. Only this morning it is with a heavy heart. There is a strong, nagging doubt in my head that this will be the last FA Cup match that Ware will take part in this season and already I miss them. It reminds me of a time when I was going to a U2 concert at Wembley. I was supposed to be going with a girlfriend but the problem was we had split up in the weeks leading up to the concert. Or rather she had split up with me. As we had the tickets and as I was still dizzily in love with her, I had suggested we still go together. As friends. And even though I looked forward to that night, I had that same nagging doubt. That this would be the last time we did something together.

It isn't nervousness. It isn't butterflies in the stomach. It is a subtle blend of excitement, misery and realism. In fact if it isn't for the fact that I *have* to go to this match, I probably would bottle it. That's another of my methods for dealing with the big occasions, especially ones where I can't face the outcome. Vanessa describes it as my ostrich-in-the sand-approach. I first discovered it when I went to see Derby play in the Championship play-off final against Leicester in 1994. At half time, with the scores level at one-all, it suddenly occurred to me that the heartache of seeing Derby lose would be compounded by the misery of trying to battle through the post-match Wembley traffic. And so with forty five minutes still left to play, I got up from my seat in the grand old stadium and left. On the way back I observed complete radio silence and arrived home completely oblivious of the outcome. Of course Derby lost. But I had the bittersweet relief of not being stuck in that traffic.

I take Evie and Jonathan to their swimming lesson and have thirty minutes of pondering time sat beside the pool wondering what will happen. I wish I'd brought a book to take my mind off it. Back home the nerves kick in and I watch the clock for the next two hours. There is the minor diversion of getting to see Ware on Sky Sports' magazine programme *Soccer AM* taking part in the Crossbar Challenge, a regular feature where players take it in turns to try and hit the crossbar of a goal from the halfway line, usually with comical outcomes. It's great to see the lowly surroundings of Wodson Park on the telly, but the feature just heightens my anxiety. The Ware performance is one of the worst I've ever seen on the programme. How can these same footballers stand up to a professional side?

Last Sunday I bought two tickets for the game and so Eden accompanies me to the match. We set off at a ridiculously early 12.30pm, partly to get there in time so I can find somewhere to park and partly to just have something to do. The weather outside of the car reflects my mood. Dark clouds hanging low and heavy in the sky. Rust-coloured autumnal leaves being whipped from the trees by the blustery wind to reveal the skeletal branches beneath. My stomach churning. We've sat in silence for about fifteen minutes, parodying the journey I made earlier in the cup run with my father and I realise that it is *me* that is the uncommunicative one. I break the silence.

'You getting nervous?'

Eden looks at me bemused: 'No, should I be?' I give a half smile.

'No, but I am. I've watched Ware so many times now that I'm starting to like them and I think we're going to lose today.' Eden gives me a long, hard look and I wonder what she is thinking. You never expect your parents to show any frailties, any weaknesses. Eden is moving towards her teens, one term at senior school and she has already shed all semblance of childhood. Not quite a teenager, but no longer my little girl.

'It will be all right,' she says reassuringly, our parent-child roles momentarily reversed.

We make quick work of the journey to Ware, arriving at Wodson Park at a quarter past one. The car park is closed off to the public today so we have to hunt around some side streets near to the ground for a suitable space. A number of *Bleeding Harriers* fans are doing the same, their cars bedecked with red scarves and jerseys. We find a space and walk to the ground, which is eerily quiet. The calm before the storm. Unlike me, most sensible people have decided *not* to factor ninety minutes of contingency time into their travel arrangements. We pass through the now segregated turnstiles and enter the familiar arena. There are only three other people already in the ground. I feel fairly ridiculous as Eden asks: 'So what do we do now?'

However the *other* thing that I did last Sunday when I picked up the tickets, purely on a whim, was put in an order for a commemorative T-shirt being created by the Ware Supporters Club. So we walk over to the stall where they are being distributed and pick up my one-size fits all garment. Beaming like a child on Christmas morning I pull it over my head. Eden reaches over, pulling the shirt down around me and arranging the arms, like the mothers in the changing rooms at swimming this morning, organising their five-year-olds.

Suitably bedecked, we then walk around the ground to where a giant marquee has been erected to handle the catering for the flood of 'glory-hunters' who have deigned to grace us with their presence today. I regard these fair-weather fans with a strange mixture of anticipation and loathing. It will be great to see the stadium packed and yet where have all these people been hiding for all these games? And actually who am I to comment? I'm not much more than a cup glory hunter myself.

The normal tea bar has been relegated to a back-up role to handle the couple of hundred segregated Kidderminster fans who will make the journey. We buy a couple of burgers and then walk back around the ground to the far terrace and sit down to eat and wait.

Slowly the minutes tick by and slowly the ground begins to fill.

With half an hour to go there must be over a thousand people in the stadium as the two teams come out to perform their warm-ups. The Ware players come right over to where we are now standing on the rail around the pitch. I pick out each of the players for Eden and can even tell her in what order first team coach Matt Allen will make them do their warm-ups. 'How do you know them *all*?' Eden asks rhetorically, teenage sarcasm another thing she is developing at a pace. But I take it as a compliment.

For the last twenty minutes a group of small boys have been marching around the ground chanting a handful of Ware songs, to the amusement of the fans and security guards, and their latest effort: 'Come on Ware boys, Come on Ware boys,' is suddenly echoed by a chorus of gruff, deeper voices as the Ware Home Support make their triumphant entrance into the arena waving their chequered blue and white flags. I wonder how *they* feel about the 'other' Ware fans who have arrived today, who are standing in *their* places on the terraces and who will be conspicuous by their absence next weekend when Ware are back to the day job of Isthmian Division One North action against Maldon Town. But I don't have time to think for long as the bulk of the *Bleeding* Harriers fans suddenly emerge from the main bar into their segregated pen, like a herd of red and black cattle, draping their flags over the temporary barriers and piping up a quick chorus of 'Who are ya, who are ya' at the Ware Home Support, who return the chant in kind.

By now the Ware players have moved on to the stretching section of the warm-up. Usually when they drape their legs along the guardrail to loosen off the old hamstrings, it is to an empty terrace. Now they have to be careful where they place their studded boots in case they gouge out a fan's eye. They are nodding and winking and hello-ing to friendly faces on the terraces. It all seems too familiar to me, too friendly. Like a works' outing to Southend rather than the biggest day of their footballing lives. I'm thinking they need to get some focus when centre half Stuart Hammonds suddenly starts bellowing the familiar rallying cries about 'getting up for it' and 'switching on'. That's more like it.

Allen orchestrates a handful of sprints and then manager Glen Alzapiedi, who has been forced to go from unknown taxi driver to local and national media darling in the short space of a week, whistles them back into the changing room for the pre-match team talk. Just then the announcer gets on the tannoy to bring the burgeoning crowd the team line-ups. At this point I realise that in my haste to leave for the ground I have come completely unprepared. No pen, no pad, no watch, only my trusty camera. But in a twinkling I realise that I don't *need* to record the minutiae of this match. All around me are media outlets who will do this for me. My cup odyssey has taken me from the minor tributaries to a fast-flowing stream. The BBC cameras are high up in the stands and the goals at least will be on *Match Of The Day* tonight. Journalists in the press box will be recording the stats and reporting the action in tomorrow's newspapers. If, *if*, I ever get this book published, then there will be a library of photos from the legion of snappers from now until the final which will be available for inclusion. And anyway, in the excited hubbub of a crowd of two thousand people, and standing on the far side of the ground, I can barely hear what the announcer is saying.

The *Bleeding* Harriers fans are having a field day, taunting the newly-born Ware legion with an array of organised chanting: 'You're supposed to be at home!' The home fans are ill-equipped to match them. Only the Ware Home Support know the appropriate songs about John Frendo, Danny Wolf and Chris Ellerbeck and they number too few to make a ripple. 'John Frendo My Lord, John Frendo!'

But as the referee Mr D J Phillips leads the teams out we finally get a raucous, uniformed cheer from all sides of the stadium. Ware are wearing a quartered blue and white FA Cup special shirt with their names on the back. A lovely touch.

Both teams are quick to their marks as the captains toss up and then Ware retreat to the now customary huddle. I can sense the anticipation in the air on all sides of me but inside I am tense and fretful. I pray that there are no early goals. If we make half time level then who knows what may happen, but a brace of early strikes from the *Bleeding* Harriers would burst the carnival atmosphere inside Wodson. Just as the match kicks off, a shaft of sunlight suddenly beams out from a gap in the grey, pregnant clouds.

The first twenty five minutes absolutely fly by. Faster than any match so far. I'm completely absorbed in the game, muttering encouragement to the players under my breath as they tackle, pass and challenge. 'Come on Bezza!' 'Get there Ellers!' 'Go on Joe!'

'You really *do* know them all,' says Eden as I offer up another prayer to the Wodson Park Footballing Gods. The home team are matching the visitors in effort and endeavour, much as Great Wakering did against them, but you can see that the *Bleeding* Harriers have an edge. They are quicker to react. Their positioning is so spot on that any loose ball inevitably ends up at a Harrier boot. And they are *just* physically stronger. Stronger than any team so far. The Ware players bounce off them, are barged off track, forced off possession. But they are holding their own. And the *Bleeding* Harriers are threatening little. In fact the best chance of the first half falls to Ware, the result of an exquisite passing move which harks back to every match I have seen them play and the style of football that they obviously relish. Little passing triangles, one touch play, pass and move, pass and move, working down the wing before a cross into the box right into the path of Ellerbeck. The goal hero of so many rounds. Formerly on Tottenham's books. A chance which unfolds before me in slow motion. The ball bounces up off the surface and Ellerbeck has to angle his body across it, a *Bleeding* Harrier sniffing at his back. Ellerbeck strikes. From where I'm standing I have no perspective of where the shot is going, it will either be snagged by the net or flash past. The groan from the crowd speaks volumes before the ball raps against the barrier.

Then in first half injury time the *Bleeding* Harriers actually get the ball in the back of the Ware net and as their fans erupt in delight, a second, louder roar reverberates around Wodson as the referee spots his flagging linesman and rules the effort out for offside. It is virtually the last effort of the half. As the teams disappear down the tunnel I find myself yawning involuntarily, but it is not sleepiness, just sheer emotional fatigue. I've tackled, passed and challenged for every ball from my position on the touchline, and despite the fact that Ware have comfortably survived the first forty five minutes, I still have that heavy heart. For Ware to emerge victorious everything must go right. The ruled-out goal was one that did; the Ellerbeck chance was one that didn't.

There's no chance of going to the toilet or for some sustenance at half time, because losing our place by the guardrail will see us relegated to a viewing position three people back. So we stand there for the fifteen minutes. Eden says she's cold so I give her a cuddle, enjoying the intimate contact, so familiar when she was a baby, but which is disappearing from our lives as she grows older.

Eventually the teams return to the pitch for the final forty five minutes.

Immediately you can see that the professionals have the legs over the part-timers. For fifteen minutes Ware are totally up against it. And yet *still* the *Bleeding* Harriers offer no real threat to the Ware goal. Their fans have been restricted to the odd chant every now and then, but there is no inspiration from their team to galvanise their vocal cords. But at the same time, there is no twelfth man on the pitch for Ware. The home crowd are unable to rally their team. They just don't have the tools. They can't muster the appropriate chants.

Then comes the turning point. A through ball sees John Frendo scudding off towards the *Bleeding* Harriers goal, hotly pursued by away skipper Stuart Whitehead. Their bodies clash and Frendo goes down just outside the box. The referee is on the scene in a heartbeat. Now the Ware fans *do* have the required vocabulary. 'Off, off, off,' we cry, cheering as Mr Phillips yanks the red card from his pocket and then 'Cheerio, cheerio, cheerio' as Whitehead is banished to an early bath.

Bleeding Harriers! Down to ten men! And Ware with a free kick right on the edge of the area. From where I am standing I can see exactly where Sam Berry needs to hit this one to find the top corner. But after a lengthy delay while Frendo's collision injuries are administered to, Berry goes for power. The ball ricochets off the edge of the wall, clips another defender and stings the hands of Harriers goalkeeper Chris Mackenzie, but it stays out.

Almost immediately the *Bleeding* Harriers turn defence into attack with Russell Penn making a powerful run from his own half. Ware stand off him and he bears down on the penalty box. Stuart Hammonds, the last line of defence, has to make a death or glory lunge to arrest Penn's momentum, but the Ware man misses the ball and clatters into the player. The referee is quick to his whistle and the *Bleeding* Harriers now have their own free kick on the edge of the box. Ware assemble a four-man fortification and are marched back the mandatory ten yards. It is almost a mirror of the Berry free kick just seconds ago. But Kidderminster's Blackwood is canny and rather than blasting it, he places it towards the corner of the net on the blind side of Luke Woods in the Ware goal who can only watch as the ball arrows past him into the far corner. Nil-one.

The *Bleeding* Harriers fans to my right erupt in a synchronised cacophony of ecstasy. After ten seconds of cheering and bouncing around they galvanise into one voice: 'Ten men, and we're one-nil up. Ten men, and we're one-nil up.' Jeering, heckling, crowing. Now it is *their* turn to mockingly sing 'Cheerio, cheerio, cheerio,' as they wave their arms and pour vitriol on the home fans. There is no worse sensation in football than having to listen to opposition fans celebrating a goal. There is just no contextual comeback. There are no chants which allow you to say: 'Yes OK, you may be one-nil up with ten men, but you're a professional team playing against a committed bunch of part-timers from three divisions below you who have held you for seventy six minutes.' You can't get statements like that to rhyme, let alone get them to scan to the melody of *Delilah*.

The only comeback is anger. And I think this is one of the reasons why football generates violence. On the pitch and off it. I can feel the testosterone in my body distilling into a growing hatred towards the red and black mob. I'm not a violent man, but I could easily hurl something at those baying hyenas at this moment.

Worse is to come. As the silenced crowd and the blue and white chequered players are licking their wounds, James Constable picks up the ball on the edge of the Ware penalty box, fashions some space and drives another measured shot into the same bottom corner of the net. Nil-two in four minutes. This game is over. Cue more jeering from the *Bleeding* Harriers and again it is aimed at Ware's shortcomings rather than their own team's success. Why do they do that? Where is their class? Admittedly they must be relieved that their team is not going to slip on a cup banana skin, but can they not give credit where it is due?

The atmosphere on the Ware side of the terraces is growing nastier. Tired of being ridiculed by their opposite number, there are now grumblings and mutterings about 'meeting them outside,' peppered by a string of profanities. A couple of policemen assert a border guard at the point where the segregated sections meet. I start to wonder whether I am in the wrong part of the ground to be standing with an eleven-year-old girl and so we move further around the pitch to a gap in the crowd vacated by some of the glory-hunters who have decided that enough is enough. The *Bleeding* Harriers have spied them too: 'We can see you sneaking out! We can see you sneaking out!'

Just as the mood threatens to descend further, the atmosphere is lightened by the introduction of a hardy streaker, who dashes onto the pitch from the far side of the ground and starts galumphing around in the centre circle with that unique gait of the exhibitionist which ensures that all appendages are flailing to the maximum. The thinly-spread steward army is slow to react and after taking the cheers from both sets of fans the streaker realises that he has an opportunity to escape. He turns tail and heads back to the far side of the pitch at a fast lick, vaulting the barrier and disappearing through a side gate into the woods beyond the perimeter fence before the orange-jacketed marshals have a chance to apprehend him. Now everyone is chuckling and smiling, the intervention has had a cathartic effect on the growing tension. The interlude has allowed the Ware fans to accept that defeat is imminent.

But while others are coping with acceptance, we still have nearly a quarter of an hour of the game to endure and for me it is a miserable time. For me the journey is not destined to end with this final whistle. I will have to progress with the *Bleeding* Harriers on to the next round. In my mind I am half thinking of kicking the whole thing into touch. I'm sore at losing, I'm already missing Ware and I cannot find anything in my heart to endear me to the *Bleeding* Harriers and their bleeding fans.

Then after seven minutes of extra time, we are finally put out of our misery. Kidderminster striker Justin Richards has just been brought down right in front of Eden and me, and instead of blowing for the foul, Mr Phillips draws out three long blasts on his whistle to signify full time. Richards picks himself up from the turf, picks up the match ball and throws it directly to me in the crowd. I catch it, confused, and am about to toss it back when the rangy striker says 'No mate, keep it, keep it.' And in that single moment, the pain clears. My hatred wiped away like raindrops from a windscreen.

'That's a nice touch,' says the spectator to my right and it doesn't end there. As the Ware players embark on a slow, tired lap of honour around the ground, the Harriers form a guard of honour at the tunnel entrance and applaud the plucky part-timers off the pitch. This *is* class. The recognition withheld by the Harriers fans has been repaid in spades by the pros on the pitch. Perhaps they're not so bleeding bad after all.

We wait for the last player to leave the pitch and then I hand Eden my new prized possession, a scuffed and muddy FA Cup match ball and we leave Wodson Park for the very last time.

Ware 0
Kidderminster Harriers 2 (Blackwood 76, Constable 80)

Attendance: 2,123
Money Spent So Far: £80.00
Miles Travelled So Far: 815
Winners Receive £16,000

1990
The Replay

One of the requirements for a team's position in the Non-League Pyramid is the standard of their ground. You cannot progress from junior football to intermediate football unless your pitch is 'enclosed', even if this means just hanging a rope around the pitch. You cannot move from intermediate football to senior football unless you have floodlights. With Braintree & Bocking United playing at the lowest Saturday afternoon level, it meant that our matches started at 2pm to make sure there was enough daylight to complete them. If someone humped a Row Z defensive clearance off the pitch, the opposition had to go and retrieve the ball themselves. It was an excellent tactic we often employed in the dying stages of a close match when we were playing down the hill. Our attendance was generally one old man who lived in a nearby house and his obligatory dog. So you can imagine the excitement which spread through the Braintree & Bocking team when we played at Chelmsford City's New Writtle Street stadium in the cup final. Proper changing rooms, a grandstand, even ball boys. But that excitement escalated to delirium for the replay as it was an evening match under floodlights. There is just something about the brilliant illumination of a grassy green arena which heightens the senses.

In the build up to the match, nerves were on a knife-edge at Hall Mead School. The players who would take part in the decisive fixture passed each other in the hallways exchanging silent nods with one another that transcended the usual student-teacher relationship. We knew that this one would have to go the distance. There had to be a result. If level at full time, it would be extra time. If still level, it would be penalties.

James Lovett and I were discussing this as we walked the pitch, minutes after arriving at New Writtle Street early in the evening of Tuesday April 24th 1990.

'Will you take a penalty?' He posed the question as we stood in front of the goal at the top end of the pitch, just as the twilight began to cast long shadows of the grandstand across the turf.

'Of course,' I replied. Throughout my career I'd been the penalty taker for most of the teams that I'd played for. I'd missed my first ever one, when playing for Roma against Mornington Boys, and had spent the remainder of that match crying. I had only been eight-years-old mind. But then I'd won an end of season Penalty King competition when I'd started playing for Upminster Park Rovers, which had boosted my confidence for the one-on-one challenge of the spot kick. I'd learnt then that penalty taking was a confidence thing. And I learnt never to be afraid of it.

'Will you take one?' I asked.

'No chance,' replied James. 'What will you do? Blast it or place it?'

'I always do the same thing,' I said, 'I take a long run up, at least from the edge of the penalty box, shape to go to the right and then stick it in the bottom left.'

'Do you think it will go to penalties?'

'I hope so. It's the only way we're gonna beat this lot.'

By the time we were led out for the match by the referee and his linesmen, darkness had descended and the pitch was lit by those glorious floodlights from the four corners of the ground. The pitch was tacky but not as sodden as the previous game. The natural smell of mud and turf mingled with the medicinal tang of liniment rubbed into leg muscles. There was a much bigger crowd in the grandstand for this match. Possibly a hundred people or more. Easily the biggest crowd I had ever played before and all making a fair bit of noise, at least relative to the one man and his dog from our normal games. But just as the professionals say, once the game got going, the occasion and surroundings drifted to the back of my mind and it was just another match.

Miraculously we actually opened the scoring.

After a combined two hours of resolute defending, Mr Morgan (all right, *John* Morgan) fashioned an opening and found the back of the net. We were frankly rather astonished that we had the lead. It was just a shame that it had come so early in the game. It meant that we were going to have to hold out for another hour at least.

For the first half we did just that. Defending from the front and only occasionally sallying forth to try and catch Galleywood on the break. But the inevitable equaliser came and at full time we were still level, which meant another thirty gruelling minutes. I was already exhausted, having spent the evening chasing lost causes, closing down, and basically making my legs do the work rather than the ball. But while we were level there was still a chance. Another fifteen minutes of extra time was played out. Still we defended, still they failed to break us down.

We changed sides for the final quarter of an hour before penalties. We had held them for three and three quarter hours. We had to hold them for another fifteen minutes. With just four to go, they scored.

It was a bittersweet moment for me. A combination of disappointment and the recognition that as the better team they probably deserved it. I'd like to say that it spurred me to rally the team. To bellow and charge and galvanise an heroic action, but instead I just felt a relief that this emotional and physical ordeal was coming to an end. I think this is the reason why I never progressed above the level of football that I did. I have never had that drive and determination to succeed at all costs which marks the professional from the social player.

The Braintree & Bocking heads dropped. I can remember looking around the team, as Mr Morgan and I were about to kick off, at the total resignation from all positions. This was the result which had been expected, we had just managed to postpone it for as long as possible. But in the final reckoning, Galleywood's name had *always* been on the cup ever since the ten-nil gubbing earlier in the season.

Galleywood *definitely* thought their name was on the cup, because in extra-time *injury* time they went to sleep. Garry Neill, a portly Braintree midfielder lacking pace but with a fairly sweet left foot, was sent down the left wing by a raking pass from the back. Without looking up he whipped a high curling cross into the box and it was another one of those occasions for me when time seemed to switch to slow motion. Well maybe that's not true. It wasn't slow motion, it was just my brain processing information so fast that actual events seemed to be moving at half speed. My brain told me that I was unmarked and thundering into the penalty area. I could see the exact point where my path would intersect with the ball as it flashed across the box. I could see their keeper desperately making yards from his line to try and reach it and the defenders frantically back-pedalling to intercept me. I could tell immediately that none of them would make it in time and I knew that I was going to score. Before I had even made contact with the ball I knew that I was going to score. It was an incredibly uplifting feeling.

With seconds to go after four hours of football I headed the ball home.

It was a moment I have played back in my mind thousands of times. It was the *defining* moment of my footballing career. Looking back over the games recorded in my father's exercise book I played a total of 448 games between Sunday February 24th 1980 and Tuesday April 24th 1990. In that time I scored 198 goals. But the sweetest, most deliriously happy moment of my career, if not my life (yes, I told you I was shallow), were those nanoseconds of time between knowing I was going to score and actually scoring in that cup final.

By today's standards I should probably have whipped my shirt off and gone racing up the line whirling it around my head *a la* Ryan Giggs, but back then I just stood there with my hands aloft, too tired to really celebrate, as team mates came to incredulously congratulate me. A vertical version of Charlie George's celebration after scoring the winner in Arsenal's FA Cup and League double year. Galleywood barely had time to kick off before the final whistle was blown.

I was mobbed by the team. Then everyone realised that this meant penalties. But like I said before, spot kicks are just a confidence thing and right then mine was stratospheric. I offered to take the first penalty before anyone else had a chance to worry about it and my team mates stood in the centre circle as I approached the very goal that James and I had stood in front of three hours earlier. I didn't see the keeper or hear the crowd, I just waited for the whistle and strode up to the ball. I shaped to go right and tucked it away in the bottom left-hand corner. One–nil Braintree & Bocking. Galleywood also converted their first but you could tell by the posture of their players in the centre circle that they could not believe they had thrown that precious, injury time lead away. They knew they were going to get mugged on penalties by a team they should have crucified and eventually they did, the winning strike falling to Tony Clary.

The rest of that night, the presentation of the trophy, the celebrations in the bar, are all a blur. Like the Ricky Villa goal in 1981, the glare of my equaliser has blinded my memory of whatever came next. But I do remember going to bed on the night of the victory and lying awake for hours, playing that goal through my head again and again and again. I've maybe played another hundred matches since then. I've even spent a season playing a higher standard for Herongate Athletic in the Essex Intermediate League, but none of these games have been recorded in my father's exercise book. The final entry will always be: *Braintree & Bocking United two, Galleywood two (Braintree won five-four on penalties) Scored two.*

November 2007
Daggers Drawn

The morning after the night before I awoke with renewed antagonism towards Kidderminster. All right so I had decided not to refer to them as the 'Bleeding' Harriers any more, mainly because of the magnanimous way in which their players had accepted victory, but I still bore the grudge that it was *they* who had ended my fledgling love affair with Ware. But I had my match ball memento and my commemorative Ware T-Shirt and I vowed that I would wear Ware wherever the cup journey took me, all the way back to Wembley.

But before I could think about the big day out in May, there was the major task of the seven preceding rounds and in particular the Second Round Proper. The draw took place on Sunday afternoon straight after the live BBC broadcast of Torquay United versus Yeovil. Although I no longer needed my children to generate the magic of the velvet bags/Perspex bowls, we still assembled as a family in front of our TV screen in the lounge to witness Sir Tricky Trevor Brooking as master of ceremonies ably assisted by former Spurs player Steve Hodge and West Brom legend Cyrille Regis.

'It feels like we're all a part of this now,' Vanessa said, as we settled down to watch proceedings and a warm glow spread through my body. I still remembered the original tongue-lashing I received when I had first mooted my idea to her on the phone four months ago. I'd already promised that if a trip to Kidderminster was required, or some other far-flung part of the country, that we would go as a family for a weekend away. And Eden had already said that she was signed on for the next fixture although we would need to make sure she wrapped up a bit warmer.

So to the draw. We watched as Steve Hodge dropped the numbered balls into the bowl and then gave them a swirl: 'If I'd known they did that,' said Vanessa, 'I would have got the kids to use marbles.' Naturally this was music to my ears.

'Tie number one,' said Trevor.

'Number thirty four,' said Steve.

'Oxford United,' said Trevor.

'Number ten,' said Cyrille.

'Will play Southend United,' said Trevor.

'Aah,' chorused the family Stoneman. Southend United were on our wish list as we had all gone together to see a match between the Shrimpers and Derby last season at Roots Hall. And Southend with its beaches, pier and amusement arcades was a family favourite.

'Tie number two,' said Trevor.

'Number thirty nine,' said Steve.

'Swindon Town,' said Trevor.

'Number nine,' said Cyrille.

'Will play Forest Green Rovers or Rotherham United,' said Trevor.

We all looked at each other blankly. No Oohs or Aahs required there.

'What number are Kidderminster?' Asked Eden.

'I'm not sure,' I replied, 'I think they are twenty four or something like that.'

'Will play Crewe Alexander,' said Trevor.

'Who got Crewe?' I asked, 'I missed that.'

'Oldham or somebody.' And so we watched as our fate unfolded before us. We dodged a potentially gruelling trip to Barrow as they were drawn away to Millwall, that's if the Lions could negotiate a replay with Bournemouth. In fact thinking about it we also dodged an away trip to Millwall which was something of a relief.

Far-flung wildcards like Bradford, Tranmere and Torquay all came and went. The Torquay draw had a comedy moment attached to it as the cameras switched to the dressing room at Plainmoor where the recent victors of Yeovil Town were watching, still in their sweaty, muddy kits. As their number came out there were whoops of delight, but when Cheltenham Town or Brighton followed them out, you could see that they were singularly unimpressed.

Cheltenham who?

Eggsactly.

I was just explaining this to Vanessa when Trev piped up: 'Tie number eleven.'

'Number two,' said Steve.

'Dagenham & Redbridge,' said Trevor.

I hunched forward in the chair. 'COME ON, PLEASE, PLEASE PLEASE!'

'Number twenty four,' said Cyrille. Again time went into slow motion.

'Will play Kidderminster Harriers,' said Trevor.

'YES!' I cried leaping to my feet. 'It's the Daggers! Oh knees up Mother Brown, knees up Mother Brown, under the table you must go. E-i-e-i-e-i-o'. I cavorted madly around the room, the children looking at me with a mixture of bemusement and fear.

'Your father's played at Dagenham & Redbridge,' explained Vanessa, 'in a charity match.'

'Really?' said Eden.

'And I saw them in a fantastic FA Cup match against Orient when I worked on the *Redbridge Guardian*,' I bellowed. 'It all fits perfectly! Oh knees up Mother Brown, knees up Mother Brown, under the table you must go. E-i-e-i-e-i-o.' Quite why I should break into a cockney anthem is still unknown to me, but I swear it's what happened. Needless to say I was delighted with the outcome. Dagenham & Redbridge. A team that I had covered as a reporter when I worked on the local papers. A ground I had *played* at when I worked for the *Barking and Dagenham Post*. A team that I could unequivocally throw my entire support behind. And a team that was only thirty miles down the road! Even now as I write this I want to break into another chorus of *Knees Up Mother Brown*.

Just then the phone rang. It was my father.

'Did you see the draw?' He asked.

'Yes!'

'I knew it was going to be Dagenham when they pulled it out.'

'Me too!'

'It shouldn't be too hard to get tickets for that one.'

'I know!'

'And you went to see them play in that nine-goal thriller with Orient.'

'I know!'

'Can you believe it.'

'No!'

At that point I half expected *him* to encourage old mother Brown to get her knees up. Instead I had to make do with relating our adventures at Ware the day before and how I was now the proud owner of an FA Cup match ball. I could tell he was *definitely* getting a voyeuristic pleasure out of my cup odyssey and it made me feel good about myself. Amazingly from the depths of depression when faced with Ware's exit, I was now cock-a-hoop again at the prospect of a perfect Second Round tie. I imagined that from high above the clouds over Wodson Park, the Footballing Gods were looking down and chuckling, pleased with their day's work.

★

OK, get ready for one of the most complicated football history lessons there is. I make no excuses for the fact that this could get very stat-ish, but Dagenham & Redbridge are a complete historical aberration. The team which now plies its trade in League Two, having *finally* emerged from Non-League football in 2006/07, has evolved from no fewer than six previous clubs.

Back in 1881, four years before the Football League was formed, a club by the name of Ilford FC emerged in east London. They were one of the original entrants in the FA Amateur Cup and founder members of the Isthmian League in 1905. They played their games at a ground called Lynn Road in Newbury Park from 1903 onwards.

Five years later another team was formed in east London called Cedars FC, although in 1892 they changed their name to Leytonstone FC. They spent one season in the inaugural Spartan League before themselves transferring into the Isthmian. Leytonstone played at Granleigh Road, a compact urban ground which stood in the shadows of a high level, over ground railway station.

Four years after that, a couple of miles on the other side of the Lea Bridge Road, another team was created in east London, this lot called Walthamstow Avenue. The team was derived from members of the Pretoria Avenue school team who stayed together when they left. They started off in local leagues before progression to the Spartan, then Athenian and finally the Isthmian League directly after the war. So at the cessation of hostilities in 1945 we have Ilford, Leytonstone and Walthamstow Avenue, all minding their own business and ensuring plenty of local Isthmian League derbies.

Four years after that and a little bit further to the east of London, another team was founded under the name of Dagenham FC. They progressed through the Metropolitan, Delphian, Corinthian and Athenian Leagues before finally arriving in the Isthmian in 1973. For three seasons between 1974 and 1977 all four teams fought alongside each other in the Isthmian Division One, with Dagenham posting the best record with three successive third-placed positions. The following year after a major league restructuring, Ilford dropped out of the top division leaving the other three behind. And two years after that they sold their ground in Newbury Park to take part in the first of a series of mergers and acquisitions that would make Gordon Gekko blush.

A combined Leytonstone & Ilford FC had immediate success, gaining promotion into the Isthmian Premier as Division One champions at the first attempt. But eight years later the merger and acquisition vultures were circling again with the struggling Walthamstow Avenue being absorbed into the fold.

Leytonstone & Ilford upped sticks for Walthamstow's historic Green Pond Road ground and a season later changed their name to Redbridge Forest to reflect the combined histories of the teams from the boroughs of Redbridge and Waltham Forest.

In season 1991/92 Redbridge Forest were promoted to the Football Conference but in order to reach that level of football, they had been required to leave the lower grade stadium at Green Pond Road and ground share with Dagenham. The following season the combined forces of generations of east London football finally emerged as Dagenham & Redbridge FC when landlord and tenant came together.

The club is probably best known for being the unfortunate victim in the 2002 Conference title race when they were pipped at the post by Boston United, only to see the Lincolnshire club found guilty of inappropriately making illegal payments to players in that title-winning season. After that disappointment the Daggers went into a slight decline, but last season they got the combination right again and gained promotion to league football for the first time in their history before the end of April.

Here was a team that I had a shared history with. There was not one iota of doubt as to who I would be cheering for come December 1st. The day the tickets went on sale at Victoria Road, I drove down to the ground on the way home from work and secured my own place in the Second Round Proper.

Saturday December 1st, 2007:
Second Round Proper
Dagenham & Redbridge v Kidderminster Harriers

For the first time this season I wake up on match day and my first thoughts are not of the game. Don't get me wrong, it's only a matter of seconds before I *do* remember it, but I'm conscious of the slight delay and feel a tad guilty. A month ago I would wake up on match day with a big beaming grin, would be counting the hours until I could sneak away. Today it feels like just another match. It reminds me of when I split up with the U2 concert girl and James Lovett arranged a blind date 'to get me out of my misery'. Only I didn't really *want* to get out of it. The misery was the last thing I had left of the relationship to hold on to. I feel like that now. I know that I have fallen in love with a football team called Ware, and while Dagenham & Redbridge are not a bad blind date, I'm just not ready to be back on the scene.

You will either understand this declaration or not. It seems there are no half measures nor grey areas. You will either recognise something of the football fan in yourself, something which has led you to make an equally ridiculous commitment to a loose collection of individuals who happen to play in the same coloured shirts, or you will think me completely insane. If you come from the latter group then I point out to you that the word 'fan' is an abbreviation of the word 'fanatic'. And we fanatics like nothing more than a good obsession to adore. Only mine has been taken from me. I've mentioned that I have a loose history with Dagenham & Redbridge. Of all the teams left in the competition at this stage they are one of my top picks, but leading up to the game I realise that they are no replacement for Ware. They are my rebound team.

The length of the scheduled gaps between cup matches is expanding now after the early rounds when they came fortnightly thick and fast. I am at a crossroads in the competition. The intriguing Non-League adventurers are slowly being picked off by the league teams and the new names on the fixture list have a familiar ring.

There is also none of the hype or excitement of the previous round. There is no sixteen-page pull-out in the *Barking and Dagenham Post* ahead of this match, as there had been in the *Hertfordshire Mercury* last time out. The clubs' respective websites and message boards are low on content surrounding the game. A second round match between Dagenham and Kidderminster means little to either team or their fans. Their inclusion in the competition at this stage is *expected* not dreamt of.

Also I will no longer be able to meander around the periphery of the matches choosing with wilful abandon where to stand and take pictures. From here on in I will be penned into designated sections and seats. For this reason I bought terrace tickets rather than go into the seats at Victoria Road just to prolong the freedom. I will be queuing to get in, queuing for the loos, queuing for a burger and a programme and it will only get worse as the size of the stadiums and attendances inevitably increases. The combination of misery and pessimism has cooled my enthusiasm for the match, for the whole project, during the three week wait.

Vanessa's criticism of my obsessions is that they burn fierce and bright, but more often than not quickly fade away. I've come to recognise it too. My cupboards are full of discarded equipment from those obsessions – football boots, sailing kit, baseball jerseys – all hanging from the rail as a constant reminder of my inability to stick with something. Is this to be another case in point?

Fortunately amid all of this despair there is another motivation at work. And this is the thing which is driving me on. Revenge. I want revenge for my beloved Ware. I want to see the Kidderminster team having to trudge forlornly around the pitch on a lap of honour after ninety minutes, but more importantly I want to see the Kidderminster fans suffer the misery of a last-gasp defeat so that *I* can crow at them as they did at me. This may sound a touch melodramatic but there you are. This season's FA Cup has become a ridiculously huge part of my life.

None of which I have time to reflect on as we make the journey to Victoria Road, Dagenham, because for once I have a full car. All three children – Eden, Evie and Jonathan – are strapped in the back, while my friend Nick is beside me in the front. Nick is an American, born and raised in New York, but who has lived in the UK for over ten years and who has developed a child-like love for the right type of football.

His knowledge of the game is admirable for one who was first introduced to it in his twenties. His appreciation of tactics, skill and endeavour is sound thanks to *Match of the Day* and EA Games' *FIFA 96*, but he lacks the historical depth. He's a football immigrant rather than a football native. I imagine this is how the star of Gerry Anderson's puppet show *Joe 90* would be after one of his brain dumps.

A thorough knowledge of any subject, but without the context of experience, still bearing a child-like naivety. Unfortunately this highly perceptive analysis will be lost on anyone born after 1980 who has no idea who *Joe 90* is.

Our journey to Victoria Road takes us on a fairly circuitous route as I promise to take Nick the long way round to show him the post-apocalyptical, industrial journey which is the A13 from Thurrock to Dagenham. I compare it to the New Jersey Turnpike just without the twelve additional lanes of traffic. We work our way through the Ford plant to ascend into Dagenham from the southern side. This part of the world has changed drastically since my newspaper days when I regularly passed through, but occasionally I spot familiar landmarks like Dagenham East tube station, The Railway pub and Dagenham Police Station, before finally passing a coned-off Victoria Road which leaves us searching for a side road in which to park.

There is a distinct lack of crowd. Nick is looking at me with the quizzical face of someone whose first live football matches were the sell-out crowds of Euro 96 and whose subsequent diet has been dominated by the tens of thousands that make their way around north London, previously to Highbury and now to the Emirates Stadium. This is a whole new ball game for him.

The weather is grey and gloomy, matching my mood. We all wrap up in coats, hats and scarves. I have some pocket handwarmers, purchased from an outdoorsy-kind of shop, which I give to the kids to stave off cold hands. In fact it was the promise of this gadget which was the clincher in six-year-old Jonathan's decision to come along.

We make our way down Victoria Road and the recently over-named London Borough of Barking and Dagenham Stadium appears before us. Apart from the name, nothing much else has changed since the last time I was here for that *Barking and Dagenham Post* charity match, where the highlight of my day was nutmegging Tony Hadley from Spandau Ballet. Again possibly a reference lost on our younger reader.

My fears of massive queues are completely unfounded. There appears to be fewer people here than there were at the last Ware game. We're through the turnstiles and programmed-up in a heartbeat. Victoria Road is a stadium of many parts all stuck together like a Lego kit. There are a few rows of terracing at either end, one for the home fans, the far end for the away. A long covered terrace runs across the far side facing the main stand which has the players' tunnel sandwiched by nine or ten rows of seats and a sort-of bolt on corporate box.

An enthusiastic announcer, as cockney as the proverbial sparrow, is encouraging people to visit the ground on Sunday week for a Fun Run which offers free admittance to anyone dressed as Santa. He is continuously apologising about the weather and suggesting we visit the tea bar for a warming drink. It's not *that* cold so perhaps this is just part of the sales pitch. I imagine him in May apologising about the sun and suggesting we all go and by a cooling can of pop.

The two teams are warming up on an undulating pitch which is possibly the second worst I have seen on my travels. I *think* it is the Harriers at the far end with a smattering of fans spread out across the terrace. Before me are the Daggers, at least I assume it is the Daggers. I can't actually tell which team is which as they warm up in their training jackets. I don't know the players or their kits well enough. This *really* is a blind date. Dagenham should be wearing red carnations in their buttonholes.

As we find a position on the far terrace which offers enough shelter and room for the kids to see clearly, the players disappear into the tunnel ahead of their pre-match team talk. The jovial announcer brings us the team line ups but I don't have the enthusiasm to make notes in my programme, I can check the line-ups online when I get home. I don't know who's who anyway. The only name I recognise is that of Dagenham & Redbridge striker Paul Benson and this is because my father is a distant relation to his mother and Dad's mentioned him to me before.

'Predictions?' Asks Nick.

'I really don't know,' I reply, 'I would imagine this should be a home banker for the Daggers. But I haven't seen them play this year. They are a division higher than Kidderminster although they only got promoted last season. Apparently the danger man is a guy called Paul Benson. My dad is vaguely related to his mum.'

'So we're cheering for Dagenham right?'

'We're actually cheering for a result.'

'What do you mean?'

'Well you know I've been following all the matches from the early rounds? I've potentially double-booked myself a fortnight on Tuesday night. I've got to go and speak at some event for work. There's no way I can get out of it. And if they draw today the replay will be on the same night.'

'And there's no way you can miss that game.'

'Right. So we need someone to win, preferably Dagenham. Hey you see that bit of turf there?'

'Yes.'

'That's where I nutmegged Tony Hadley.'

'Really?'

Before I can relive any more eighties New Romantic glory, Jonathan tugs on my arm with the look of the child who realises that he's been sold a pup as far as an afternoon's entertainment is concerned.

'I'm bored,' he says.

'No you're not. Remember that conversation we had in the car when we agreed that you wouldn't say you were bored today?'

'Yes.'

'Well you're not bored.'

'Can I have some chips?'

'Yes.'

This bribe has the desired effect and he and Eden disappear off to the snack bar with a crisp five pound note in hand. Before they have a chance to return the jovial announcer advises us to 'make some noiiise, for the boyyys,' and the two teams march out. The ground has filled but is nowhere near full. The Dagenham Hard Core are away to our right and they have a drum. I can't see the Kidderminster fans very well, they are too far away. With the minimum of pomp and ceremony we are soon underway and again it's like that on-the-rebound blind date. You sit there at the table making small talk with somebody but your heart's not in it. You don't really want to be there and your brain is running on parallel trains of thought, one side processing the conversation and serving up automatic replies, the other side screaming an internal monologue – 'What am I doing here?'

It doesn't help that the opening exchanges between the two teams are fairly bland. Dagenham are playing with that arrogance that I've now seen so many times. The higher division superiority complex. They're playing like they have a God-given right to win the match. Even Nick spots it – 'Dagenham don't look like they want it today.'

Kidderminster are playing the part of the underdog just right. They are working hard for each other, closing down quickly, denying Dagenham any time on the ball. They are completely worthy of a thirteenth minute opener. A free kick taken by Andy Ferrell by the touchline on the grandstand side of the ground, just outside the penalty area, floats into the box and is met by the towering head of defender Mark Creighton. One of those goal attempts where from my viewing position I am directly in line with the trajectory of the ball and can see where it is headed before anyone else in the ground – into the back of the net.

The Harriers fans away to my right erupt in a cacophony of delirium. The Dagenham fans around me begin muttering and swearing. I give Nick one of

Dagenham & Redbridge v Kidderminster... My first visit to a 'league' ground

Both teams had their eyes on the prize of a place in the Third Round Proper

Chris Moore went close for the Daggers, but Paul Benson went closer

Southend v Dag & Red...Adam Barrett's appeals echoed around Roots Hall

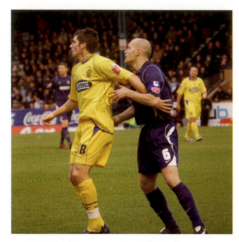

Barrett got close to Ben Strevens

Jon Nurse (right) is congratulated

The scoreboard told the murky story for the visitors as Southend marched on

Liverpool v Barnsley... After defeating Southend, the Tykes faced the mighty Kop

Dirk Kuyt's opener was wiped out shortly after by Barnsley's Stephen Foster

After his last-gasp winner, skipper Brian Howard salutes the Barnsley hordes

Barnsley v Chelsea... Kayode Odejayi beat Cudicini in the air for the vital goal

Quite simply, it was the longest twenty three minutes of my life

Somewhere in all this, Nick the American was enjoying his first pitch invasion

Queue Sera Sera... Standing in line for seven hours for semi final tickets

Barnsley v Cardiff... The two teams lined up ahead of the semi final at Wembley

Shortly after these two shots, the batteries in my camera ran out. Schoolboy error.

Abide With Them, Katherine Jenkins and Lesley Garrett helped to raise the roof

Nwankwo Kanu scored the game's only goal but was told to keep quiet about it

Countdown to the celebrations...

That's it! Referee Mike Dean blew, while Harry consoled Cardiff's Dave Jones

Portsmouth heroes... Sol Campbell at the back and Nwankwo Kanu up front

A delighted Harry Redknapp and the closest I'll ever come to the FA Cup

The author, standing beside the Bobby Moore statue outside Wembley Stadium

those looks. My brain is calculating. This means that Dagenham now need *two* goals if I am to avoid a replay *and* get revenge. Right now they don't look like getting one.

But the goal has snapped Dagenham out of their lethargy. Like a slap to the face or a glass of wine over the head as penance for not paying enough attention during the blind date. They now sense the shame of defeat to a lower league team and they generate more bite in their tackles and zip in their legs. They press without looking overly dangerous, but a left winger called Chris Moore catches my eye. He is huffing and puffing and running at the Harriers' right back with some success.

Half an hour into the game and the Daggers get a deserved equaliser. A real opportunist's goal. A deep cross is brought down on his chest by Paul Benson and he turns and rifles home a volley from outside of the box. Nick, the home fans and I raise our arms involuntarily and cheer in that way that only a goal can bring. The combined ingredients of surprise, relief and delight parceled up in a split-second of emotion. But once we have all high-fived and applauded and the burst of adrenaline has run its course, a dim and distant beacon of angst starts to flare up. We are all square again. I need a clear result, not a draw. What if Kidderminster now roll out the fortifications and go for a replay back at Aggborough? What if Dagenham are unable to convert their superiority into goals? What is Vanessa going to say if I get fired for skiving off work to go to a football match?

Half time comes and goes and we stamp our feet to keep out the cold and each have a turn on the hand warmers. While not a huge crowd, there are enough people descending on the snack bar to rule a cup of tea out of the question. Eden and Jonathan start to play a game which involves chasing each other in and out of the smattering of spectators in our section. I tell them to stop, so instead they start climbing on the handrail by the touchline.

The two teams come back out for the second half with the Daggers now attacking the goal furthest from us. If they score any winners we will barely be able to see them. Two or three rounds ago I would have just walked down to the other end of the ground. I could still move further down the terrace but the kids would lose their sightline so we are grounded where we are.

The match restarts. The minutes tick by. Nobody seems to be taking an upper hand although Dagenham are comfortable in defence and possibly shading it. Evie spots the digital clock above the home goal terrace.

'How many minutes are there in a football match Daddy?'

'Ninety. Forty five in each half.'

'Then there are thirty six minutes to go.'

'How do you know that?' She points her answer up at the clock, the numbers showing fifty four minutes gone. Thirty six minutes for someone to score. I'm started to think about how I can get out of this work event and the options are limited. I could pull a sickie, but then someone would need to cover for me and nobody would want to have to do this. Giving a speech for forty five minutes in front of two hundred and fifty city executives. If I just blow out the event organisers my bosses will find out. No, I need a goal. Back on the pitch Dagenham make a substitution. Moore is replaced by Jon Nurse. I'm mumbling to Nick that I need a goal. The tension is starting to work its way up my back into my shoulders.

'Twenty four minutes to go Daddy,' says Evie. Jonathan and Eden have disappeared from sight so I crane my neck over the people in front of me to see them. They have worked their way down to the corner flag now. I figure they will be all right so again turn my attention to the game. There just doesn't seem to be any sign of either team making a breakthrough.

The minutes tick by. It suddenly starts to pour with rain but Kidderminster have weathered the early half dominance of the home team and are starting to come into it again as the game stretches with tired legs. They get a couple of breakaways which call for some last line of defence work. One tackle in particular by a Dagenham centre-half is reminiscent of Bobby Moore on Pele in the 1970 World Cup, such is the perfection of its timing. All right, maybe I'm exaggerating, but it is definitely a sweet challenge.

With Evie pointing out there is just nine minutes to go and my beacon of angst now flaring brightly, Kidderminster get another breakaway. Striker Iyseden Christie untangles himself from a Dagenham defender and finds himself one-on-one with keeper Tony Roberts. He must score. Again the speed that my brain works amazes me. I've already computed that the Harriers will be going through and that I am off the hook as far as work is concerned as Christie's right foot triggers off. But Roberts' brain is one jump ahead and he pulls off a brilliant reaction save.

It is the turning point. Almost immediately the Daggers go up the other end and Jon Nurse on the left wing drills a ball across the face of goal. Ben Strevens is piling in from the right wing. This is absolutely it. The defining moment. If Strevens can find the back of the net the match is won and the team I want to win will be going through, my football/work fixture congestion solved. Strevens connects and the ball races past Kidderminster goalkeeper Scott Bevan and into the far corner of the net.

The terrace around us erupts with a delighted roar. Evie leaps into the air and then turns around to check with me that it is indeed a goal. Jonathan and Eden appear from among the crowd for a high five each. For the first time this afternoon I feel my spirits lift. I can just about see the Kidderminster fans at the far end of the ground, standing still and looking grim. The rain has been pouring down on their exposed terrace, they are wet through and now their team has suffered a mortal blow. As the match kicks off again I think back to the match at Wodson Park when their side brought Ware's cup run to an end. Now *they* are the ones being barracked by the dominant fans. For the first time in three weeks I am at peace. My revenge being served both cold and in this case wet.

The fourth official shows three minutes of injury time to be played but it holds no fear for me because Benson has picked up the ball in acres of space on the right wing as the Harriers press forward for an equaliser. Benson runs in at the Kidderminster goal, drifts to the right of a defender and then drills the ball into the right hand corner of Bevan's net. A third and decisive goal.

Just as the referee blows his final whistle the downpour ceases. The Daggers have won, the Harriers fans have seen their hopes dashed, I've had my revenge and now I'm not going to get wet on the way back to the car. Boy's Own stuff (Again a reference possibly lost on our younger reader).

Dagenham & Redbridge 3 (Benson 32, 90, Strevens 84)
Kidderminster Harriers 1 (Creighton 13)

Attendance: 1,493
Money Spent So Far: £97.50
Miles Travelled So Far: 887
Winners Receive £24,000

1992
Legend Of The Orient

The greatest FA Cup match I have ever attended in person took place on November 11ᵗʰ 1992. It was a thrilling rollercoaster of a game at Victoria Road, a First Round Proper clash featuring Dagenham & Redbridge against east London neighbours Leyton Orient. Just as in the earlier Woodford Town versus Orient match, the local rivalry and short distance between the teams ensured a big crowd, a Victoria Road record attendance at the time of five thousand three hundred. And while I was no particular fan of either team, the event was heightened for me as I was attending in an official capacity.

When I left Hall Mead School in 1990 I walked straight into a job as a trainee reporter for the Guardian, Gazette and Independent Group of newspapers based in east London. When I say I walked straight into it, I mean I finished school on the Friday and started work on the Monday. Actually getting the job had been a triumph of persistence over rejection, which had its roots in one teenage evening when I'd watched the Watergate journalists' epic *All The President's Men* with Robert Redford and Dustin Hoffman and thought I'd like to do that.

I managed to get a couple of hours of work experience on the *Evening Echo* in Basildon and then, with my A Level exams approaching, I'd written hundreds of letters to local and regional newspapers up and down the country. Of over one hundred and fifty letters sent, I got eleven 'no thank you' replies and just one asking me to attend an interview. Fortunately, as I've said, I like interviews and I did enough in the two hours at the newspaper offices in Walthamstow to talk my way into the job.

I was incredibly lucky. There was a recession brewing in the economy at the time and local newspapers, with their dependency on the advertising spend of small, local companies felt the pinch as hard as anyone. I was the last trainee reporter that the newspaper group took on at the offices in Fulbourne Road for the entire time I was there and a year into the job, I was fortunate to dodge a wave of job cuts that decimated the newsroom. My starting wage of £6,600 per year obviously left me well underneath the redundancy radar.

I was also lucky to have got such a completely cool job. While my friends from school had almost to a man followed the Essex boy career path of working for a bank, broker or trader in the City — swapping Romford Market for the financial markets — I was roving the streets of east London sniffing out stories and features and getting paid to write about things. OK so it wasn't exactly Watergate, but in amongst the ruby weddings, fete openings and cats stuck up trees, there were some good stories to cover and you can't beat meeting people, watching things and then writing about them as a way to earn a living.

The routine of a local weekly paper is focused around deadline day. That fixed point in time when whatever you've accumulated for that week's edition has to go off to the printers in order to go through the presses and get out to the shops. In the case of the *Redbridge Guardian*, H-hour was Wednesday lunchtime, allowing the paper to be in the newsagents on Thursday morning. When the deadline passed we would invariably slope off to one of the nearby Walthamstow pubs, a mixed-bag editorial team of ambitious, young, journo climbers on the way up and cynical, weary, old hacks who had long since spiked any desires for the bright lights of Fleet Street.

Wednesday afternoon, slightly beery, would be spent back in the office catching up on reading, unwinding or making a couple of calls. Next week's deadline a dim and distant milestone and the pace reflecting this. Thursday would perhaps be spent at one of the courts. Redbridge Magistrates in Barkingside would be a battery farm of minor offenders from around the borough, so we would sift through an endless line of hearings for petty crimes like shoplifting, burglary and assault, waiting for that one glint of gold in the bottom of the pan. Something with an angle. Something which was funny ha-ha or peculiar, something which tugged the heartstrings, anything which would make good copy. Court reporting cranked up a notch at Snaresbrook Crown Court, where the violence intensified, the sum swindled had more noughts attached to it and the criminality became more professional. A more subdued journalistic high came from the Coroners Court in Walthamstow where the grief of the loved ones left behind cut through the clinical investigation of the circumstances of death.

One evening a week we would be on council duty. Redbridge, Waltham Forest, Havering and Epping were all borough and district councils which fell under our news area and the mechanics of local government made substantial if somewhat stodgy material for the printed page. These tedious meetings, focusing on local issues but fought over party political lines never failed to amaze or frustrate me. Your average local council is made up of a combination of either worthy do-gooders or self-serving, small pond, big fish. The sort of person that would have been branded a 'dork' or 'boffin' at school, obsessed with scoring political points over each other in debate and bogged down by the reams of paperwork which clutter the running of a regional administration. And yet the sums of money that are distributed by these minor mandarins is staggering. I would find myself in the press box biting my lip at the inadequacies of these people. My job was to report, sometimes to comment, but never to interrupt. And yet I don't blame the councillors for their inadequacies. They were doing a job that no one else wants to. I blame the apathy of the people that award the power. The electorate which either fails to vote, or fails to find out *who* they are voting in. I strongly believe that if everyone in the country had to attend at least one council meeting in their life, turnout rates for local elections and the quality of those voted for would soar.

Anyway off my soapbox and back to life on the newspaper. By now you were at the weekend, a time when the perks of the job really started to pay off. With the rough comes the smooth. For every council meeting press gallery I sat in, there were an equal number of sporting press boxes just waiting. And the key that unlocked these coveted locations was the mythical National Union of Journalists Press Pass. Within the boundaries of my news area were seats at Tottenham, Arsenal and West Ham. One call to a club's press officer, one fax of your credentials and you were watching top flight football from some of the best seats in the house, rubbing shoulders with the big boys from the national papers, radio and TV.

If you wanted to try your hand at any sport, one call to a press officer, one fax of your credentials and you were training with Jurgen Klinsmann, or facing 100mph deliveries from Curtley Ambrose. In my time on the papers I have abseiled down buildings, bungee jumped over the River Lea, raced speedway bikes, wing-walked on a biplane and watched a number of England matches and a pair of League Cup finals at Wembley. All thanks to my beloved Press Pass.

By Monday morning the deadline had suddenly reared into view. You'd *never* done enough reading or made enough calls, and while the sports pages were filling nicely with the reports coming in from the weekend, and the middle of the paper was filled with human interest features, the real meat of the paper – pages one through five – were still glaringly empty and the pressure was mounting. You had two and a half days to come up with that massive splash for page one which would hurl the paper off the shelves and into the shopping bag. The page three lead had to be almost as good, to pull the reader further into the paper, while page five could legitimately be the last of the really strong news stories.

The chief reporter would disappear off into the editor's glass box office for a concerned huddle before emerging and walking over to the team of reporters who were nervously smoking at their desks. His question of 'What have you got for page one then?' inevitably answered by a collection of blank looks.

By Tuesday the pressure of the deadline would be intense. There would either be an obvious candidate for the splash story or you would be desperately scrambling the phones, suggesting interviews with the local rent-a-gobs on the council who you knew would say something controversial, if lacking in substance.

By Wednesday morning, if every lead had been followed, if every source had been tapped-up, if every avenue had been investigated, there was only one last resort. Deep Throat. A covert call to a good friend on a rival paper and in a telephone stage whisper… 'What have you got on page one?' Twenty minutes later, copy filed, editor and chief reporter satiated, it was off to the pub and the weekly cycle would start again.

On the Saturday in question I had made my way to Victoria Road and filed into the away end flashing the beloved Press Pass. I had gone in with the away supporters because my colleague Sumit Bose was a lifelong Orient fan, born and raised in Leyton. He'd convinced both myself and another good friend and newspaperman Mark Poulter to discard the loose allegiance we had for the Daggers – from filling the sport pages of the *Redbridge Guardian* with their match reports – and stand with the Orient mob. As we'd started off two hours earlier in the Railway Pub adjacent to Victoria Road, neither of us was particularly inclined to disagree and it was a good choice, because there is just something magical about standing with away fans. They tend to be the most hardcore and so the most vocal. The atmosphere they generate engulfs you and before you know it, you are clapping and stamping along and finally picking up the words to the songs, especially with a couple of lagers on board.

I'm sure that the O's fans were convinced that this would be a formality, that old Goliath syndrome. Newly-merged Dagenham & Redbridge were in the Conference, two divisions below Orient. The mood on the away terrace was very much 'what a jolly day out in Dagenham we are having.' That's until the home side scored. Not once, but twice and in the first twenty five minutes. The O's pulled one back twelve minutes later but then Dagenham struck again three minutes after that. We were barely catching our breath and looking forward to a respite after forty five frantic minutes when the O's netted in first half injury time. Three-two going into the break.

Five minutes after the restart it was all square again when Orient defender

Mark Cooper headed home a free kick and he produced a carbon copy twenty minutes later for Orient goal number four. The visitors looked to have tied things up when a seventy eighth minute free kick came off the bar to be slotted home for a fifth Orient strike. But that just galvanised the home side further and they pulled one back with an immediate response from ace marksman Paul Cavell. Despite ten furious minutes of attacking the Non-Leaguers were unable to break down the Orient defence and it finished five-four to the visitors. Dagenham boss John Still described it thus: *'It was the best game I've ever been involved in. I now know I'll never have a heart attack as a football manager – if I survived today, I'll survive anything.'*

It had been everything that the cup should be about. Passion, pride and pulsating action. Local rivalries, good-natured banter and above everything, football came out the winner. John Still left Dagenham & Redbridge in 1994 to take over as manager of Peterborough United, then had coaching and managerial spells at Lincoln City, Barnet and Bristol Rovers. But in an interesting twist of fate, he was now the man back in the hot seat at Victoria Road who had masterminded Dagenham's defeat of the Bleeding Harriers. Another omen perhaps?

December 2007
Back To The Seaside

My favourite films during my teenage years were the *Back To The Future* trilogy. The comic familiarity of the characters as they transcended different generations and eras, the subtle complexity of the plotlines and the paradoxes which unfold from the smallest of actions, all contrived to delight my juvenile mind. And of course it didn't hurt that the stainless steel, gull-winged DeLorean was a schoolboy's fantasy of a car. And with the approach of the Third Round Proper, my FA Cup adventure echoed the plight of Marty McFly and Co.

There was the familiarity of the process. Match leads to victor, victor leads to progression, progression leads to draw, draw leads to match. A chance goal here, a last minute save there and my future could be thrown down an unexpected path. While the events had a familiar, repetitive nature, each one was slightly different from before. And after the draw for the third round, I had my own paradox which would see me travel back in time.

I now had an extended family showing interest. On the day of the Third Round Draw, my sister had travelled up to our house with my brother-in-law Ross and her two daughters Alice and Ruby for Sunday lunch and to see where I would be going next. My brood was sat around the TV waiting in anticipation and my father was on the end of the phone. The draw was officiated over as usual by Sir Trevor Brooking, while Kevin Beattie and Sammy Nelson had the honour of retrieving the numbered balls from the bowls. I had printed off a list of all of the teams that were going into the hat and it had an ominous bias, because the Third Round Proper is when the FA Cup gets serious. The Premiership and Championship teams were joining for the first time and my anticipation was heightened by the prospect of a trip to Old Trafford, Stamford Bridge or Anfield. Of course I was desperately hoping that Dagenham & Redbridge avoided any of the 'big' teams, as this would only increase the difficulty of obtaining tickets for future rounds. No, I was looking for a mediocre league side, with a middle to low attendance and not too far away. As the balls came out I drew a line through each of the teams, waiting for the Daggers' number fifty five to emerge. I'd struck through forty names and dodged the bullets of Liverpool, Manchester United and Arsenal, when a team appeared which piqued my interest.

'Number forty five,' said Kevin.

'Oxford United or Southend United,' said Trevor.

'Go on,' I cried, 'I'll take that.'

'Number fifty five,' said Sammy.

'Will play Dagenham & Redbridge.'

'Wahey!' The fates had produced another dream result. Potentially an all-Essex derby match between Southend and the Daggers. Two teams that were inexorably linked to my footballing history. I say potentially because of course first of all Southend of League One would need to negotiate a replay with Conference League Oxford United. This meant that while my destiny was already in the Third Round, I would need to go 'Back To The Second Round', before finding out where I would end up in the future. See what I mean? Great Scott!

And the fact that the Second Round replay between Southend and Oxford was being held at Southend's Roots Hall meant that it was easy for me to drive the thirty miles from my house to catch that game as well.

The journey had familiar overtones, similar yet different. It was virtually the same route I had taken for the Great Wakering replay with Ware back in September. But back then it had been a balmy Indian summer evening, warm and light. This time around it was a cold, dark, crisp December evening where gloves, hat, scarf and three layers of clothing (including my Ware T-Shirt of course) were the order of the day. Too bad I didn't own a DeLorean. It was also a journey bereft of the stress and anxiety of previous matches. I really didn't care who won this game because I already had the Daggers safely tucked away in my back pocket. If Oxford won it would be a nice away day to a ground I'd never visited and against a team that I fancied Dagenham to beat. If Southend won through then I was guaranteed an Essex team to root for in the Fourth Round.

Eden was sat alongside me wrapped up in multiple layers against the cold. Vanessa and the other two children were in France (again) on a pre-Christmas visit to her parents, so a midweek football fixture, despite school the next morning, had been granted by the remaining (lax) parent incumbent. We arrived at the ground with about forty minutes to go until kick-off and Roots Hall was just as I remembered it. I'd first visited in 1984 during that stint as a ball boy, the next visit saw a then first division Derby humbled by a then fourth division Shrimpers in the league cup of 1987. I remember on the way to the ground on that occasion telling my father it was just a case of how many Derby would score. We'd sat high in the East Stand and watched as Southend recorded a competent one-nil giant-killing without really breaking sweat. Derby had been terrible, exhibiting the now all-too familiar higher division complacency. Following that embarrassment I had borne a grudge against Southend for years.

It was heightened in 1993 when I was courting Vanessa. We had stolen off to Stratford-upon-Avon for a weekend break and to my delight she had agreed to my suggestion of a visit to the Baseball Ground, especially when she heard that Southend were playing. It's amazing what people will do when romance is blossoming. Nowadays she would rather pull fingernails than come to a football match with me and I'd rather cut off an arm than ask her. We funnelled in to the confined terrace of the Baseball Ground's Popside, deep in Rams territory and she had raucously cheered every one of the three Southend goals as they went in to only one Derby reply. With our Thames Estuary accents it's a miracle we got out of there alive.

But my turning point with Southend came in January of 2000 when I decided one Saturday to take myself off to Roots Hall to watch them play Rochdale. This was the first live football match I'd been to in six years and I'm not really sure why I went, although if you look at the match date, 15th January 2000, it can probably be assigned to some sort of miniature mid-life crisis. Three weeks prior to this game my middle child Evie was born. I imagine that the sudden desire to disappear on a Saturday afternoon was directly linked to the enforced domestication of double fatherhood.

Anyway, I had settled down in the West Stand among the Southend fans desperate to see the Blues and their supporters suffer a slice of humiliation to soothe my Roots Hall grudge. And Rochdale went about their job with gusto, scoring three times in the first half to go in at the break apparently with the three points in the bag. The Southend manager at the time, Alan Little, must have been hurling the teacups because the Blues came out in the second half a changed side. They immediately pulled one back and I was swept up by the glorious release that a goal brings to a packed terrace. There was nothing else I could do but stand up and applaud. When the second goal went in I was on my feet cheering in unison with the crowd and when they pulled off a dramatic last gasp equaliser I was hooked.

I went back a fortnight later and saw them beat Swansea two-one and then the following week I went on an away day with the Southend fans to nearby Leyton Orient where they lost by the same score. At that point something must have cracked at home because the matches dry up. Again I can't remember exactly what it was, but I suspect it was something to do with my two-month old daughter, or rather my apparent neglect of my two-month-old daughter. I wouldn't visit another live match until 2005 when Eden started to develop an interest for football and I took her to Portman Road for a pre-season friendly between Ipswich and Rangers.

However as the Back To The Future cup clash at Roots Hall played out in front of us, it was very apparent to me that I *wanted* a Southend win. And they duly obliged scoring twice before half time and then wrapping things up with a third goal in second half injury time. The all-Essex Third Round derby between the Shrimpers and the Daggers was set up, but where to go? In with the away fans from Dagenham or in the Southend home seats?

Saturday January 5th, 2008:

Third Round Proper
Southend United V Dagenham & Redbridge

We set off for the ground at 9am. Admittedly an early start for a thirty mile journey to a 3pm kick off but the reason for this is that *everyone* is going. Me, Vanessa and all three kids. So first we have to go to swimming lessons, then on to a mid–day party for school friends of Jonathan and Evie, and then on to Roots Hall. It's a beautiful winter's day. The sky is bluer than a Coventry home kit, the sun a deep orange like an old–fashioned winter football and the cold snap from the Urals which brought a smattering of snow to the streets of Essex earlier in the week has long since departed.

I'm excited to be going to a match as a family. There's an implicit acceptance that I've proven to Vanessa that this is not just some hare-brained scheme and that I will get complete support and more importantly, her approval from here on in. Especially as distances and costs begin to increase. When *she* woke up this morning, *her* first words were 'Football today'. My heart soared. Of course there are trade offs. She's negotiated a full day of household tasks for Sunday, a trip to the bottle bank, one to the tip, a curtain rail which needs to go up with accompanying tie-backs, but these are for tomorrow.

The morning streaks past in a blur. We pick up the two little ones from their children's party in Chelmsford and head off to Southend on the now very familiar journey. I'd checked back in my records earlier in the week after it occurred to me that I've probably visited Southend more times than any other league ground. I was right. The only stadium I've visited more often is Wembley. Nice omen.

The decision that the whole family will accompany me to this match has also decided whether we sit with the home or away fans. There are five tickets for the Family Enclosure snuggling in the back pocket of my jeans, partly because Vanessa is more aligned to Southend than I am to Dagenham, but mainly because the tickets are wickedly cheap. Forty pounds for a family of five.

All right so I imagine you are thinking what has brought about this big change in Vanessa. All of a sudden she is a football fan accompanying me on matches and not someone I need to be furtively sneaking around. I've been thinking about this and I believe the explanation is a combination of events. First of all I made our children happy with the staging of the mock draws. And when her children are happy, she is happy. Secondly and more bizarrely, Southend have drifted into the equation and she *really* has something going with Southend. I'm sure she will never admit it, even and especially to herself, but I can see a Shrimpers fanatic in denial.

Anyway back to the action and despite leaving home at 9am we only reach Southend with about half an hour in the bag. We park on Prittlewell Avenue and make our way into the ground, the children each being handed an ominous-looking plastic package titled 'Bam-Bams'. A quick trip to the loo each and we head for our seats.

Roots Hall is an old ground. An old-fashioned old ground. Four disparate grandstands loosely connected by a rectangle of green grass. Small, compact and atmospheric. Wedged between the main road into Southend and terraced houses. The Blues have their own ambitions to move to a cookie-cutter stadium, with the mandatory shops and hotels attached, but then the Blues have had ambitions to move for as long as I've been following Essex football. For now, Roots Hall will have to suffice.

We are in the Family Enclosure section of the West Stand, five rows up from the front and eight seats in from the corner. I have an excellent view of the corner flag, the south goal and little else. Opposite me is the East Stand where Eden and I sat for the Oxford United replay. The main stand of the ground. The players' tunnel flanked by rows of seats, below the corporate boxes with their winking TV screens, covered by an arch of grey, corrugated 'stuff'.

To my (far) left are the Dagenham supporters in the Muddy Fox stand. Named after the sponsor, an Essex bicycle manufacturer. Muddy Fox has a bizarre advert in the match day programme showing a crescent of young models in high-heeled shoes, Southend United shirts and their knickers, sat astride Muddy Fox cycles in front of the Muddy Fox stand. With that and the (inaccurate) reputation of the 'Essex Girl', it's no wonder the Oxford United fans were singing: *'Town full of slappers, You're just a town full of slappers.'* I'd half expected the Southend fans to respond with: *'Town full of slappers, We've got a town full of slappers.'* But they'd disappointed me. They're not the most vocal or imaginative of fans.

To my right is the most modern stand, the South Stand, a twin deck affair (only about ten rows in each tier mind) which abuts on to a block of flats behind.

Our stand is similar in fashion to the East Stand only with a double arch of that grey, corrugated 'stuff'. From our low position all I can see beyond the ground are two towers. One of flats and one of a church. At each of the four corners of the ground, looming up into the sky are a set of floodlights, proper ones. The sort of pylons that came in the Subbuteo Floodlight Edition or in the opening titles of the BBC programme *Sportsnight*. The glare of the lights stands out against the darkening winter sky.

Now that we are moving up in standard of playing professionalism, so too are the production values of the pre-match build-up. With fifteen minutes to go the PA system is blaring out a slow, rhythmic backing track of dance music which is building in impetus and pitch, heightening the anticipation. The two teams are warming up and the crowd is bustling around us. People stand by their seats with their backs to the pitch looking up into the stands, searching for and acknowledging familiar faces or drinking in the atmosphere, like meerkats on sentry duty. The two Southend mascots, Sammy the Shrimp and Elvis the Christ Knows But He Looks Like A Horse And It's Not Obvious Why, are doing the rounds, getting great value from the patrons of the Family Enclosure. And it is then that the objective of the packages handed out to the kids becomes apparent. All the children surrounding us are waving a pair of white, plastic, inflatable Bam Bams badly beating out time as the musical background increases like a demented South Sea Island band.

My three kids look at the other childrens' Bam Bams, look at their own cellophane packages, and then look up at me. Without a word they offer me their packages, their sentiment implicit yet unspoken: 'Father. Inflate us.'

'This is Roots Hall, home of Southend United,' bellows the announcer to a great roar and hammering of Bam Bams. 'But before the teams come out, first a word from our Chairman Ron Martin.' A man takes the microphone from the announcer, the music dies and the stadium quietens. Mr Martin speaks: 'First, I want to apologise for Tuesday's performance.' A guarded round of applause. 'This is not the sort of performance that we have come to expect from a Steve Tilson side.' More applause, this fellow's good. 'I will not accept it and Tilly will not accept it. We need to make amends and funds *will* be made available in the coming transfer window. This is a great club, with a great future and we need to work together to make this happen, starting today.'

Martin gets a giant cheer and rapturous applause as he heads back down the tunnel. So it would appear that the Blues are in something of a funk, this bodes well for the opposition and it is at this precise point that I realise where my loyalties lie today. I want the underdog, I want the Daggers.

The music restarts as the two teams emerge from the tunnel. After the players from each team are announced to the crowd the PA blares out a rendition of The Beatles' *Hey Jude* which I remember from the Oxford match. This is apparently the Southend anthem and the demented Bam Bam band has suddenly found their rhythm, beating in time with the music. Finally the referee, Mr A Bates, blows his whistle and we get underway.

As the first half unfolds I look at the players on show and realise that I barely know a single face. I recognise Tony Roberts in the Dagenham goal and sort of remember their strikers Ben Strevens and Jon Nurse, but unfortunately and more concerningly, it looks as though Paul Benson, by far the Daggers' most dangerous striker against Kidderminster, isn't playing. I assume he must be injured. On the Southend side I can generally pick out their long-serving captain Kevin Maher in a line-up, but *he* isn't playing either. So it's going to be another one of those impersonal games where I merely want a Yellow to beat a Blue to the ball.

The opening exchanges are scrappy, a theme which runs throughout the first half. Southend score after just ten minutes but it is right down at the other end and virtually impossible for us to see from our low, far position. The distance of our viewpoint means that any action down at that end is monochrome attacking. It's either a goal or not. You can't really see the build-up or the closeness of an effort. The first you know of what has happened is from a feint billow of the net and the reaction of the crowd. When the goal goes in we react because of the cheers not because we've seen it properly. Vanessa and the kids leap up to cheer the goal and I stand slowly and reluctantly, obliged to clap because I'm in a Southend stand and with a pro-Southend family. But inside I'm grumbling. I can feel that old Southend antagonism starting to emerge from the depths of my brain.

Despite the setback Dagenham come back into the game after the restart. There is only one division of difference between the two teams, so they are fairly well matched physically and it is only the Southend attack which is slightly cuter than the opposition's. But on the half hour mark the visitors snatch an equaliser when Nurse gets the right side of his defender in the six-yard box to steer home a low cross from right in front of us. By comparison to the previous strike this is a Technicolor goal. At this end our proximity means we can see *everything*. The movement of the players, the flight of the ball. I can't resist a subdued 'Yesss' and low fist clench in the direction of Vanessa and the kids. All four eye me warily. I've shown my colours now.

All in all though it is a poor half and I'm wondering about the sanity of bringing Vanessa along as she can't be impressed by it. Jonathan takes out his

Nintendo and spends the rest of the half squabbling with Eden about who gets to play it. Evie sits on her mother's lap watching the game studiously, but without enthusiasm. I am dispatched to the snack bar with five minutes to go to half time for refreshments, returning with burgers and two coffees which are so ridiculously caffeine-strong that before long both Vanessa and I are hammering out a beat on the Bam Bams with wide-eyed craziness.

So to a second half as rich in incident as the first has been bereft. The darkening sky is now an inky black and the floodlights stand like giant flares against it, pouring brilliance onto the arena, making the green of the grass glisten, shining luster onto the yellow shirts of Dagenham and the dark blue of Southend. Across from us the faces of the fans in the East Stand are cast into relief with just the dim lights of the press boxes showing through. Vanessa leans over and whispers to me, 'I like it when it gets dark.'

I start to think about the possible outcomes. A win for Dagenham seems unlikely. A win for Southend tears against my heartstrings, a draw and return to Victoria Road would be my preference now. I've grown to dislike the longer gaps between matches in the latter rounds and I crave replays for the additional action they bring.

Twelve minutes in and an unexpected turn of events. Another black and white goal at the far end. I can see a Dagenham striker squirming along the goal line, I can't tell who. I can see him rifle off a shot and the ball seem to bulge the net. I see the Dagenham fans erupt before I hear them, only momentarily, but then the celebrations synch and I see Mr A Bates pointing to the centre circle. Rather bizarrely the Daggers have taken the lead. Again the clenched fist and again the family glares. It's only when the PA announces his name that I discover that it is Ben Strevens who has found the back of the net.

Now the tempo of the game really cranks up as Southend come out looking for the equaliser. The visitors have already been to Roots Hall in the Johnstone's Paint Trophy this season and stolen away with a win on penalties. There is more than a place in the Fourth Round at stake here, there's Essex pride. I start to calculate what needs to be done. There's about thirty minutes to go. Thirty minutes of resolute defending required. I've been here before of course, when Ware went ahead against Thurrock. Ware had the luxury of extending to a two-goal lead when they snatched a third. Dagenham need to do the same.

Just as I finish making a note of this in my trusty notepad, Southend score and I curse the Footballing Gods for letting me jinx the visitors. A fabulous one-two on the edge of the area is finished with aplomb by Dean Morgan. Again I have to wearily get to my feet and clap with gritted teeth as the Bam Bams waggle furiously around me. It's disappointing but at least my favoured outcome of a draw and replay is now in play.

Both teams then play out a cagey ten minutes, neither prepared to probe too far and risk anything at the back. Southend force a corner. The ball goes long and drops down at the far post to the feet of Simon Francis. He shapes to cross but then cuts back inside the defender and hammers home a low drive which somehow misses a battalion of legs in the six-yard box and slams into the back of the net. My heart plummets as my legs push me upwards, out of my seat and into the now mandatory applause position. Vanessa and the kids are jubilant. I am thoroughly despondent.

Behind me in the Family Enclosure I can hear a father and son. They have been discussing the match throughout the first half, the father pointing out the finer points of the game. For most of the match he has been saying *exactly* what I have been thinking. Now he speaks again, the words drifting down a row into my ears: 'They'll have to chase the game now and Southend will get another one on the break.' It feels like he is some sort of Essex-accented Jiminy Cricket. Reading my thoughts and acting as my conscience, while I, a fifteen-stone Pinocchio still dream of the 'wrong' result.

With barely five minutes to go it looks hopeless but the Daggers force a corner. With nothing to lose even goalkeeper Roberts goes up for the attack leaving his untended net gaping like an open mouth. The ball swings over and Roberts hurls himself at the ball, missing by a couple of inches and crashing into the Southend defender Peter Clarke. As the ball breaks clear, Roberts and Clarke start tangling for a spot of afters in the penalty box, meanwhile Southend are flooding forward towards the open Dagenham goal with two Daggers defenders in desperate pursuit.

Mr A Bates is trying to disentangle Roberts and Clarke. The rest of the stadium are twisting their heads like spectators at a tennis match, first to the fight at one end, then at the breakaway open goal chance at the other. No one knows which way to look. I finally drag my head away from the far end and watch in disbelief and then delight as first one effort on the Dagenham goal is blocked on the line by the flying rearguard action and then the rebound is shanked wide of the net. Back at the other end Mr A Bates has finally got to the bottom of the punch up and red cards the Dagenham keeper. The Southend faithful's disappointment at the missed open goal is assuaged at seeing red and the ground is alive with a chattering outburst of excitement. 'What happened then?' Vanessa asks. 'What was the goalie doing in that half?' I can do nothing but shrug my shoulders, teeth still gritted. This is going from bad to worse.

When the dust finally settles and the game restarts, amazingly with a goal kick for Dagenham, the fourth official hurls a lifeline with four added minutes of extra time, and equally amazingly this signals a frenzied attacking spell from the visiting ten men. They force two corners, the second of which falls to the feet of Danny Foster. He is on the edge of the six-yard box and the Southend goal is at his mercy. Again that sensation of slow motion in my brain. He must score. His left foot cocks like the hammer of a gun and he toe-pokes the ball up towards the top corner of the goal, but somehow, despite the short distance it has to travel, the ball curves away, missing the post by inches and disappearing into the Muddy Fox stand. My head literally and I mean literally sinks into my hands at the miss. My stomach plummets as if on a rollercoaster. I feel almost physically sick. I hear the jubilant words of the conscience Jiminy Cricket behind me: 'That's their last chance.'

When a team is chasing a game with ten minutes to go there is always at least one more 'last' chance. When the chance passes it's as if everyone in the stadium, in the dugouts, on the pitch, knows. I recognise it from my playing days. Dagenham know it too, as do Southend, and the home side starts playing with a renewed confidence. A stinging, long-range shot is brilliantly parried by the substitute goalkeeper Ed Thompson but the ball loops up twenty feet in the air and slowly falls back to earth towards the Dagenham goal to be bundled over the line by Morgan. Four-two.

At that moment all of the hatred for Southend that I've bottled up over the years is finally uncapped. The embarrassing league cup defeat against Derby in 1987, the three-one reverse in one of my rare visits to the Baseball Ground in 1993, it's like my later admiration for the team was just a plaster I stuck over those wounds which has now been ripped off again.

To add insult to metaphysical injury, Southend bag a fifth minutes later. A slick passing move which is tucked comfortably home from close range. This time around I don't even bother getting out of my seat. I've given up caring if some Family Enclosure firm of ten-year-olds want to give me a Bam Bam battering for being a Dagenham fan in a Southend seat.

Finally Mr A Bates puts me out of my misery, blowing his whistle to a thunderous cheer. After five defeats on the spin the Shrimpers have responded to Chairman Martin's pre-match plea and delivered on their end of the bargain. For Dagenham it is a short, sharp conclusion to a bittersweet, (or should that be sweet then bitter) cup campaign. Anyway my mob are happy. Vanessa says excitedly: 'We'll come to the next one if you can get tickets.' I start to think about the next one. Getting tickets will be one problem, but sticking the plaster back on my Southend hatred wound may be a bigger one. Right now I hope they rot in hell.

Southend United 5 (MacDonald 10, Morgan 63, 90, Francis 76, Bailey 90)
Dagenham & Redbridge 2 (Nurse 31, Strevens 57)

Attendance: 6,393
Money Spent So Far: £109.50
Miles Travelled So Far: 947
Winners Receive £40,000

1993
The Thin End Of The Wedge

Two weeks after the Dagenham versus Orient thriller in 1992 I moved out of my parents' house in Harold Wood. After eighteen months of on-the-job training and a three-month block release course at Harlow College in Essex, I was now a fully trained and certified journalist according to the National Council for the Training of Journalists and that meant the tight arse bean-counters at the Guardian, Gazette and Independent Group were obliged to give me a miserly pay rise. I decided that the most important thing to fritter away that additional cash on would be rent money.

I'd tapped up the Orient fan in the office Sumit Bose, who was also living with his parents, to see if he was interested in flat sharing and we found a two-bedroomed place on the top floor of a terraced house in Daisy Road, South Woodford. Forty minutes from Harold Wood, fifteen minutes from the offices in Walthamstow and rather poignantly just a five minute walk from my Gran's house at Twelve Lilian Gardens. Grandad Joe had died in July of that year aged ninety one, his funeral at the City of London Cemetery being the first I had attended in my life. I can remember a deep sense of nothingness during the service, no misery, no grief. If anything there was just a mild annoyance at the informal tone used by the vicar during the eulogy. I was aware that he never knew my grandfather and yet he spoke about him in terms which bestowed a lifelong friendship. However I held no real malice towards the holy man, as I'd interviewed and written a feature about him in the newspaper a few months previously. He was a well-known figure around the parish because he tended his flock from the back of a motorbike. Naturally our chief headline writer Mick McGlinchey had dubbed him the 'Revving Reverend' and indeed I was pleased to see him retrieve his crash helmet from behind the lectern on the way out, having pressed the button which dispatched Grandad Joe's earthly remains to the furnace.

So Granny was now living alone in that familiar old house which started to loom around her as she began to shrink in that way old people do. Now that I lived closer by I was able to visit more often, although in retrospect probably not as much as I should have done. And indeed she was one of the first people to visit me in Daisy Road once I'd moved in. The freedom of living away from home was a jarring experience, equal measures of liberation and loneliness. I'd imagined that keeping my own hours, playing my music as loud as I wanted and generally being my own boss away from the influence and rule of my parents would be somewhat more fulfilling then it actually was. Instead I found I missed the comfortable, social interaction of the family home. But I was comforted to be living in an area which my grandparents had taken me around when I was a small boy.

Work was going well. I was progressing up the hierarchy of the newsroom, continuing to enjoy the perks of the Press Pass and mixing with a new circle of friends developed from my working environment and change of scene. A sub-editor called James Hislop became a very close friend spending many hours in the flat, hanging out, listening to music and we developed an unhealthy penchant for obscure war-based board games and Trivial Pursuit competitions.

On the footballing front my new location meant I had cut all of my ties with previous clubs and entered something of a vacuum playing-wise. My weekends had become somewhat busier as I was often out covering events in the news area or reporting on matches concerning the local teams. Almost out of the blue came an unexpected trip to Wembley to see Derby play in a cup final, albeit a very minor one – the Anglo-Italian Cup Final against Cremonese in March of 1993. My father and I celebrated the momentous occasion of the Rams at Wembley by buying the most expensive tickets on offer and yet for some reason we still found ourselves sat in front of one of the notorious Wembley pillars that obscured your view. Sumit had used his own magical Press Pass to blag a seat in the press box and taken great delight when learning of our viewing misfortune, compounded by a three-one victory for the Italians.

Derby also gave me a brief moment of FA Cup excitement that season by reaching the Quarter Finals for the first time in my living memory where they faced Sheffield Wednesday. The match was shown live on TV on a Monday night and I found myself sat in a Walthamstow pub with James and his girlfriend Jo, desperately trying to pay attention to the ensuing Quiz Night questions while The Rams and Wednesday duked out a six-goal draw. Naturally we lost the replay and in one of those bizarre quirks of the draw process, Blackburn Rovers, Ipswich Town and Manchester City all lost at that stage as well. This meant that two great footballing rivalries, Arsenal/Spurs and Sheffields Wednesday/United would contest the two semi finals that year.

Two years previously, the FA in its infinite wisdom had embarked on a process of allowing semi-finals to be played at Wembley when Arsenal and Spurs were also drawn together in 1991. And they repeated this process in 1993 rather than saving the grand old stadium for the big day itself. The matches were good ones, I'll grant you that, the Gunners and Wednesday triumphing respectively. But in my opinion, playing semi-finals at Wembley, rather than say at a neutral venue like Old Trafford or Villa Park, meant that the thin end of the wedge lodged its first chink in the glorious mystique of the grand old competition. Was the magical cup in danger of losing some of its sparkle?

January 2008
Rooting For The Shrimpers?

Southend United versus Barnsley. The names winked out at me from the computer screen. The FA had held the Fourth Round Draw on the Monday afternoon after Third Round weekend at 1.30pm. I had been sat at my desk at work unable to get to a TV or radio and unable to get the audio working on my laptop to listen to Five Live over the web. It was another massive draw anti-climax.

I had known that I couldn't wait until I got home from work to fashion one of my pseudo-draws with the kids. There were too many people by then who knew about my cup odyssey. It would have been incredibly difficult to maintain radio silence until I got home. Not in a world of email, texts and instant messaging. So I'd logged onto the BBC Sport website at 1.30pm to try and watch the draw there. Unfortunately I suspect that the rest of cyberspace must have had the same idea because the BBC site had ground to a halt. I flipped to the FA website but that too had crashed after the first tie had been drawn out of the hat and by the time I had got across to Skysports.com the draw had taken place and all of the balls were out of the Perspex. I'd drawn Barnsley.

Or rather Southend had drawn Barnsley and to add to my infuriation, they'd drawn them at home. Which of course meant a repeat visit to Roots Hall. A real pain in the arse with all of my best descriptive writing on the ageing stadium already used up in the previous chapter. On the positive side the lure of Barnsley would probably not set cup fever flooding through the streets of Southend-on-Sea so I was fairly confident of being able to get tickets. And more importantly I'd avoided the big four clubs for another round.

In fact up until now the draw had been fairly kind in limiting the threat of Premiership teams. Three major scalps had already occurred on Third Round day. Everton were unexpectedly beaten at Goodison by Oldham, Huddersfield Town had overcome Birmingham City and Blackburn Rovers were walloped four-one by Coventry at Ewood Park. Bolton Wanderers, Sunderland and Aston Villa all failed to progress while West Ham lost in a replay to Manchester City – always a reason to be cheerful.

Liverpool and Newcastle were both lucky to escape with draws away to Luton and Stoke respectively. But then 'King Kevin' Keegan arrived back as the manager on Toonside and the Magpies romped to a four-one victory over Stoke despite playing for most of the replay with just ten men. Liverpool made easy work at Anfield of financially beleaguered Luton whose better players had been firesold by the administrators in the time between the first match and the replay. And the Footballing Gods had ordained that it be Liverpool who progressed because that set up a heavenly Fourth Round game between the five time European Cup winners and the last remaining Non-League team in the competition Havant & Waterlooville who had stunned Swansea City in their own replay.

I have to admit watching the Havant result come in on the Wednesday night with envious eyes. Having followed the cup odyssey from its lowly, Non-League roots, I knew just how special both the win against Swansea and the trip to Liverpool would be for the fans of the Blue Square South team. Just as Ware had played *their* cup final against Kidderminster, Havant were destined to go even better with a trip to Anfield.

But with eight out of the twenty Premiership teams already having fallen by the wayside and three more all-Premiership ties in the Fourth Round featuring Manchester United, Arsenal and Chelsea, there was a good chance of more devastation for the top-ranking teams.

So while the draw had been fairly accommodating, I was more worried about the state of my relationship with Southend United, now destined to extend their lead as the team I have visited the most in my spectating history. It appeared that I had something of a love-hate relationship with them depending on the opposition. So I decided to do some research into the club's history to try and mend some emotional fences.

Southend was formed in 1906 by a group of football enthusiasts who were organised by a certain Oliver Trigg the landlord of a pub in Victoria Avenue, Prittlewell called the Blue Boar, just a stones throw from Roots Hall. Here's a little local knowledge for you, Southend is called Southend because it is at the south end of the village of Prittlewell. Anyway, the Shrimpers convened that night and originally played in the Southern League until 1920 when they were one of the founding teams of football's Third Division. The next seventy years of history was spent almost exclusively at this level apart from a handful of seasons yo-yoing down into the Fourth Division and back again.

Even the presence of the legendary Bobby Moore as manager between 1984 and 1986 failed to galvanise the team significantly. My wife Vanessa tells a great story of regularly seeing the 1966 World Cup idol waiting for the train to Southend at Fenchurch Street station in London of a morning while the vast waves of work-bound Essex commuters were getting off. She regrets never once having gone up and spoken to him and describes him as mainly looking quite sad. It is astonishing and indicative of the massive changes in football that a World Cup winning former England captain could move so anonymously through life while his modern-day less successful counterparts get feted by Hollywood movie stars.

Sad too that he even needed to work for a living and sadder still that he failed to make his mark. Indeed it was Moore's departure which heralded Southend's first tastes of success. His replacement David Webb, who has had four spells as manager, took Southend in 1991 up into the second tier of English football for the first time and on New Year's Day of 1992 the Shrimpers sat proudly on top of the table. Poor form in the run in saw them dip back down but their final position of twelfth was the highest in the club's history.

Webb stepped down at the end of that season and the club then had a remarkable merry-go-round of high profile managers including Barry Fry, Peter Taylor, Ronnie Whelan and Alvin Martin, none of whom could build on Webb's success and by April of 1999 when Martin left, Southend were fifth from bottom of the Football League. The club was under the threat of bankruptcy and so it was decided to sell Roots Hall to developers in preparation for a proposed relocation in 2003, a move which has still to materialise.

It was not until the appointment of former player Steve Tilson that an upturn in fortunes returned to the seaside town. Tilson and his assistant Paul Brush took the team to successive LDV Vans Trophy finals at the Millennium Stadium – losing on both occasions – but a third visit to the Welsh capital in 2005 saw them victorious in the League Two play-off final. The following year the Shrimpers were promoted back to the second tier as League One champions in a memorable season for professional football in Essex and East London. Southend were joined in the automatic promotion slots by close rivals Colchester United while Leyton Orient moved up from League Two after finishing third and West Ham made it to the FA Cup Final.

After such rapid table climbing the Shrimpers found life in the Championship heavy going and were relegated after just one season, but they did produce a memorable scalp when they inflicted a one-nil league cup defeat on a Manchester United team featuring both Rooney and Ronaldo. While Roots Hall was packed to the gunnels that night, it is undoubtedly the limited twelve thousand capacity of the stadium which handicaps the team's assault on the higher reaches of football. Even if they were filling it week-in, week-out, that's still not enough revenue for an assault on the Premiership. And while they have planning permission from local councils for a new twenty two thousand seater stadium at their current training ground Fossets Farm, the final rubber stamp by national government is currently the subject of an inquiry.

Similarly the team has only ever had limited success in the FA Cup although the competition is responsible for the biggest ever attendance at Roots Hall when over thirty one thousand people packed in to watch a nil-nil Third Round draw against Liverpool. To put that into context there were only eleven thousand inside for the league cup match against Manchester United. Never having made it further than the Fifth Round, the Shrimpers have only got that far on four occasions. Whether they could make it a fifth would depend on them converting home advantage into goals against a Barnsley team sitting pretty comfortably in mid-table in the Championship, one division and twenty positions higher than Southend.

Friday January 25th, 2008
Fourth Round Proper
Southend United V Barnsley

It's Thursday morning and I'm sat in a hotel room in Boston on the eastern seaboard of America. The home of the famous bar *Cheers*, baseball's current World Champions the Redsox and the NFL powerhouse the New England Patriots. Somebody, somewhere, at the FA or at Roots Hall, has decided to bring the Fourth Round match between Southend and Barnsley forward from Saturday afternoon to Friday night and while Vanessa has organised the tickets for me, I'm on the wrong continent.

I've travelled to the States for an all-hands company meeting. I've been in Boston for seven days and was due to fly back on Friday night. It's been organised for months. But my travel plans have been thrown into turmoil. I have a full day of work meetings arranged for Thursday but I'm going to have to bunk off and make a dash to New York for the only scheduled direct flight which can get me back to Stansted in time to make it to Southend.

I finish packing my suitcase, take a last look around the hotel room for forgotten items, switch off the interminable American TV and negotiate my way around the remains of the giant breakfast of steak and eggs – a last meal from room service which is now laying heavily in my stomach. The race is officially on.

I was originally scheduled to take a flight from Boston to New York and then transfer to the transatlantic American Airlines flight to Stansted, but I only had a transfer time of forty five minutes at JFK Airport. On the way over to the States, with a similar window, I'd missed my connection. That had only meant waiting an hour for another flight to Boston, but I'd realised that if the same circumstances occurred on the way home and I missed my Stansted flight, there was no way I would make it to the match.

On Wednesday night I logged on to the internet to check my options. The simplest and cheapest alternative would be to take the Amtrak Acela Express service between Boston and New York, a four hour train ride which dropped down the eastern coastline between the two great cities. With the exchange rate hugely favouring the pound it is the sort of train ticket that I can fly under the radar of my company expense forms without setting off any alarm bells.

And so at 10am on Thursday I pitch up at Boston's South Station with my suitcase in tow after a fifteen minute, morning walk through the theatre district, Chinatown restaurants and Downtown high rises. It's a clear, crisp day. The temperature has been below zero for most of the week and there is snow on the sidewalks with the wan sun offering little relief.

Whenever I travel in America it feels like walking onto a movie set or TV show and this trip has been no different. As I sit in the giant, marbled waiting hall of the station, two characters from *The Sopranos* are sat beside me waiting for the journey back to New York State. Their thick-set, heavy Italian features and bulky frames barely masked by the large Crombie coats on their backs. They bark separately and angrily into their cell phones about some business deal which is going awry, continuing together after hanging up to the poor unfortunates on the line. 'I knew we shouldn't have let him fucking handle this,' exclaims one. 'Let's go get a fucking coffee,' suggests the other.

A call is passed over the tannoy for all passengers for the Acela Express to make their way to track seven and we shuffle over to the train which waits patiently by the platform, sleek and powerful, like a long metal snake. Now we are boarding the *Silver Streak*, the conductor singing out destinations with an east coast twang: 'Next stops Back Bay and Prrr–ovidence.' As the train pulls slowly out of the station and the skyscrapers of downtown Boston drift away we move through the poorer Boston suburbs of *Good Will Hunting*.

I find a place to sit and am immediately welcomed by a grey-haired man in his forties at the seat opposite. 'How you doing today?' he asks. As someone used to the sightless, anonymous transport of the London commuter his question catches me off guard and I stammer a short, clipped, very English response, snatching up my copy of *USA Today* to avoid any further eye contact.

The train rolls on, gathering speed as we escape the clutches of the suburbs and head into a frozen, open country. Now I *love* travelling long distances by train, especially when compared to the protracted teleportation of air travel. There is no better way to get to know a country than to see its panorama unfold in front of you from the window seat of an express train. And while I've spent plenty of time in the arid Silicon Valley of west coast America, I'm new to the graceful vistas of New England and greedily drink them all in.

Past Prrr–ovidence we enter a region which seems strangely familiar to me.

To my left is a seascape, the water incredibly still, to my right an old collection of clapboard houses and shipyards. A sign on top of one of these buildings flashes past and piques my interest, forcing me to pluck up the courage for some conversation.

'Excuse me,' I ask a woman sitting on the other side of me who has been naming places to her husband throughout the journey, 'Where are we now?'

'This is Mystic,' she replies. Another movie reference. This time the Julia Roberts film *Mystic Pizza*. I'm amazed that I can have spotted this location from a film I barely remember, or maybe it's all those reruns of *Murder She Wrote*. Gaining confidence I start talking to the woman and her husband, a retired couple from Cape Cod who are travelling down to Washington because he is now a professional bagpipe player who travels the country blowing out hot air. Talking openly to strangers is quite a strange sensation for me. Not completely unpleasant and quite the norm for all of the Americans in our compartment. Even the guy opposite me chimes in quite freely.

The miles track by as we continue down the eastern seaboard. Never straying too far from the water, crossing great rivers, charging through forests and the continual New England stream of picturesque clapboard houses. It's a long four hours but I'm in no rush. While in reality this journey is a race forward in time (zones) to a football fixture in the future, my rearranged itinerary has been purposefully designed to relieve the trip of any stress. I don't want any Phileas Fogg-style dashes for departing steamers, no constant attention to a gold pocket watch. Four hours on the train gets me into Penn Station at 3pm. I then have another four hours to get across New York to JFK airport and my awaiting jumbo.

We pass alongside the still waters of Long Island Sound and the outer reaches of New York develop with the Manhattan skyline poking needle-like in the distance, sharpening into focus like a modern version of the Emerald City from the *Wizard of Oz*. Into New York's metropolitan area and the snake burrows into one of the tunnels that will take us to the heart of the great city.

As the train comes to rest alongside the platform I bid farewell to my travelling companions and tote my luggage off the Acela Express heading off into the great bustle of Penn Station. I now have two choices. Cab or subway. A taxi will be a long, protracted drag through the gridlocked Manhattan traffic while the E-Train will take me to a connecting Sky Train at Jamaica Station straight to the airport. I plump for the latter, cheaper alternative.

I can't resist one brief glimpse at Manhattan however and ascend out of the station which squats beneath Madison Square Garden. Now I've walked up onto the set of the *Spiderman* films, the great hallways of concrete and glass, covered in yellow taxis and bustling waves of people of all races and colours. In the distance I can see the Empire State Building fortunately free of any giant apes. My brain conjures the terrible image of a plane screaming low like a banshee across this scene *a la* 9-11. A man walks past me shouting to himself and although I've been on the streets of New York for less than three minutes I decide to descend again. This personal vignette probably says more about the haunted development of my psyche than any analysis session ever could.

Back below ground I bumble around the subway system in that confused way that tourists do, looking, hoping to find the right track and train. Now you can take your pick: *The Equalizer, The Matrix* or God forbid *The Warriors*. A train marked 'E' comes along. I assume it is the E-Train and hop on, scanning the carriage for other airport-bound suitcases to offer a crumb of comfort in my choice. No such luck. But I've made note of the next station I should expect to see, 42nd Street and to my relief it looms into view. I sit back and relax for the next forty minutes, the gold pocket watch still tucked snuggly in my waistcoat pocket. The ride gives me time to reflect on the strangeness of my situation. Sat here on a New York subway train racing home to make a fairly obscure football event on a different continent.

The E-Train passes out of Manhattan and the clientele switches from one of business to one of ethnicity. Prejudice and naivety start to invade my thoughts. In the movies bad things happen on subway trains. It's the only reason for having a subway train in a narrative. In my mind's eye I see a label on my suitcase saying 'Mug Me Please'. I find myself staring at the subway map and counting off the stops. Finally it's time to alight and as I do so two large, black gentlemen jump immediately to their feet and grab me by the shoulder. I freeze as my blood runs cold.

'Airport is the next stop man.'

I'm halfway out the carriage and have to check back swiftly as the doors start to close.

'Thank you.'

'No problem.'

The train is full of different coloured faces. Mine is bright red.

I alight. I connect. I check in. I wait. I embark. We take off. I eat. I sleep. We arrive. It is match day.

It seems like no sooner are the kids back from school, nor the travel presents dished out, that we are on our way to Roots Hall again for the Barnsley game. I have the light-headedness of the long distance traveller. But whether it is jet lag or this elusive Southend factor, or whether it is this sense of distance that I seem to be feeling for the later, 'professional' rounds, I am distinctly not up for the cup. It feels like I am just going through the motions. Vanessa keeps asking me if I am OK to drive and I reply with yawned nods. If the truth be told and there's no way I would tell her, the lure of Roots Hall tonight holds little promise. If it weren't for a sense of duty to the previous rounds, I would not bother going.

Vanessa nearly doesn't. She spends half an hour deliberating. She says she is tired, that she wants a night to herself. It is only when she finally agrees to come and when she is in the car that the truth comes out. She admits that she thinks she might jinx Southend by attending. I am delighted. When you start to gather irrational thoughts like that, it's confirmation that the football bug is biting down hard.

We arrive at the stadium just ten minutes before kick off. It's testament to my subdued state that this is not causing me to panic. The familiar pre-match music ringing around the ageing grandstands is beginning to build to its crescendo. We are in the East Stand this time and in much better seats than before. Just right of the halfway line. The two teams are back in the dressing rooms leaving just the mascots Sammy The Shrimp and Elvis The Donkey warming themselves and the crowd up. Of course Elvis is a donkey, what with Southend being beside the sea and all, it just took my children to point that out. Barnsley have brought more fans than Dagenham did and the stadium is looking full apart from a swath of empty seats separating the home and away sections.

At last the teams are led out and introduced to the crowd. As the Barnsley team is called out the announcer pauses on the name of Jamal Campbell-Ryce, a former Southend winger who transferred to the Tykes at the start of the season. Having done my homework I am aware of this and let out a vibrant 'Boo' which turns out to be an unexpected *faux-pas* as the fans around me all applaud their returning hero generously while turning to stare at my outburst. I'm just relieved that it appears that my sub-conscious is permitting Southend to have my complete backing for a change.

As the opening exchanges unfold however it seems like I may be backing the wrong horse. Again. Championship Barnsley seem ridiculously adept at soaking up League One Southend's forays up field and then turning on their hosts with a steely swiftness, backed by their vocal support who are also outclassing the home fans. But gradually the Blues find their touch and both teams spurn decent opportunities to open the scoring.

Then in the twenty first minute Campbell-Ryce picks up a ball deep in the

Southend half and heads off towards the left hand corner flag seemingly going nowhere. He checks back along the line towards his own half and then cuts past across the full back, the goal looming large in his sights. Expecting a pass, the centre of the Southend defence backs off and backs off. Just as I get that nagging suspicion that this does not look good, Campbell–Ryce lets fly an absolute pearler with his right foot which lifts, swirls and dips over Darryl Flahavan in the Southend goal. One–nil.

I'm irritated by the poor defending and by the absolute quality of the strike (after all nobody likes to see their team let in a beauty) – but downright angry that only *now* do the Southend fans start booing Campbell–Ryce. After giving me a hard time. Hadn't I warned them?

Vanessa's face has gone ashen white and she keeps muttering 'knew it, my fault, shouldn't have come' beside me. I try to reassure her that there is plenty of time to go. I try to put conviction into my words but I'm lacking it inside. Southend are seeing plenty of possession but they are going sideways, backwards, sideways, backwards until the inevitable long ball is gobbled up by the lanky Barnsley defence. I've seen this scenario time and again on this journey. It's the improvement in quality. That pattern of play where it doesn't matter how hard you huff and puff, you simply don't have the invention, the creativity, the cuteness to unlock the opponent's defence. Generally in these situations you will have just one absolute gilt-edged chance. You have to take it.

The other distinction between the two teams are the names on the backs of the shirts. Southend are almost to a man domestic: Francis, Hunt, Clarke, Barrett, Black…

Barnsley have that international flavour: Muller, van Homoet, Ferenczi, Tininho, Souza…

It seems like League One to the Championship is more than just a league division.

Half time comes without Southend having that cast-iron chance, although a long-range effort from Mark Gower forces Barnsley gloveman Heinz Muller to pull off a good save, diving to his left. Muller has been something of a comedy character for the Southend fans to play with in the first half. A couple of slips from the lanky keeper leading to cries of 'Bambi on Ice'. The razor sharp wit and timing of the terraces has never failed to disappoint from Haringey Borough through to today.

We stand up through the half time break to stretch our legs and I disappoint the kids by refusing to go for drinks and burgers. There are too many people in the stadium and the queues too long to make it in time. Jonathan takes the catering knock back personally and disappears under a blanket with his Nintendo to play out the second half in his own world.

Southend come out with their guns blazing. Well perhaps maybe not guns, more like blunt instruments. The diminutive Tommy Black pulls a fine save from Muller-Bambi which stokes the embers of the home crowd. Then fifteen minutes in, the gilt-edged chance arrives. Mark Gower picks out Alistair McCormack in acres of space on the left hand side of the Barnsley goal. It's the slow motion moment. McCormack lets fly with his left foot, a low drive across Muller-Bambi's body to the far corner. From our viewing perspective there is no knowing whether it is on target or not. As the ball travels away from his boot I wait with anticipation, patience and hope for the ball to snag the far corner of the net. But instead of nestling in the corner it drags itself across the face of the goal and out for a goal kick. The despondent groan from the Southend fans ripples like a Mexican wave around the stadium.

Vanessa and I hold our heads in our hands. 'That was it,' we sigh in unison.

However there are still thirty minutes to go, or rather to endure. All of my tiredness is washed away by the jolts of adrenaline invoked by chance after chance, but Muller-Bambi in the Barnsley goal is having an inspired evening. He saves high shots, low shots, shots from distance and from point-blank range. As the minutes tick by the Barnsley defence grows in confidence and Southend crab from side to side. The tipping point comes when the first Blues supporters start to make for the exits to the delight of the Barnsley fans: 'Yorkshire, Yorkshire, Yorkshire,' they scream at us. Vanessa is furious with them. 'That's disgusting,' she cries indignantly. 'No it's not,' I reply with resignation, 'it's football. We'd be doing the same to them if we were winning.'

Four ineffectual minutes of injury time tick away and then the referee blows his whistle sending me another step further on the cup journey, out of the south east of England and straight to bed, exhausted.

Southend United 0
Barnsley 1 (Campbell–Ryce)

Attendance: 7,212
Money Spent So Far: £126.50
Miles Travelled So Far: 1,007
Winners Receive £60,000

1996–2005
Where Did It All Go Wrong?

So how did the FA Cup and indeed football itself lose its lustre? For me anyway. Up until 1996 it seems that I had happily paid my money and taken my choices, but then the magic of the game had drifted away. I've given this some thought and the simple answer is television. Throughout my childhood the only entirely live domestic game that you could watch uninterrupted was the FA Cup Final. Outside of that it was all limited highlights packages – *Match Of The Day* on BBC, *The Big Match* on ITV and the occasional midweek showing on *Sportsnight*, which was worth staying up for the theme tune alone. This meant that the FA Cup was an event in itself and whether the game was a good one or a bad one, it was the date with the big red circle on the footballing calendar. The only other live matches you could depend on were England games, but even they were irregular outside of the two big international championships every second summer. The World Cup and the European Championships were themselves rarities and even more magical for it, regardless of whether England qualified or not.

But then came the live broadcasting of league games. Like drips from a leaky tap. One here, one there, once a week and only on one terrestrial channel. Then came satellite telly. Rupert Murdoch gambled that people would take out subscriptions if they could have football pumped into their living rooms. The gamble paid off and the public lumped on. We thought we were buying choice. We thought we were buying variety.

The success of the silent satellites attracted consumers and their combined eyeballs in turn attracted sponsors. Advertising money began to pour into football. Media companies began to take more interest in the game and they searched for additional broadcastable content to attract more subscribers and more marketing budgets. What else could they pump out to rake in the cash? They looked at the internationals and realised that they were infrequent, but what the hell, they'd take them too. They looked at the European Cup and realised that the old knockout format was too limited so they expanded it. Changed it from a cup competition to a league with knockout playoffs tacked on at the end. They increased the reach of the product and they increased the frequency, the two watchwords for any marketeer.

We consumers lapped it up because again we thought we were buying choice and variety. I was sucked into the pattern, happily paying my satellite subscription because I thought I was getting as much football as I could consume. In any given week I could watch football almost every day of the week. On Sundays at least two games from the Premiership and another on Monday night. Tuesdays and Wednesdays the Champions League, Thursdays the UEFA cup. On Fridays a match from the lower leagues and then Saturday, if I wanted to go Pay Per View rather than stand outside in the cold, I didn't even need to leave my house.

They say that familiarity breeds contempt but in my case it bred apathy. When there were so many matches to consume I got my fair share of good and bad games, but I also started to get trigger happy with my remote control. If a match wasn't shaping up I flipped over, content in the knowledge that I wasn't missing anything and that there would be another game to watch either on another channel or on another day. I hadn't invested time, money and effort in getting to the game, I'd just invested a discreet, direct debit, line item on my monthly bank statement. I started to realise that there were an awfully large number of poor games, or matches where I was indifferent to the teams playing and these devalued the whole product for me. They became football muzak. Always on in the background while you bumbled around the house doing other things.

Then in 1999, three years after the start of the Premiership, I became involved in an attempt to resurrect an old speedway team that had become defunct, the Rye House Rockets. My father had taken me to the track in Hoddesdon with Grandad Joe and my sister throughout my childhood to watch meetings and although I had lost touch with the sport in my teenage years I had many happy memories of sunny Sundays at the small stadium by the River Lea in Hertfordshire.

Speedway is a summer sport which runs from the middle of March through to the end of October but the administration of a team is a year-round business. I found that my weekends and spare evenings were taken up with a large variety of required tasks such as writing the programmes, producing press releases, reams of official paperwork that needed completion, and conspiring with my collaborators on how we were to get the team back into speedway's third division.

Attending the weekly race meetings gave me that fix of live sporting entertainment that I craved and because I had a major, personal investment in events it was all the more exciting. The big difference between speedway and football at that time was that you couldn't see much speedway on the TV, and so you had to attend the meetings, you had to invest time, effort and money to go along and the rewards you got for doing that, win, lose or draw, were all the more heightened. I travelled up and down the country with the Rockets, including two memorable there and back in a day journeys to St Austell in Cornwall and Linlithgow outside Edinburgh. There is something exhausting and exhilarating in spending eighteen hours travelling to watch fifteen minutes of racing. Vanessa would probably say exasperating.

Added to that my family responsibilities were ever increasing with the arrival of my third child Jonathan in 2001. Now there were three little Stonemans either running or crawling around the house so Vanessa and I had to move from man-to-man marking to a zone defence. I'd left the newspapers and my job description had morphed from journalist, through business development manager, to being a sales director working in the internet advertising business. Naturally I railed against these professional and domestic responsibilities in true man fashion and found diversions in the shape of training to run those two marathons, which for the record were Stockholm in 2003 and Rome in 2004. I did the first one in four and a half hours, and was rather irritated to shave just seven seconds off my time in the second.

I still followed football to a certain degree but it was more restricted to checking the Derby result at ten to five on a Saturday afternoon or listening to a game on the radio if I was sat in the car with nothing else to do. I stopped watching *Match Of The Day* on a Saturday night and only kept up my Sky Sports subscription because of the increasing number of speedway meetings that they were covering. In the ten seasons from 1996 to 2005 I went to just four live matches. The three Southend United games at the start of 2000 and that year's League Cup final between Leicester City and Tranmere Rovers at Wembley and only then because it was a corporate freebie.

Football had drifted away from me like one of the canal boats that glided down the River Lea past Rye House Stadium, partly because of a lack of available time, partly because of the predictability of seeing the same 'big four' teams dominating the domestic game, but mainly because with so much choice to switch on to, I found myself switching off.

January 2008
Tykes, Touts and Tickets

I threw a sickie on Fifth Round Draw day. Partly because I was ill and partly to make sure that I could watch the draw live on TV at home. The effect of my transatlantic travelling added to the late night in the January cold of Roots Hall had lowered my defences and I was struggling with a solid dose of man-flu. I wonder to this day whether a Southend win would have given my immune system the boost required to fight it off.

So having slept through a fever all morning, at 1pm I dragged myself out of bed for a bowl of Vanessa's chicken soup in front of BBC2 where Sir Trevor of Brooking was on station with an ironic choice of designated ball-men – Ray Wilkins and Jimmy Case. Ironic because both men had been involved in that first FA Cup Final that I remember being unmemorable – Man United versus Brighton in 1983.

Barnsley were ball number seven and emptied into the Perspex bowl alongside six Premiership teams, seven more from the Championship and two from League One. My aims for the draw were simple. Avoid the top four, hope in fact that they draw each other, while achieving a dream tie of an away trip to Southampton. My friend James Hislop's father was a season ticket holder at St Mary's so I figured I could call in a favour there.

In the earlier, heavily populated draws, the proceedings could last for some time, but with just sixteen names left in the hat, this would be a short, sharp hit of cup action. It would also be decisive because for the first time in over fifty years there had been no drawn matches in the Fourth Round Proper and so no replays were pending.

Sir Trevor got things underway and Ray and Jimmy pulled out the first teams. Bristol Rovers versus Southampton. Crap. That was my dream tie gone then. Next out was Cardiff versus Wolves, an all Championship affair. Then Sheffield United against Middlesbrough. My mind was doing rapid fire odds, the sort of stuff that a bookmaker dreams of. Ten teams left in the hat, four of which were big guns. The odds of getting a top four team had shortened from three to one, to two and a half to one.

Just as I was digesting this Ray pulled out ball number six.

Trevor: 'Liverpool.'

Vanessa: 'Ha, yes!' She knew I didn't want a big four club. In an instant I began to suspect that her apparent acceptance of my quest was merely a thinly-drawn veil over her true irritation.

Jimmy: 'Number seven.'

Trevor: 'Will play Barnsley.'

Me: 'Crap.'

As I was trying to come to terms with this turn of events, the blow was softened by the next pair out. Manchester United given a home draw against Arsenal. Good. One top four casualty confirmed for the quarter finals. Preston were then drawn at home to Premiership Portsmouth – who were shaping up to be my dark horses for this season's race to the final* – Coventry drew high-flying Championship leaders West Brom and Chelsea fluked a home tie against League One side Huddersfield.

What a nightmare. Liverpool. At Anfield. Whether it was the tie or the man-flu, I felt totally despondent. I'd known it was inevitable that I would cross paths with the top four at some point and I suppose I should have been grateful that it had been delayed for so long, but now it had happened, I was faced with the prospect of getting myself into a match featuring one of the best supported teams in the world. A team with a waiting list for season tickets, with a set of ticket allocation rules as complicated as any in the country. One look at the ticketing section of the Liverpool website illustrated my difficulty. First dibs went to Priority Ticket Holders. Then came Season Ticket Holders who had been to both the Luton AND Havant & Waterlooville games. Then Fancard Holders with both of the previous teams. Next up were Season Ticket Holders with Luton OR Havant & Waterlooville, then Fancard Holders with either or. Presumably once they were all done, there may be some available for general sale. Fat chance.

I immediately hit the phones. The first call was a blast from my journalism past to the Liverpool Press Office where I explained my plans for a book about the FA Cup and asked about the possibility of a press pass. I was told to fax off an application stating my case but was warned that because the press box at

---

* I know what you are thinking, how convenient that he has picked Portsmouth at that early stage, but I checked the date modified time on the computer file for this chapter and I wrote that in January 2008, so there!

Anfield was quite small, I would be in a pecking order behind the national and local papers which would be decided by the amount of column inches I could guarantee. As this was a total of nil, my chances were slim. Nevertheless a fax was dispatched.

Further research on the Liverpool web site provided another route. Corporate Hospitality. The prawn sandwich brigade so loathed by the terrace fan. This looked interesting. There were two levels of Corporate which had promise. The Reds package and the Executive package. Tickets in the region of fifty to hundred pounds respectively. I called the Corporate Hospitality line and was informed that pricing and availability for these tickets would not be known until the date of the match was confirmed. But if I wanted, I could complete an application form and send that in so that when the details were finalised I would already be in a holding pattern. Once again, a fax was dispatched.

At that moment, one of my former bosses Scott Beaumont, pinged up on Instant Messenger.

Scott: *Have you seen the draw yet?*

John: *Yes.*

Scott: *OK, just checking. Didn't want to spoil the surprise!*

John: *That's OK. Could have been worse I suppose…*

Scott: *I have a friend who is a big Barnsley fan. Want me to see if he can help out with tickets?*

John: *YES PLEASE!!!*

Scott: *OK, leave it with me.*

Three avenues open however nothing decisive. So I typed 'Liverpool Barnsley Tickets' into *Google* just on the off chance. One result caught my eye. A posting on a message board website offering tickets to the game. Bearing in mind that the tie had only just been announced, I was slightly surprised to see someone *already* offering tickets. I glanced over both shoulders, got up from my chair and walked over to the study door and shut it tight. Then I walked over to the windows and slowly pulled down each of the blinds. Back in my chair I glanced around again before clicking on the link…

The message, from someone called 'football_tickets', was simple:

'Tickets in all stands, email or PM.'

Someone called 'ian333333' had already posted a reply:

'Isn't it a bit pointless selling tickets before they have even gone on sale? Counting your chickens and all that…'

And someone called 'peanut' had responded:

'It's not counting his chickens if he has credits from all previous rounds. Then he is guaranteed tickets.'

I decided to email for further details and almost immediately got a response.

'Hi, ok, they're forty five pounds each all stands – call if you want.' This was followed by a telephone number. I called and a Scouse accent answered.

'It's about the tickets. For the Barnsley match.'

'Ah right mate. Forty five pounds all stands. Where do you want one? In the Kop?'

'Err, yes I suppose so.'

'OK, how do you want to pay? Paypal?'

'Err, yes I suppose so.'

'OK, I'll email you the details.'

The line went dead. I checked my email and the payment details were already there waiting. I have to admit to feeling slightly nervous. Forty five pounds was a bit steep and totally unguaranteed. The tickets were likely to have a face value of half that. And I'd not even asked where they were coming from. Actually I didn't want to *know* where they were coming from. I had a decision to make. Ten minutes later I'd wired the money to a complete stranger.

Five minutes after that, another email arrived: *'Hi John, got money thanks but had to refund – please don't put any mention of tickets etc – just put events – sorry should have mentioned it.'*

A hot flush welled up inside me. Basic schoolboy error in online ticket touting. I re-sent the money, this time removing all reference to the word ticket. Five minutes later and another email arrived simply saying: *'Thanks.'*

I assumed that I had just bought at least one ticket to the Fifth Round Proper. However it was clear that I was going to have to wait and see if I was actually getting into the game. So in the mean time I decided to go into research mode. One look at the respective routes to Wembley and you could argue that Liverpool were having something of a charmed life in the competition so far, having faced cash-strapped Luton and then Havant & Waterlooville in their earlier rounds. But the fact was that the Reds had been struggling. A slightly fortunate draw at Kenilworth Road kept them in the competition and they had twice gone behind against the Non-Leaguers before recording a five-two win. Also in the league that season they were making hard work of clinging to any of the league positions which befitted a member of the 'Big Four'.

Outside of their recent cup run I didn't bother to research Liverpool any further because I didn't feel I needed to. For most of my football watching life I'd seen first hand what they'd done. Their dominance of the English game and European glory had all coincided with my early, informative years. They were the first team that I had grown to dislike *because* of the overwhelming success that they had generated and yet, if you sat me down and told me to write out one list of men who had played for Liverpool and another of those who had represented Derby, I'm embarrassed to say that the Reds list would probably be the longer. Plus I could do some more digging into Liverpool's history in the next round after they'd brushed Barnsley aside.

But the Yorkshire team were almost as much of a mystery to me as any of the Non-League clubs I'd seen so far. I didn't even know where Barnsley was, not precisely, and had to look on a map to confirm that it's up the M1 a bit to the right of Sheffield. I visited *Wikipedia* and the club website and learnt that the football team of Barnsley St Peter's was established in 1887 and joined the Football League in 1889 under the shortened name of Barnsley FC. They were the first out of all the teams I have encountered to have actually been to an FA Cup Final, having visited Wembley on two occasions, as runners up in 1910 and winners in 1912. Then for most of the remainder of the Twentieth Century, they drifted between the lower divisions never quite able to make it into top flight football. The closest they came was apparently in 1922 when they missed out on promotion by a goal difference tally decided by a single goal.

But in the 1996–97 season they finally achieved that illusive promotion and that was when my own personal radar picked them up. I remember that season as a plucky but ultimately doomed attempt to stave off relegation, and naturally once they dropped back down to the second division, they also dropped off my scope.

The websites filled in the gap between then and now. Barnsley were badly burnt by the collapse of the ITV Digital deal and spent a torturous financial period in administration before a current period of stability in the Championship. Apparently Barnsley have spent more seasons in the second division than any other team in the leagues.

Outside of that I knew nothing more about the club or the town and it occurred to me that for the first time in my cup odyssey I would be visiting a match and watching teams that I had no personal or geographic link to. My first match out of the south east. My first encounter with one of the potential cup winners that I had been desperately hoping to avoid. My first visit to a truly unknown part of the country. For some reason instead of exciting me, it left me feeling a bit empty. Maybe it was the lack of emotional attachment, or maybe just a reflection on my age. I've spent the last ten years building a career, raising a family and trying to structure some order around the chaos of life. Now I was faced with a journey into the unknown and instead of a boyish anticipation I was feeling the indifference of older age. Unwilling to confront the uncomfortable. There was also the nagging doubt of whether I would even *get* to the match. For that I would just have to wait and see if any tickets materialised.

Saturday February 16th, 2008:

Fifth Round Proper
Liverpool v Barnsley

Eyes open. Match day morning. Spirits soar again. But no time to waste as I've got a game to get to. I jump out of bed and run upstairs to Eden's bedroom to wake her up. It's half past seven and I want to get away by eight o'clock for the long trip up to Liverpool. I shower and get dressed and meet her downstairs. All the rituals have been observed. I've packed my reporting kit of camera, notebook and stopwatch and am wearing my Ware T-shirt. I give my treasured FA Cup match ball a kiss for good luck and we head out of the door right on time.

In my back pocket are a total of *three* tickets for the game. The Corporate Hospitality package came through for two of them and Eden jumped at the chance to come along. It seems never to have occurred to her that it may be a bit weird for an eleven-year-old girl to want to go all over the country to football games with a varying degree of randomness. She's never once said 'You know what Dad, I don't think I fancy the M25 today, I might just stay at home with Mum.' I think it's a reflection on how modern-day football has broken out of the old-fashioned, male-orientated, working class stereotype.

The third ticket nestled in the pocket of my jeans comes courtesy of my scouse, internet ticket tout. We've nicknamed this anonymous vendor 'Kenny', after one of the Liverpudlian characters from the Guy Ritchie movie *Lock, Stock and Two Smoking Barrels*. It *looks* official enough but you never know. Because this third ticket is for a different section of Anfield and because there's every chance it could be a fake, I can't possibly take either Evie or Jonathan and so have invited Nick the American to come along for the ride and to *hopefully* get in.

We set off on a crisp, clear February morning. Not a cloud in the azure sky. Global warming definitely appears to be taking the chill off the British winter. This may have huge ramifications for the British nation if not the globe, but it does make perfect conditions for a game of football, even one that's seven hours and over two hundred miles away. Hopefully the additional kilograms of carbon dioxide I pump out on the M6 will sharpen conditions to a fine point.

We drive down the M11 on the same route that took me to Haringey Borough, Wembley and Dagenham & Redbridge. Past the M25 which took me to Hythe Town and drop down into Stoke Newington to get Nick. By nine o'clock we are picking up the M1 at its source and passing up through north London. Off to our left we can see the great arch of my ultimate destination. The new Wembley. Only two matches away now with both the semi finals and final being played there this year. I'm inwardly delighted that my anticipation is tremendous, both for today's game and the matches ahead. I'd been concerned that apathy was starting to enter my quest after the chore of the Southend and Barnsley fixture, but now I know I am right back on track.

The car gobbles up the miles as we follow the spine of the country. Towns flash past. Watford, Luton, Milton Keynes. Each has more of a significance to me now. Watford made it to the Fourth Round before going out to Wolves, MK Dons fell at their first hurdle to Crewe and of course had Luton converted their chances against Liverpool in the Third Round, then today's destination may well have been Kenilworth Road. The whole country has been knitted together for me by this year's FA Cup, I even know where Barnsley is now.

As we cruise past Coventry I look across at the Ricoh Arena where the Sky Blues will be playing West Brom in a tasty all-Midlands tie this afternoon. When we stop at the motorway services we are immediately surrounded by a posse of blue and white striped shirts. Huddersfield fans on their way to 'their final' against Chelsea. They have about as much chance of progressing as Barnsley do at Anfield. I see that some fans have printed their own *Terriers On Tour* T-Shirts charting the progress of their team from the First Round to Stamford Bridge. A trifling four-game run. Amateurs. This will be my sixteenth FA Cup match of the season, not including the ones I've watched on TV or listened to on the radio.

It's only when we pass Stoke that we hit our first traffic jam. Until that point we had seemed to lead a charmed life with the radio reporting a ripple of M1 and M6 accidents that were following us up the country. I keep a constant check on the sat-nav's estimated time of arrival as the two hour safety cushion that I've factored into my travel plan is slowly being eaten away. We stop-start our way for almost thirty miles until we reach the M62 and the grip of the jams releases us. As a result it's just approaching two o'clock when we arrive in Liverpool and find a side-street off Townsend Lane and park the car.

'You want me to hide the sat-nav in the glove compartment?' asks Nick, 'not that the car will be here when we get back.' I smile and tell him that I'd read on a Liverpool fan website that the stereotype of car-nicking Scousers is as much maligned as the white-stilettos of the ladies from Essex.

He gives me a 'Yeah, right' look.

'So who we supporting today? You hate Scousers more than Jocks right?' Nick's *other* stereotype is of British people hating anyone from a different region. As I am a southerner he assumes I hate anyone north of the Watford Gap. I've pointed out in the past that as a north Londoner, I also hate anyone from south of the Thames but this cuts no ice. 'Where is Barnsley anyway?' He asks.

'Yorkshire,' I reply, 'so I probably "hate" them more than I "hate" Scousers. They have this conceited opinion that Yorkshire is "God's own county", you'll hear them singing today. "Yorkshire, Yorkshire, Yorkshire." I actually don't care who wins today. I just want a result. It's going to be *very* hard to get tickets for a match in Barnsley. If I had to pick a team then it would be Liverpool but only because it's been easier than I thought it would be to get today's tickets.'

As the words come out of my mouth it occurs to me that this sounds as though I am just here to do a job. As though all of the excitement and anticipation at the start of the M1 has fizzled out at the end of the M62, but nothing could be further from the truth. I don't *care* who wins, in fact it's fairly obvious who will, but I can't *wait* to see it unfold. I just can't afford a drawn game.

We march up Pinehurst Avenue beside a gigantic line of parked coaches. Into Utting Avenue and the small stream of fans suddenly becomes a torrent as we move into the sightline of the stadium. Anfield. One of the great cathedrals of English football. The huge modern structure juxtaposed against the old-fashioned, red-brick terraced houses of the surrounding streets. Red-shirts and scarves everywhere alongside the heaviest police presence I've seen so far, everything from motorbikes and mobile camera vans, to officers leashing barking German Shepherds. Street vendors selling memorabilia, small shops selling chips and gravy or curry sauce, and a constant Scouse backing track of the chattering, excited Liverpudlians. The accents heighten the adventure. This really is a different world to the previous games, where everyone has sounded exactly like me.

Eden says she wants the loo so we try and cram our way into the heaving crowd of The Arkles pub on Arkles Lane but once through the door an oppressive wave of body heat and the reek of beer does as much to prohibit our progress as the crushing crowd itself. I tell her to hold it in.

We pass through the Paisley Gates and look over to the statue of Bill Shankly. I'd wanted to take a picture of myself alongside this for the book, but there are just *too* many people about to make this work. The surrounds of the stadium are like the chaos of an ant hill with people scurrying in all directions and then disappearing through the portals of the Anfield turnstiles.

Just at that point we hear an announcement over the external tannoy.

'Ladies and gentlemen we would like to remind you that this is an all-ticket game and would strongly advise people not to buy any tickets from sellers outside of the ground, as there is a good chance that they may be fake.'

Eden, Nick and I look anxiously at each other.

'Kenny…'

'Well this is it,' says Nick, 'wish me luck.' He's sucked into the crowd and quickly disappears from view. Eden and I make our way to the Corporate entrance in the Lower Centenary Stand where we are welcomed by our hosts and then shown through to the Reds Bar. Inside there is a swarm of red–scarved patrons queuing for the complimentary food, propping up the bar, sitting at tables and staring up at the giant TV image projected on the wall showing the early kick–off between Bristol Rovers and Southampton. Just as Eden disappears off to the toilet, Rovers striker Rickie Lambert hits a deflected free kick into the back of the net to set up what would probably be the upset of the day if the League One side can hold off their Championship opponents.

Eden returns and we consider getting a drink or something to eat, but decide against both and leave the comfy confines of the Reds Bar. The bowels of the stadium are dark and dingy in comparison and there are swathes of ant supporters busily making their way around the Anfield ant hill.

We find our block and climb the short steps up into the arena. This is one thing that the big stadia have in their favour over the smaller grounds I have visited. That moment of anticipation as you walk up the steps into the light of the great arenas. A Technicolor moment of blue sky, green pitch and the banks of red seats. The famous Kop end looms like a gaping cavern directly to our left. To our right is the away end and directly opposite the Main Stand. I check the seat numbers on my ticket and to my delight realise that we are in row one, pitchside about twenty yards away from the corner flag. It's a bit of a tight fit leg–room wise, I've barely enough space to swing a gnat, but it's a prime camera position. A steward even welcomes us as we sit down and points to the players warming up.

'That's the team that's going to start. Kuyt and Crouch up front.'

Looking around me I can see the massive impact that mobile phones have had on the community of big sporting events. People are texting each other, they are standing in their seats filming the Liverpool warm-ups. They are calling people, asking them where they are and then turning around to wave at each other. Just then I get a text.

Nick: *'I'm third urinal from the end at the pub down the street.'*

Me: *'Are you serious? You didn't get in?'*

Nick: *'Of course I did. I'm down by the Barnsley fans. I'm the one shouting* YORKSHIRE.'

Me: *'We are front row in the corner by the Kop.'*

Nick: *'I've even put some bets down already. Torres to score first from twenty first to thirtieth minute.'*

Me: *'Steward says he's not playing.'*

Nick: *'Dalglish is though, right?'*

'What's he saying?' Asks Eden.

'Nothing worth while.'

Just then there is another ripple of applause from the home supporters as Steven Gerrard emerges from the tunnel wearing his tracksuit. Looks like he's not starting either then. But Peter Crouch and Jamie Carragher are. There's John Arne Riise and Xabi Alonso. I realise that for the first time on this journey I actually *know* some of the players from a new team. It's an exciting moment. My cup run is approaching the sharp end.

With five minutes to go until kick off the ground is nearly full and the spectators in the Kop have started to pass one of their giant, historical banners around over their heads. It's a far cry from the flag that the Ware Travelling Support hooked up behind Lee Pearce in the Wembley FC goal back in September. Then the two teams are led out onto the pitch to a great roar from both ends of the ground and the Liverpool supporters hold their scarves aloft for the singing of *'You'll Never Walk Alone'*. As the famous anthem rings out around the ground I realise that the hairs on the back of my legs are standing up. I can't imagine what it must have been like for the players of Havant & Waterlooville to have to put on a performance after this kind of reception – light years away from their usual pre-match build-up. Almost before the final words of the song die out, our referee Mr Martin Atkinson blows his whistle and we are underway.

It takes me about five minutes to discover my loyalties for today. Barnsley get a chance. A good chance, but drag the ball wide across the Liverpool goal. I feel a wave of relief. Liverpool then almost immediately reply with an effort from Crouch which bounces inches wide of the Barnsley net. I have to check my disappointment. So it seems that without making a conscious decision, I have thrown my lot in with the home team. It's the first time I've not instinctively rooted for an underdog. Maybe because of the ease with which I was eventually able to get the tickets and with one eye on the same task for the quarter finals. Another Liverpool home tie and I could play the corporate card again, or give a call to my mate Kenny. But of course first we need some Liverpool goals.

I'm studying the match with the keen eye of the FA Cup veteran. There have been recognisable patterns of play at every level of the competition. The danger for Liverpool would of course be the *Goliath Complex* as displayed by Ware and Dagenham & Redbridge in previous rounds. Then there is the *Siege Engine*, where a higher level team throws everything at a minnow but fails to break down the invisible, rectangular forcefield thrown up across the goalposts by an eleven-man defence. Perhaps today would be the *Only A Matter Of Time* pattern, where technical superiority and a steady stream of chances leads to a comfortable multi-goal victory – think Southend versus Oxford.

Barnsley are busy and industrious and backed by a tremendously vocal support of six thousand Yorkshiremen off to my right. They are by no means daunted by the occasion and are denying Liverpool time on the ball in defence, pressing tightly whenever the ball crosses the halfway line. The home team are moving the ball around neatly and another comparison of the levels of quality I've seen is in the ability of the Reds' back four to play a ball out of defence, rather than applying the Danny Wolf School of Defending's trademark hoof upfield.

A curling, twenty-yard effort from Alonso addressed to the top, righthand corner of the net is intercepted in transit by a fine save from Barnsley goalkeeper Luke Steele, who according to the preview on TalkSport we heard in the car, is making his debut today having signed on emergency loan from West Brom just two days ago because of injuries and ineligibilities.

But Liverpool then make a complete hash of the resulting corner, in fact they seem to be making complete hashes of all their set pieces. I find it bizarre that despite fielding a man who is literally head and shoulders above the rest, they don't seem interested in trying to hit the head of Crouch in the box. Every corner and free kick around the area is played short, Barnsley press and then the Liverpool player under pressure hits a poor ball into the box which is comfortably dealt with by the defenders in white. In fact one quickly taken free kick is pressed so well by Barnsley that the ball ends up way back with Charles Itandje in the Liverpool goal, to a chorus of boos from the home support.

I'm just explaining to Eden what a waste of money I think Dirk Kuyt is when he scores. Ryan Babel employs some wing trickery, roasting Barnsley's Bobby Hassell to reach the byline. He pulls the ball back to Kuyt on the edge of the six-yard box and the Dutch international traps it and then toe-pokes it home. We erupt. A great cacophony of cheers. I'm doubly delighted because the entire goal plays out in front of me and my Nikon is clicking furiously. I'm still not convinced about Kuyt mind, Eden could have scored that one.

Just before half time Liverpool do sling a high one into the box which Crouch wins easily and powers a header goalbound, but Steele again pulls off the kind of save that sees multiple defenders walk over to him afterwards to ruffle his hair. A second goal on the stroke of half time would have put the game into *Only A Matter Of Time* territory.

On the whistle we shuffle out of our seats and return to the Reds Bar to use the toilet. The convenience of these particular conveniences is very apparent as the queues for the main stadium loos go snaking down the corridor. The other hospitality patrons are tucking into their complimentary tea and biscuits, or again propping up the bar for something stronger, but we return to our seats to avoid the rush. I don't fancy the prospect of having to edge past a full row of people right at the front when the match has restarted.

'We just need a nice early goal to kill the game off now,' I tell Eden as the second half kicks off. We actually have to wait twelve minutes for the goal, only it doesn't kill the game off, it ignites it. Because the wrong team score.

A fantastic cross from wide on the right by Martin Devaney is met by an equally spectacular leap from Barnsley defender Stephen Foster, who climbs highest of a group of players to head past the flailing figure of Itandje. One–one. All square. Crap. As Foster celebrates in front of a silenced Kop and with the cheers of the away fans rolling like waves up the pitch from the far end, I instinctively crane my neck to the stadium clock behind me to check the time. Half an hour to go. All right. Calm down. Plenty of time. Liverpool just need to score again.

Almost from the restart they very nearly do. Benayoun is put in behind Barnsley by a cracking, defence-splitting pass and he skips past the advancing Steele. He *must* score, the net is gaping in front of him, but a last ditch block by Foster and Hassell keeps it out and then Tykes skipper Brian Howard blocks the follow up from Crouch. The away fans celebrate as if they'd scored again, I have my head in my hands. That absolutely should have been a goal. Somehow it wasn't. I've seen this scenario before. This is the *Siege Engine*.

Liverpool then proceed to hurl the kitchen sink at Barnsley for the next twenty minutes. With every miss, every fluff, every chance, every save, the gnawing sensation in the pit of my stomach grows larger. Steele definitely has cast a Jedi forcefield over his goal today. The ball is simply not going to go in. I get a text message from Scott Beaumont saying: *'Err, I don't think you want a draw do you?'*

I refuse to look up at the stadium clock as the minutes tick down. Rafa Benitez brings on Harry Kewell and Steven Gerrard and the introduction of the talismanic Liverpool skipper brings a sigh of relief from the crowd. They believe that their midfield maestro will rescue this game but I have my doubts. There are larger forces at play here. The Footballing Gods have decided to test my ingenuity. This game is destined to be drawn so that I will have to somehow magic a replay ticket out of thin air. Finally I can resist no longer and I cast a glance up at the clock. Eighty eight minutes played. The fourth official pops up and shows four minutes of time added on. It will not be enough, especially when Kewell hammers a shot which is tipped onto the bar by the Jedi Master Steele.

Home fans are starting to stream towards the exits, especially when the Barnsley supporters raise *their* scarves into the air for a rendition of *You'll Never Walk Alone*. The Liverpool support is stunned into silence by this blasphemy in their back yard. Barnsley pump the ball clear time and again and deep into injury time, one of these last ditch clearances suddenly turns into an unlikely attack. Skipper Howard finds himself with the ball at his feet in the area and about to pull the trigger when Sami Hyppia snags his cocked left foot.

'Penalty!' I scream, then realise my error and in a loud stage whisper to Eden I try and cover my tracks. '*We* were lucky that wasn't given as a penalty.'

Howard is equally furious and remonstrates with the referee. But the ball is still in play and he suddenly realises that again he is in space with the ball at his feet. He shrugs off a challenge and beelines towards the goal unleashing a low, left foot drive which races across the surface and tucks itself neatly into the gap between the goalpost and Itandje's despairing dive. The net billows unexpectedly. Howard wheels away unbelievingly. The Kop disperses almost instantly. I am struck mentally dumb.

There is barely time for Liverpool to restart. Their kick off looks more like a rugby match as virtually the entire team masses on the halfway line to race into Barnsley territory, but even as the ball is lofted deep into the early evening sky, Mr Atkinson the referee blows his whistle to signify the conclusion of one of the great cup upsets. Championship strugglers Barnsley have mugged the mighty Liverpool at Anfield. Brian Howard's goal has netted £120,000 in prize money and a place in both the quarter finals and the back page of every national newspaper.

As the stadium clears, Eden and I stand and applaud the Barnsley team, alongside it must be said a large proportion of sporting home supporters. I realise that at not one point during this game or its build up had I given Barnsley even the slightest chance of winning. I hadn't even considered it. Eden and I look at each other and are both speechless. It's the same when we meet up with Nick outside Anfield. The only thing all three of us can muster, as forty thousand disappointed Liverpool fans stream by, is a bemused 'Wow'.

Liverpool 1 (Kuyt 32)
Barnsley 2 (Foster 57, Howard 90)

Attendance: 42,449
Money Spent So Far: £185.25
Miles Travelled So Far: 1,495
Winners Receive £120,000

2006:
Epiphany Part One

After ten seasons in the wilderness, my footballing epiphany came in 2006. Maybe not an epiphany, maybe a resurrection. I already loved the game, I'd just forgotten I did. I'd forgotten what makes it the most amazing experience in the world. Joyful, painful, rewarding, cruel, exhilarating, dispiriting, passionate, dramatic, I could go on, but then *thesaurus.com* would want a donation as well. Three things happened to me in 2006 which reversed the apathy, the malaise that had set in. The first was totally unexpected.

I had been forced to organise a business trip for my American boss. It was a European tour of customers, partners and prospects from four different countries. We started off in London meeting advertising agencies, then Audi in Milton Keynes and then two of the major publishers that ran on our advertising network. Then we flew to Paris for a whistle-stop one day tour, meeting with the *International Herald Tribune*, the French equivalent of *Yellow Pages* and then more advertising agencies. A one-off hop through Amsterdam meeting with KLM airlines and then off to Hamburg in Germany, one of the media capitals of Europe.

The widespread nature of German business meant further meetings in other cities; Berlin, Munich, Frankfurt, Ingolstadt, and so in total we had a whole fortnight's travel planned. This meant I had to spend a weekend in Hamburg away from family, friends and any respite from my travelling partner. An American. A loud, repetitive, irritating American, as red, white and blue as any flag-waving, blindly patriotic, Mom's apple pie, good old U. S. of A. stereotype you could find. The prospect of entertaining him for a fortnight had led me to devise a strategy of going out every night and getting him blindingly drunk to divert me and disorientate him.

But it was impossible to suggest a strategy of getting blindingly drunk on a Saturday morning and going on a bender clean through to Sunday night. So I had to come up with something else. In desperation I turned to football. I knew there was a local team, SV Hamburg – any child brought up in the 1970s with Kevin

Keegan as an idol knows that – so I logged on to their website praying for a home fixture. I was in luck. A Bundesliga match against some mob called Arminia Bielefeld. I called the ticket office and booked us in.

It was the first time I had ever been to a football match abroad, so I was intrigued to see what it was like. What the subtle differences would be. As we approached the stadium, my irritating American in tow like a kid on a school trip, there appeared to be none. Apart from the fact that no one was speaking English, it was the same male dominated, lager-fuelled, colours-wearing, boisterous march of tens of thousands of people streaming toward a stadium. After a slight crush at the turnstiles we eventually entered with slightly *less* German efficiency than I had expected and made our way to our seats, passing the stadium vendors who were fully loaded with *wursts, pretzels und bier, aber keine* Bovril *oder* meat pies.

HSV's home, the AOL Arena (as it was then, now named the HSH Nordbank Arena) was as impressive a stadium as I'd seen up until then. It was built in 1998 and had a fifty thousand plus capacity which was almost the average gate for a Hamburg home match. In the taxi on the way to the game my American 'friend' had been in fine form, asking questions like, 'Did we flatten this city in the war, or was that Frankfurt?' and the slightly more embarrassing, 'What is it that can make a bunch of people get so fanatical that they rise up behind one madman?' I could feel the steam building in the cab driver's ears. But a glimpse of light was thrown on the answer to the second question five minutes before kick off.

The Germans still have some terracing sections in their stadiums. Cheap seats behind a goal where the hardcore fans congregate. Just before the two teams were led out onto the pitch, a giant platform began to rise behind one of the goals in front of that hardcore support. They immediately responded by starting to rotate their scarves in that way that Jonny Foreigner does and the noise levels cranked up a number of notches. The platform was raised what seemed like sixty feet in the air before a singer and guitarist on top led the entire stadium through the HSV anthem. What they sang was lost on me, my German is *nicht so gut*. What was not lost on me was the fanaticism of the German fans. Even the Prawn Sandwiches in the corporate boxes behind us were hammering it out.

More was to come when the goals started going in. Bielefeld scored first, which the home fans weren't too impressed by, but then shortly into the second half the ball was squared to some cat called Piotr Trochowski who curled a wonderful shot into the top corner of the net. The Germans were up on their feet in a heartbeat, nothing different there, but then they went through this delightful ritual where the stadium announcer bellowed out the goalscorer's name with the

crowd in unison: 'TRO–CHOW–SKI, TRO–CHOW–SKI, TRO–CHOW–SKI…
HAMBURG, EINS! BIELEFELD NULL!' Now I'm not sure why they said
'Null' for Bielefeld, as it was actually one–all at that point, but maybe I'm just
splitting Herrs. Apparently it's just the way it is, like saying, 'we got one, you didn't'.
Anyway the result was spectacular, uplifting. When the second goal went in, a
winner from Sergei Barbarez, I was up on my feet too: 'BAR–BAR–EZ, BAR–
BAR–EZ, BAR–BAR–EZ… HAMBURG, EINS!…' You get the picture.

As the dust settled and we all stood around smiling at each other, divided by
history, language and borders, but united by the sight of a cracking goal, an
irritating, sulky, American voice piped up from the figure sat with folded arms
beside me. 'I once saw Pele score the bicycle kick at the Giants Stadium in New
York. How about that?' I pushed the irritation to the back of my mind, I'd get my
own back at the restaurant that night with the forty per cent proof Schnapps, but
right then I was busily going through my first stage of footballing resurrection.

February 2008
Compliments Of The Season (Ticket)

We arrived home from Liverpool on Saturday night just in time to catch *Match Of The Day* on TV. Vanessa and the other kids had already gone to bed. The first match up was the Liverpool game and after some furious button work on the remote control I was delighted to freeze a frame which showed Peter Crouch attacking the Barnsley goal with Eden and me caught in the front row of the crowd back drop. Then I sat and watched the match unfold for the second time that day. It was still very difficult to take in. But it led to the question of what would happen in the subsequent draw on Monday?

I went to bed on Saturday night and lay awake, tossing and turning, unable to sleep as the question of quarter final tickets rolled around in my head. Then I had a sudden, blindingly obvious idea. A lightbulb above the head moment. The teams left in the competition were almost an equal combination of Premiership teams and lower league outfits. If Barnsley drew either of the big two away – Manchester United or Chelsea – then I could try the corporate route for a ticket, or go back to my online touts. But if Barnsley drew anyone else, either at home *or* on the road, then there was another way. Rather expensive, morally corrupt, but a work of criminal genius that Lex Luthor himself would be proud of. On Sunday morning, having finally got to sleep at around 3am after the adrenaline had run its course, I went online and toured the websites of the remaining teams in the competition, creating an elaborate spreadsheet containing the appropriate information. Then I waited.

I made sure I was in the office on Monday morning in case I needed to use the fax machine to send off any application forms and then busied myself with work for the next few hours. The morning dragged by interminably. Finally at 1.25pm I went to the BBC website to watch the draw unfold. I didn't need to see it live, by now it was just eight balls coming out of the Perspex, so no great suspense or drama. I just needed to see the results and then scramble for the phone lines.

After plenty of frantic web page refreshing the first three draws emerged. I'd avoided the unresolved silver bullet of Sheffield United / Middlesbrough, these two still had to replay and with two potential names in the hat it would have left my criminal strategy untenable. In fact the only names not out were Barnsley and someone else. For a moment I couldn't think who. I refreshed the page again and then there it was. Barnsley versus Chelsea.

A quick check of my spreadsheet and I punched in the appropriate number for the Barnsley ticket office into my mobile phone. I reached an automated answering service, hit button three and was told that I was in a queue of one. After twenty seconds the line answered and put me straight through to voicemail. Gah. I redialled, hit three again and this time was told I was in a queue of five. It seemed I was not the only vulture to be spiralling. Three minutes of pacing up and down, in both a real office corridor and a virtual phone queue, and the phone was finally answered by a human being.

'Hello Barnsley Football Club can I help you?'

'Yes, hello, I'm phoning up to see if there are any season tickets available.'

'There are sir,' said a croaky, Yorkshire-accented, female voice, 'but they aren't cost effective any more.'

'Yes but are they *on sale*?'

'Yes sir, but it's sixty pounds more expensive than buying individual tickets at this time of the season.'

'That's OK, I'd like one please.'

'O-Kaaay, are you a member?'

'Of what?'

'I mean are you on our system?'

'No.'

'Have you ever been to a game before?'

'No, I mean yes, I went to the Liverpool game on Saturday.'

'So the *only* game you have ever been to was the Liverpool game.

'Yes, I mean no, I went to Southend versus Barnsley as well…'

'Are you even a Barnsley *fan*, sir?'

'Yes, yes of course,' my Essex accent hung heavy on the line between London and Yorkshire.

'I'm sorry, I'll have to speak to my manager.' The woman put me on hold. I paced furiously for another three minutes. Workmates sitting in neighbouring meeting rooms stared up at my agitated state with concern. Finally the ticket woman came back on the line.

'OK. I've spoken to the General Manager and he says it's not a problem. So just pop down to the ticket office and we will issue you with a ticket.'

'Erm, I can't actually do that you see I live in Essex. Is there any chance we can do this over the phone.'

'Hang on.' On hold again. More pacing.

'Ok sir, that's fine we can process the application now. Where would you like to sit?'

'I don't know. Where do you recommend?'

The conversation continued in that vein until finally the transaction took place and I became a fully signed-up member of the Tyke Army. I was told the season ticket would be available for collection a week Tuesday on the night of Barnsley's next home match against QPR. I was elated. At just over two hundred pounds I admit it was a bit steep. And it would take my FA Cup spend so far perilously near to the four hundred pound mark, but if you average that out over sixteen games, and in the wider context of what I was trying to achieve, I thought it was a small price to pay.

Twenty minutes later I had a sudden, nagging doubt. What if she thought I was just a crazy psycho fan and had told me the ticket was being processed just to get me off the line? I dialled again. This time I was in an automated queue of eight people listening to some irritating non-descript dance muzak. I waited for the number to dwindle until the same croaky voice answered. I explained that I was the person who had called earlier, omitting the crazy psycho fan part, and asked when was the soonest I could come and pick up the season ticket. This involved even more fabrications about being on a business trip near Barnsley later that week. She told me that the payment had been processed and the ticket was available for me to come and collect whenever I wanted.

I came off the phone with relief washing over me but vowed to find space in my calendar for a secret trip to Barnsley later in the week to get confirmation in person. To make sure that the season ticket was *actually* in my hand. But things were looking good. As a season ticket holder I would automatically be eligible to buy two tickets to the cup match against Chelsea. And while the morality of buying a season ticket was in doubt, after all this was mean that a pair of *true* Barnsley fans would be denied places at this historic game, I was one step closer to Wembley. The only thing left to do now was to break the news of this latest spend to Vanessa.

Que sera sera,
Whatever will be, will be,
I'm going to Barnsley...

Saturday March 8th, 2008:

Sixth Round Proper
Barnsley V Chelsea

I wake up terrified in a cold sweat. For the last hour I've been running around the outside of Villa Park with the game about to start, trying to find a tout who can sell me a ticket having left mine at home. The relief that floods through me as I realise it was just a dream is palpable. The irony of course is that I wasn't even at the right ground. Not so much a dream as a nightmare. Why do our brains do this to us?

Vanessa looks sleepily over at me. 'Are you all right?' she asks. I reply a breathless yes and she tucks her head back under the covers. It's still dark outside but the digital clock shows it's coming up for 7am. I get out of bed and walk downstairs, my mind playing back edited highlights of the vivid dream before I flush it from my memory.

In the kitchen I make Vanessa a cooked breakfast to have in bed. It's a transparent attempt to earn some Brownie points to make up for the fact that once again I will be an absent parent for a whole Saturday. Quarter Final Saturday. It's also an attempt to assuage my feelings of guilt because I *still* haven't told her that I've bought a Barnsley season ticket, paid all that money just to earn the right to buy a cup ticket for this game. The appropriate moment to raise this delicate subject has just not come up yet. Perhaps that's the reason why my subconscious has been putting me through this recent torment.

'What time is kick off?' She asks as I place her breakfast before her.

'Five thirty.'

'So what time are you leaving?'

'Half eleven.'

'That's a long time.'

'Well I don't want to miss it. What if I'm caught in traffic?'

She pauses, inspecting her breakfast. 'You're going to be home really late then.' I ponder what the right response should be. 'It shouldn't be too bad, maybe elevenish,' I lie.

Things have been a little tricky between us lately, especially in relation to the football. When I reminded her earlier in the week that I was going to be out all day Saturday, I picked the wrong time to say it and it led to an argument. I'd then made the mistake of using the defence that there were only three games to go. She'd countered that by dragging up every obsession I have ever followed where I always claim that this will be the 'last thing' I do before settling down to her version of idyllic domesticity and fatherhood. We both know these are false claims. Her sarcasm-heavy final comment of 'Do what you want, you always do,' is still ringing in my ears.

But the bacon and eggs go down well on two counts and as we lay back in bed sipping our mugs of tea she lays out the terms and conditions negotiated for her approval today. A circuitous trip to the tip, the dog kennels and to the camping shop for a variety of errands that are outstanding. I finish my tea, hurriedly get dressed and set off to complete them. After all there's no better way to kill the three hours before I can depart.

Throughout the morning the air is heavy with cup quarter final expectation. I listen to TalkSport in the car as the breakfast show presenters lay out the matches for the weekend. The first game up is Manchester United versus Portsmouth at midday, which is perfect as I can listen to this on the way up to Barnsley. Then comes the clash at Oakwell, just make sure I don't go to Villa Park or forget the tickets. On Sunday Cardiff travel up to Middlesbrough while I will be cooking Sunday dinner and then West Brom are hosted by Bristol Rovers after we've eaten it. A perfect weekend.

At five to eleven I give all the family a kiss goodbye, sneak into the study to give my FA Cup match ball a good luck kiss, and then head out of the door. My season ticket gave me automatic entitlement for two tickets, but as they are in separate parts of the ground, it again means that taking a child along is out of the question, so Nick the American is again my wing man. I pick him up from his north London home and we head out of the city on the A10. As we are approaching the North Circular Road, I suddenly recognise where we are and make a left hand turn into White Hart Lane.

'Where are we going?' Asks Nick.

'I'm going to show you something. It's just up here. There's the Bridisco factory and this magnificent arena is where it all began. Haringey Borough.' Nick peers underwhelmed through the entrance to Coles Park. Inside a car boot sale is just about winding down.

'Jesus. How many does that thing hold?' Asks Nick, pointing at the dilapidated grandstand.

'Four banks of sixty six seats.' I reply, remembering the count I had made at the time.

'It's a long way from Anfield.'

I put in a three point turn in Bridisco's entrance and then we are back on the A10 heading north. I negotiate the suburban traffic and we reach the M1 just as the match at Old Trafford kicks off on the radio.

'So who do we want today?' Nick asks.

'I think it depends on what happens in *this* match,' I reply, pointing at the radio. 'If Man United win then they are probably going to reach the final. And if that happens then I think I want Chelsea to win today. I think it would be good for my cup run if the final is played by two of the big clubs, to see some of the best players in the world up against each other. But if United lose then I want Chelsea to lose as well. I don't want one of the big teams getting an easy match at Wembley.'

'Like the final a few years ago with Millwall.'

'Right. But I honestly can't see United *and* Chelsea both losing.'

Neither can the Five Live commentator Alan Green. He's waxing lyrically over the airwaves that the only result he can see from the United–Pompey game is a three–nil home win. And when Ronaldo is barged to the ground in the penalty area in the opening minutes, he berates the referee for not awarding a penalty, while Nick and I grin with glee.

We gobble up the miles on the M1 with ease. The traffic is light and even the roadworks at the southern end of the motorway offer little resistance. Up in Manchester, United are bombarding the Portsmouth goal. Each time Green's voice rises an octave we wait for that crowd roar which will signify the opening goal, but each attack ends with a groan from the Stretford End and amazement from the Belfast-born commentator. 'How did that stay out!' He cries.

'Come on Harry, get them in to half time at nil-nil,' I cry as we pull off the motorway services for a break. I expect to see some Chelsea fans milling around as we run to the loo and grab a burger, but the services are as empty as the motorway. Back in the car they have kicked off for the second half and still the Portsmouth rearguard action is holding. We hear Carrick miss a chance, then Evra hit the post. I'm desperate to say to Nick that it sounds like it could be one of those games where United will never score and Portsmouth may mug them, but I keep quiet because I don't want to jinx Pompey.

Then we hear Portsmouth on the break, we hear Baros in the area, and then that beautiful phrase as the tall striker is bundled over: *'Penalty!'*

'Yesss!' We both cheer involuntarily. We hear the referee showing keeper Tomasz Kuszczak a red card. He only came on at half time as a substitute for the injured Edwin Van Der Saar.

'They've got no keeper on the bench!' I realise. My hands grip the steering wheel tighter, foot pressed hard down on the accelerator. We're doing eighty miles an hour in the fast lane of the M1, the countryside flashing past us. My eyes are focused on the road ahead, ears glued to the radio. Way up ahead of us in Manchester, Rio Ferdinand is donning the goalkeeper's jersey and gloves, the Portsmouth fans are waiting expectantly in the rafters of Old Trafford. Sulley Muntari is lining up to take the crucial penalty kick.

'*And Muntari steps up, and scores…*'

'Yesss!' We cheer again, delight washing over both of us like a wave crashing onto a beach.

'Errr, John, do you know how fast you're going? Asks Nick. I check the speedometer. 110mph.

'Oops.'

The next fifteen minutes are a torturous grind. The problem with listening to football on the radio is your complete reliance on the intonation of the commentator's voice and the ebb and flow of the backing track from the crowd. Quiet crowd and slow-paced commentary tones – good, high pitched squawking and crowd roar – bad. But Portsmouth are a man up and boast a defence chock full of experience. The minutes tick down without another serious effort on the Pompey goal and then suddenly the referee blows the final whistle and an unlikely lunch time upset lights up the day. Manchester United are *out*.

'I bet the Chelsea fans are licking their lips,' I say, as we reach the outskirts of Sheffield and Nick greedily drinks in the giant chimneys of the city's famous steel works.

'They must think their name is on the cup,' he replies, 'now I *definitely* want Barnsley.'

'I just want a result,' I say, 'I'm *really* in trouble if this goes to a replay. I've got to go over to Paris for three days for a work thing with my boss when the replay will be on. And I *absolutely* cannot get out of it this time. I'll have to tell them I've got chicken pox or break my arm like that goalkeeper in *Escape To Victory*.'

'Sylvester Stallone?'

'No, the proper one.'

Fifteen minutes after Sheffield and we are pulling off the motorway and heading into Barnsley town centre. It's a familiar route for me. This is the third time I've been here in the last fortnight. Once to pick up the season ticket, then to get the quarter final tickets and now finally for the big day itself. I point this out to Nick and he gives me one of those half looks which asks the pitying question: *What kind of obsessed moron are you?* We park by some council buildings and as we exit the car we immediately hear a great roar and the chants of a big football crowd.

'Is that the game?' Asks Nick.

I check my watch. It's only half past three.

'It can't be. The ground is on the other side of the town centre.' We follow the noise through the high rise buildings and find its source. A herd of Barnsley supporters outside a large pub called The Courthouse. With time on our hands we plough in amongst them, past the bouncers on the door, and force our way up to a heaving bar for a couple of pints. The atmosphere in the pub is heavy with the heat of a hundred bodies, the reek of beer and the constant chattering of the expectant punters. The Portsmouth victory or the pints of lager are bouying the underdogs. It takes ten minutes to get served.

'Two Stongbows please,' I ask the small, bald man behind the bar.

'Halves or pints?'

I look at him incredulously.

'Pints, of course.'

'All right, all right. I'm not a fooking mind reader.'

I tense up. My southern accent has obviously got me pegged as a Chelsea fan. That and the Stamford Bridge blue of my Ware FA Cup T-shirt which is peeping above the neckline of my jumper. I zip up my anorak to cover the shirt, despite the heat of the pub, and pull out the woolly Red Sox cap that I bought in the freezing-cold Boston winter back in January. I figure that the big, red 'B' on the hat will provide perfect camouflage. But obviously the trick will be to keep my mouth shut today. I could always try and affect a Yorkshire accent, but that could only make things worse if I drop an aitch in the wrong place.

After drinking up we head out of the town centre and walk down towards the railway crossing, following the path of the red-shirted mob. A heavy police presence also act as beacons, blazing the appropriate trail. There are occasional gaggles of Chelsea supporters, but there is no ugly mood, they obviously think that today will be a formality.

Crossing the railway line we march up a sloping road towards Oakwell beside rows of red brick houses. The weather has turned grey and cloudy, but the air lacks any wintry bite and the home fans are exuding a warm excitement which is contagious. Then after cresting the top of the hill we see the stadium for the first time (that day…). Oakwell is a curious combination of the old and the new. It has the high sides and the angled metal of the modern arena, but up close you can see the weariness of weathered age.

Our tickets are in the East Stand. I'm in the upper tier (my usual season ticket place of course) while Nick is in the lower. We march around to the far side of the ground where the views across a Yorkshire valley roll off magnificently into the distance. Ever the parent, I find the right entrance for Nick before looking for my own.

'OK, you go in that one, and I'm in over there,' I say pointing to the signs for the Lower and Upper entrances respectively. We shake hands poignantly, wish each other a good game and then move off to our turnstiles. It's only once I'm through that I realise that the ceremonious farewell has been a touch melodramatic. Both entrances spill out into the same hallway beneath the East Stand. No sooner are we through than we are back together again.

'Fancy a swift one?'

'Why not.'

Standing in that concrete hallway, surrounded by the strikingly different accents of the Barnsley faithful, the enormity of the task facing the home side is brought into focus by the glowing television screens of 'Tykes TV' which has announced the line ups. I'm still not familiar enough with Barnsley to pick out anyone beyond captain Brian Howard, goalkeeper Luke Steele, Southend-killer Jamal Campbell-Ryce and the blond-haired Bobby Hassell. But Chelsea have brought the big guns. Terry, Cole, Carvalho, Essien, Ballack, Wright-Phillips and Anelka. The only possible chinks in the armour are Carlo Cudicini in the sticks instead of Petr Cech and the absence of Frank Lampard and Didier Drogba.

After three successive visits to the toilet, a sure sign that I am nervous, we make our ways to our seats, and as I step up the stairs into the arena, the significance of the event is all too apparent by the virtual sell-out status of the ground. All stands are fit to burst, barely a seat left in the house. A familiar tune is ringing out around the stadium speakers. Incredibly familiar and yet nothing that I can remember hearing on the radio or TV. It takes me a full five minutes to work out that it is the same muzak that I listened to on an endless loop when I was in the automated phone queue of the Oakwell Ticket Office.

I have a wonderful viewing position just to the left of the halfway line. This is my first live, televised game of the cup run and across to the left on the far side of the ground I can see the hastily-erected portable studio of the BBC *Match Of The*

Day team. Using the zoom on my camera I can see into the studio and recognise the grey hair of Gary Lineker, the slouched demeanour of Alan Hansen and the stocky shoulders of Alan Shearer. The sole figure on the pitch is the Barnsley mascot Toby Tyke, who is taking great delight in scoring a goal in front of the Chelsea fans who pack into the entire North Stand to my far right. The person to my immediate right makes a friendly comment along the lines of 'Here we go, then,' but I can only grunt and nod back, desperately concealing my southern dialect, so it's a relief when the two teams finally walk out onto the pitch to a great roar from all four stands. The coin toss, picture poses and other preliminaries are quickly completed and just past the half hour mark we get under way.

As I sit there in the stand, watching the vibrant reds, blues, greens and whites of the game develop like a slowly emerging ink-jet picture from a printer, I think for a minute about the possible outcomes. My allegiances are vague. I'm still sore at Barnsley for knocking out Southend. I begrudge Chelsea the free ride they look like having straight to the final itself. Neither team has really piqued my imagination, and while I would love a Barnsley upset, it just doesn't seem likely. A Chelsea win would almost guarantee them a place in the final now with Man United out of the way. I try to play the emotion game. Where you watch one team attack and wait to see if you are pleased or disappointed if it comes to nothing. And if anything it is Barnsley who just about shade my impassionate heart. But if I am honest, neither of these teams are as appealing as a clear result, to get another round out of the way. That sounds like a terrible statement. After all this time, all these matches, have the games really become such a chore? Am I at the equivalent of 'hitting the wall' in a marathon? Or am I just lacking the passionate involvement of the fan?

I busy myself with trying to get some decent pictures, but while my lofty position is an idyllic one for spectating, it is too far away for crisp, clear photos. The darkening sky is too gloomy, despite the floodlights, and my feeble lens can manage no more than the occasional blurred effort. But I persevere right up until half time, after forty five minutes in which both teams have hustled and bustled, but neither threatened to take control.

I hop out of my seat and edge my way past the long row of Barnsley fans who are chattering eagerly amongst themselves, obviously delighted to be going in at half time nil-all. I then press myself through the throng in the upper corridor to find the loo. Inside it is apparent that Oakwell was never designed with capacity crowds in mind because the queue for the toilets is five deep at each urinal. The pee-er being pressed to the porcelain by the would-be pee-es. A truly unpleasant experience which only the mad (football) fanatic would endure. It takes virtually the whole of half time before I emerge again.

The first half has been dispassionate, workmanlike. The second half is very different. In the second half I find myself starting to grumble at every decision which goes against the men in red. I mutter at every misplaced Barnsley pass, and find myself jeering with pleasure, albeit quietly, when Shaun Wright-Phillips shanks one over the bar. Chelsea have come out in the second period with slightly more purpose and perhaps it is this dominance which galvanises my emotions. The appropriate top dog-underdog roles are suddenly being played out as Chelsea exude an arrogant class while Barnsley hook away clearances and scramble to block shots. And as we all know, I'm a sucker for the underdog.

And yet when Barnsley score a goal; a precious, beautiful, unexpected goal, my heart sinks.

My eye is glued to my camera's viewfinder and I track a deep cross from Martin Devaney, watching the ball through the small square of zoomed-in vision, seeing striker Kayode Odejayi and goalkeeper Cudicini challenge for it, crashing together. Odejayi makes contact with the ball, Cudicini flaps at fresh air. At first I think the referee is going to blow for a foul, but he doesn't, he just backpedals away as the stadium around me erupts with delight.

But my brain is calculating in overdrive and it doesn't like it: *A Barnsley goal on sixty six minutes. This is too early. This means Chelsea will have to come out now and try harder. They've got time for an equaliser, they'll probably get an equaliser and the game will probably end in a draw. A draw is bad. Had Chelsea scored first then the tie would be over. There are twenty four minutes to go. This is too long for Barnsley to hang on. At Liverpool they did it just right by sneaking a winner in the last minute, but this is too long for them to hang on… But of course if they can hang on, if they can… If they can hang on, then my Barnsley season ticket will become a passport to Wembley…*

And right at that point I make a conscious decision. One of the strongest most positive decisions of my footballing life. Forget about jinxing a team by wanting something to happen too much, forget about sitting on the fence and forget about playing for a result. I've spent too much of my life avoiding matches because I was too frightened of the result. Too many matches where I've switched off the television or the radio rather than endure the action. And of course there was the ultimate shame when I left Wembley at half time rather than watch Derby lose in the play off final. No, enough is enough. There are twenty four minutes of this game left and I *will* support Barnsley through every second. I will pass every ball, make every tackle and block every shot.

It is a liberating moment. I can actually feel the shackles of fear falling away from me. My cup odyssey, with its various highs and lows for Ware, Dagenham & Redbridge and Southend, has educated me, equipped me with the strength to face the hideous responsibility of fandom.

I leap to my feet with a bellowing roar of 'Come Onnn,' and smile, slightly embarrassed, at the people sat around me who have almost fallen off their seats with shock at the anorak–clad statue who has suddenly burst into life. I sit back in my seat, the seatbelt of impartiality unbuckled, and wait for the rollercoaster to begin.

If the fifteen radio minutes at the end of the United game had been torturous, then this is virtually terminal. I look at the stadium clock then look back at the action on the pitch while counting to sixty, then look back at the clock to check that another minute has gone, then turn back to the action and count to sixty again. Slowly but surely the minutes tick down. Chelsea are hurling the kitchen sink at Barnsley, but the Championship side are blocking, tackling and hooking the ball away. When Chelsea go close, the ball falls to the wrong person in the box, or they snatch desperately at a shot and it disappears off into their fans behind the goal. A fan base which is thinning with every sixty seconds that I count down. We get to the stage where the fans around me begin to theorise on how many minutes the fourth official will be adding on.

'They'll get one chance,' I mutter, 'there's always one more good chance.' Barnsley are just seconds away from Wembley, and so am I. The season ticket is beginning to look like the bargain of the century if the referee would just blow.

'Come on, blow your whistle,' I scream to the tiny figure on the pitch. My accent is out of the cage, but ever since my defining moment of clarity, I've cheered, hollered and sworn at all the right moments and it's obvious that I've been accepted. The referee does blow, but only for a free kick which is misinterpreted by some of the Barnsley fans who flood onto the pitch. They think it's all over. It isn't. The stadium announcer comes on to the tannoy, tells them they're a disgrace to Barnsley and urges them to clear the pitch. One of the fleeing fans gives Cudicini a cheeky pat on the bum as he disperses. Finally the game restarts.

'BLOW YOUR WHISTLE!' I bellow at the tiny man in black. Chelsea have had their last chance, he blows. We *all* erupt. I hug both of the people beside me in the upper tier, one man and one woman. Everyone is clapping and cheering with incredulous delight. I don't think I can ever remember a time like this, certainly not at a football match, where so many people around me have been so suddenly delighted by a result which no one had even entertained as a possibility. Everyone is grinning like the Cheshire Cat. I get a text message from Nick saying he's joined the pitch invasion and that right now he's waving at Gary Lineker. We all stand around clapping madly, unwilling to leave this magnificent scene. Finally, amid hand shakes and hair tousling with complete strangers, I make my way to the exit and walk down the stairs from the upper tier with the strains of *Que Sera Sera* ringing around me.

Que Sera indeed. Whatever will be, will be, *I'm* going to Wembley.

Barnsley 1 (Odejayi 66)
Chelsea 0

Attendance: 22,410
Money Spent So Far: £433.25
Miles Travelled So Far: 1,835
Winners Receive £300,000

2006:

Epiphany Part Two

My second revelation of 2006 came in May, three months after the magnificence of Hamburg and this time around it was the old faithful that delivered, the FA Cup Final. Contested by Liverpool and my old arch nemesis West Ham United, it was a game played at the Millennium Stadium, Cardiff, an arena which played the understudy role so successfully while the new Wembley was being built, that it was almost a shame to see its last staging of the showpiece event. I sat down to watch it on television, partly because it was the last Cardiff final, partly for the anticipation of watching West Ham get gubbed, but mainly because after Hamburg, my footballing antennae were twitching again. It was a game that has gone down in the record books as one of the all-time classics.

The details are probably still fairly fresh in people's minds, but the final was another alleged mismatch. West Ham had produced a reasonably successful season by their standards, finishing ninth in the Premier League, but still the vast gulf that had developed between the haves and the have-nots in English football pointed to a formality. Someone forgot to tell West Ham that. By the half hour mark, the Hammers were two-nil up thanks to a nightmarish own goal from Jamie Carragher and a bizarre effort bundled over the line by United striker Dean Ashton.

And it was at that point that I experienced one of the strangest sensations of my footballing life. I started to *want* West Ham to win something. It pains me to type that phrase but it's true. I hated what had happened to English football. I hated the fact that every season it was a three (four if you are being blindingly charitable) horse race, and that the league and cup had been devalued by the divide. I used to laugh at Scottish Football and the Celtic-Rangers stranglehold, but you only needed to look at the stats to see that England had mimicked that stalemate, only to the power of three rather than two. From 1996 to the present day the same three clubs had been crowned champions of the Premier League, while only Liverpool could be added to that group to account for the FA Cup winners of the same period. It just wasn't healthy.

But all of a sudden, here was an outsider with a two-goal lead just sixty minutes away from causing what could only be described as a major upset. A West Ham win would be a win for football, real football, for the millions of players who turn out week in, week out, on miserable pitches in miserable parks the length and breadth of the country. An entry in the record book which could never be overturned. A chink in the dominance of the fat-cat braggers on Millionaires Row.

Anyway trust West Ham to cock it up.

Djibril Cissé pulled one back before half time and then ten minutes into the second half, Steven Gerrard equalised. That was it, the dream was over. The millions of park players were pulling off their sodden, muddy shirts and stomping back to the changing rooms for a freezing cold shower before going out on the lash.

But wait, what was that? The flukiest goal you were likely to see in aeons, when Paul Konchesky crossed deep from the left, a cross which sailed over José Reina's head and into the Liverpool net. I was on my feet leaping into the air. It was a Ricky Villa-esque moment. The dream was alive.

Suddenly West Ham were thirty minutes away from scoring a victory for all of football. The clock ticked down. The thirty became twenty and then ten and then five minutes to hang on. Five minutes to fill the boots of every player in teams below that top four divide with belief for the future. Into injury time, the claret and blue ribbons were being unraveled, ready to go on the cup. The referee was looking at his watch...

And then? *That* thirty five yard screamer from Gerrard. Three-all. I was dashed between the rocks of desperation for football and admiration for the most gargantuan effort from a team captain you are ever likely to see. Cometh the hour, cometh the man. Boy's Own stuff! And in one of the biggest of big games. The only goal that comes near it for me is David Beckham's free kick for England against Greece in the World Cup qualifiers.

I knew there was a reason I hated the Hammers. I had given them a chance and they had blown it. But as I reeled back on the sofa, too stunned to watch or even care what happened in the penalty shoot-out, I realised that I had taken the second dose of my redemptive medicine. Football was coming home.

March 2008
Queue Sera Sera

The journey from Oakwell Stadium to where my car was parked across the town centre was one of the happiest experiences of my life. It wasn't just that *I* was happy, but rather that *everyone* around me was ecstatic. I've never seen so many people walking with such springs in their steps, such glee in their faces, radiating joy from every pore. At one point we were held at the railway level crossing which leads back into the town centre in a huge mob of red-shirted happiness and as the train pulled past us, everyone was cheering to the passengers, who in turn were all waving frantically back. It was surreal. Even the police were grinning behind their riot gear helmets.

The main cause for *my* euphoria was the knowledge that as far as the semi final was concerned it would not now be a question of *if* I could get tickets, but rather how *many* my season ticket would deliver. It was a huge weight off my mind. For the previous fortnight I had been fretting over the question of getting tickets for a Chelsea semi-final, dredging my memory for Blues-loving friends or colleagues that I could tap up. All of that worry had drifted off into the Yorkshire night sky the minute that the referee blew the final whistle. That relief, mixed with the romance of Barnsley's double acts of giant-killing and stirred with the infectious enthusiasm of the red-shirted fans, had produced an exquisite cocktail of delirium and we were all dancing around like loved-up ravers.

There was also now the real chance that Barnsley could go all the way, with the remaining two Premiership big guns both falling on what had been a Black Saturday for the cream of English football. But that of course would depend on who the Tykes drew in the semi final, which in turn was dependent on who made it through Sunday's games. And the shocks didn't stop in Yorkshire. Premiership Middlesbrough were embarrassingly turned over on their own turf by an authoritative performance from Championship team Cardiff, and it was only when West Brom thrashed League One side Bristol Rovers on Sunday evening, that the appropriate order of things was restored.

So to the draw at 1.25pm on the following Monday. I was working from home because of the bad weather that was lashing the country, but I sat in front of the TV with a foreboding sense of anti–climax. There were only four numbers going into the bowl so there was no great anticipation, plus for once, my ticketing situation was totally in the bag. Added to that we all *knew* where we were going this time. North London. Any of the four remaining teams had a chance of winning on current form, so the only minor point of interest was who I would get. I didn't have long to wait. Barnsley were first out followed by Cardiff. If you took league positions as an indication then this was the draw both teams would have wanted, as Portsmouth and West Brom were both higher up in the charts, but like I said, at this stage it really didn't seem to matter.

There was further good news from the Barnsley website which announced that my season ticket and Oakwell Centenary Club membership (sorry – did I forget to mention that I shelled out one hundred notes to join this too) would put me in the running for six tickets to Wembley for the semi final. So my whole immediate family would get a day out at the National Stadium. I realised then that *this* was the benefit of holding the last three games at Wembley. I had previously moaned about the semi-finals being staged there, rather than saving it for the big day itself, but with the way the competition had turned out this year, it seemed a fitting tribute for all four clubs and their supporters to be rewarded with a memorable day out at the great stadium rather than the fear of missing out by virtue of a semi-final loss.

So the only thing that stood between me and an easy ticketing ride to the FA Cup Final was Cardiff City, or Clwb Pêl-droed Dinas Caerdydd to give them their Welsh title. The Bluebirds were formed in 1899 as Riverside AFC and were a spin-off from a cricket club which wanted to keep its players fit through the winter months. They were one of a handful of Welsh clubs that play or have played in the English leagues and they were the only team to have taken the FA Cup out of England when they beat Arsenal one-nil in the cup final of 1927.

Cardiff's journey to Wembley had started in the Third Round with a visit to the potential banana skin of Non-League Chasetown, who actually went ahead in the tie before the Bluebirds scored three in the second half. To put this match into perspective, Chasetown were from a similar level of the Non-League Pyramid as Ware. To put it into context, I listened to the game on my way to Southend versus Dagenham & Redbridge. Following that, the Welsh team had to withstand a twenty minute battering at legendary FA Cup giantkillers Hereford United in front of a sell-out crowd of nearly seven thousand people before emerging with a two-one victory.

But it was not until the Fifth Round that Cardiff eventually hove-to in front of my attention when they hosted Wolverhampton Wanderers at Ninian Park. And this was because they crossed the path of another Road To Wembleyian called Andy Ollerenshaw who had been writing an internet blog about his experiences called *Wick To Wembley*. Andy's journey had started with an Extra Preliminary Round replay between Chertsey Town and Wick – a replay mind, he missed the first game(!) – before visits to Sittingbourne, Dartford, Camberley Town, Bromley, Eastbourne Borough, Cambridge United, Wolves and Watford.

Throughout his journey I had been reading his reports and debating long and hard with myself on whether to reach out to him over the internet. At one point I sent him an email to which he briefly, but positively replied, but in the end I decided not to take things any further. I think this was due to some sub-conscious desire to keep my experience special and unique to me. Alternatively my disinterest may have been more related to jealousy, as his blog had been featured on TalkSport Radio and ESPN TV. I had so far shunned publicity as I wanted to keep my book project under wraps lest I give anyone else the idea of getting a similar thing published. It was probably the same jealousy that had led to my 'hatred' of the Three Wise Monkeys from ZigZag Productions who I presumed (with delight) had failed to get any TV moguls interested in the early footage they had taken at Haringey Borough and Wembley.

On the day that the semi final tickets went on sale I woke up at four in the morning, got dressed and headed straight off for the three hour drive up to Barnsley. The tickets went on sale at 8am and I needed to be back in Essex by mid day for a work-related conference call. There was very little traffic on the road at that time of the day and I made the journey to Oakwell in record time, but as I turned into the road approaching the stadium, I was shocked to see the car park already full. It was still only half past six, but there were already hundreds of people in line for their tickets.

I jumped out of the car, a sense of dread washing through me, and rushed over to the queue for the fifty five pound tickets. I estimated that there were maybe two hundred people in front of me, but that when the turnstiles opened this would soon shorten. I could not have been more wrong. Eight o'clock came and went and we only shuffled a couple of places forward. I looked up at the dark, threatening skies and around me at my fellow queuers who had all come prepared for the long haul with foldaway chairs, Thermos flasks full of coffee and Gore-Tex anoraks. I was wearing just a T-shirt, fleece jacket and track suit bottoms and was already frozen to the bone. It seemed somewhat ironic that amongst all these northerners, it was the soft southern jessie who was undressed for the elements. I thought *they* were the ones who were supposed to be hard as nails.

The problem was it just hadn't occurred to me that I would need to queue. I hadn't needed to for the Chelsea match, I'd just pulled up in front of the office, popped in for my tickets and then driven straight off. But this was different. With four separate bands of ticket price available, it seemed that *everyone* was trying to guarantee that they got what they wanted. And most people wanted the good seats.

At my end of the fifty five pound line, there was consternation among my fellow queuers that we would get to the turnstile to find them all gone, and having decided *not* to join the shorter queues for the forty fives or thirty fives, we would find ourselves stuck with the lowest-priced twenty five pound tickets which only gained access to a place high up in the Wembley Gods. One Gore-Tex-wrapped, woolly-hatted, middle-aged gent who was stood next to me, had been canvassing opinion on how many tickets everyone around us were hoping to buy, in order to try and calculate demand against supply. Eventually he turned to me, his Yorkshire accent thick and broad.

'Ow many for thee?'

'Pardon?'

'Ow many for thee then?'

'How many tickets do I want?'

'Eye.'

'I'm hoping to get six.' My Thames Estuary accent was again courting queer looks from my fellow queuers. I'd considered trying the Yorkshire accent, but having listened to the conversations around me I'd known I would be completely out of my depth. Then came the question I had feared.

'You'rent from round 'ere then. Where've tha from?'

I decided to round Braintree up a decimal point.

'From London.'

Gore-Tex Man considered me for a moment with a light frown.

'Why'd ya support Barnsley then?'

It was that inevitable moment. An innocent enough question, but posed in front of two thousand cold, miserable people who were already fed up with queuing, it had an air of menace. It was one thing blagging the woman in the ticket office over the phone, but this was the real thing, in front of real fans. I was faced with the choice of coming clean or fashioning a lie. My wife and my mother will instinctively know which way I went.

'Well you see my father is from Barnsley, grew up there all his life, but then he had to move down south for work, which was where I was born. But I've always been a Barnsley fan,' I lied. I even got my season ticket out and waved it for added impact. My answer seemed to satisfy Gore-Tex Man, in fact I became something of a local attraction, as whenever people went past who knew any of my fellow queuers, I was introduced to them as 'He's come all the way up from London.'

But while I stood there grinning and shivering, I was thinking about a post on the *Wick To Wembley* blog from Andy Ollerenshaw which questioned the right of Road To Wembleyians to take tickets away from the long serving, long suffering, *real* fans of teams. I was hoping for a family-sized portion of tickets for the semi final, but my family only had allegiance to me, not to Barnsley. I'd only made the decision to back Barnsley with a quarter of the Chelsea match to go. So I'd only been a Barnsley 'fan' for about twenty four minutes. So was it actually fair to be taking six of those sought after places?

My guilt was tempered by the plain maths of the situation. Wembley Stadium holds ninety thousand, but Cardiff and Barnsley only received an allocation of around thirty thousand each. That left *another* thirty thousand which would probably fall into the hands of neutrals. And listening to the people around me, the common consensus was that Barnsley has around seven thousand season ticket holders. So if you equate the ownership of a season ticket to the concept of being a true fan, it meant that there were twenty three thousand glory hunters – like me – who would be turning out for Barnsley's big occasion. Ticketing is no democracy. He who pays the money, gets the ticket.

At 9am, I soothed my guilt further by buying a round of coffees for myself, Gore-Tex Man and his daughter. At 10am I walked to the front of the queue to try and work out what the hold up was, while Gore-Tex Man saved my place. The problem seemed to be that people were able to buy four tickets per season ticket book, but also take through four books at a time, a total of sixteen tickets per person. But then people were clustering together to buy large multiples of sixteen which were all seated together. The turnstiles were only selling two hundred tickets at a time, before returning the money to the office and then waiting for another batch of tickets to be sent down.

At 11am, now frozen to the marrow, I had lost all feelings of guilt about taking tickets from a true fan with the realisation that only a true fan, or mug, would have stood in a queue like this for four and a half hours for a semi final ticket.

At mid day, after watching a Sky Sports Outside Broadcast team conduct an interview with some of us mugs, I bought a round of burgers from the van that had hastily arrived, parked up and started a roaring trade. Then I got a text message from my boss asking why I hadn't joined the conference call, and I realised with horror that I had forgotten all about it, and that I would have to dial in from the queue. For another forty minutes I stood in the cold with my mobile phone to my ear, occasionally coming off mute to spout on about advertising banners, click through rates, fill rates and revenue recognition, in clipped Thames Estuary tones, and to the total bemusement of the Yorkshire locals around me.

Finally at 1.15pm, having stood in line fifteen minutes short of seven hours I was summoned to a turnstile, and with the help of a season ticket holder who did not want their full allocation, I bought three adults and three children for the FA Cup Semi Final between Cardiff City and Barnsley. I emerged from the turnstile, shook hands with Gore-Tex Man and the other rag-tag band of queuers, wished everyone good luck for the game and then headed back to the car for the long drive home, only turning the heater off full blast when I reached the M11 outside Cambridge.

Sunday April 6th, 2008:
Semi Final
Barnsley V Cardiff

My morning starts with two bombshells. Overnight, a thick layer of snow descends on the south east and six-year-old Jonathan wakes up deciding that he doesn't want to go to football. Vanessa chooses to stay at home with him, we have a brief, but heated discussion, and I back down after she points out that not everyone agrees with my argument that a family trip to Wembley will be a 'life-defining moment.' This means a late call up for Vanessa's father Stan, who is visiting from his home in France, and Eden's school friend Molly. My dream of taking the family unit to a sell-out match at Wembley lies in snowy tatters.

I'm still sulking as we pick up Molly and drive down the M11 towards London, destination Wembley Stadium, via Stoke Newington to pick up Nick the American. We travel through sleety showers under a low, overcast sky and with the temperature outside the car showing as just one degree. It's the weather I was expecting for the midwinter rounds, not the semi final.

I've factored in plenty of time for the journey. In my experience, driving to Wembley can be a long, drawn out affair despite the fact that it is only fifty five miles from my house. On top of that, the Olympic Flame is being marched through the streets of London today, a goodwill precursor to the Beijing Olympics, and the radio is reporting that protestors, calling for the withdrawal of China from Tibet, are determined to disrupt the parade. The last thing I want is to get caught up in all that.

I'd thought long and hard about the logistics of getting six of us to Wembley. Rail, tube, road, or any combination of the three? In the end I managed to get my hands on a car park ticket right outside Wembley and so decided to drive all the way. With Nick safely on board I shoot up the A1 to the North Circular and we make our way toward the stadium. It is a Sunday afternoon and the traffic is incredibly light. Travelling up through central London means we avoid any of the coach routes from Wales or Yorkshire and it turns out to be the easiest journey I have ever made to football's spiritual home. Maybe things are looking up. Even the sun threatens to peep out from the clouds.

As we pass over the Brent Cross flyover, the giant stadium emerges before us extracting suitable sounds of awe from my passengers. I'd experienced those same emotions when en route to Vale Farm Sports Centre last August for Wembley versus Haringey Borough, so I know how they feel. And even though this is the fifth time I've seen it over the last ten months, it is still truly breathtaking. The huge structure with sleek curves like an Italian sports car, and that imposing arch which is just as eye-catching as the famous, old twin towers.

Driving towards the car park is like entering a riot zone. A heavy police presence containing a riot of colours from the reds of Barnsley outside one pub and past the blues of Cardiff spilling out of another. Everyone is shouting and chanting. I park the car and we walk through the coach park to the stairs which lead to the pedestrian walkway surrounding the ground. We pay a brief homage to the statue of Bobby Moore and I snap some pictures over the wall of the multicoloured crowds marching up Olympic Way from Wembley Park tube station. There is an air of expectation which warms the soul against the chill, wintry wind which is whipping around the stadium, and I realise that it is the location of Wembley which generates this excitement. Situated as it is, far removed from the neighbouring, residential locales, there is this feeling of pilgrimage which will always be attached to Wembley. Which makes it different, somehow special.

Although there is still an hour until kick off, we pass through our allotted turnstile and enter the underbelly of the stadium. I remember the old Wembley with its dank, dark concrete tunnels, punctuated by the odd burger bar or set of toilets, but this modern atrium casts that old memory into shadow. We are surrounded by a sea of red-shirted fans and bordered by armies of concessions, bookmakers and attractive public conveniences. I'm delighted when a programme only costs me a fiver – I'd been fearing worse here – and horrified when chicken and chips and a drink costs me eight quid per kid.

Once we've scoffed and gulped, we flash our tickets at the stewards and pass through the portal of Block 141 into the arena. It doesn't have the same magic for me as a ground I've never visited, because I've seen enough of Wembley on the TV to have some expectations, but the sheer scale of it is awesome. I don't think I've ever visited a ninety thousand capacity stadium before, not even some of the US baseball stadiums I've been to on my travels. Wembley is just *so* big. The twenty five pound seats high in the Gods seem *so* far away. The pitch looks green and lush and the wintry showers have lifted the smell of the turf high into the air, so you can almost taste the pitch as well as see it. Just then the giant screens at each end burst into life with a montage of famous events that Wembley has hosted – football, boxing, speedway, politics, rock concerts – and I stand rooted to the ground drinking them in. Everything points to a great occasion, Wembley has so far delivered on all its promise.

Ever so slowly, bit by bit, person by person, the collage of fans begins to flesh itself out, so that with thirty minutes to go, Wembley is half full, with forty thousand souls, standing, staring and singing. My fifty five pound tickets that I queued for seven hours to obtain have deposited us on the tunnel side of the stadium, parallel to the penalty area. I begrudgingly admit that they were worth the wait.

'What chance does Barnsley have? Asks Nick the American beside me. I love the way he refers to a team in the singular. Grammatically of course it is correct, but it sticks out like a sore Yankee thumb here in England, where we tend to refer to a team as 'they' or 'them'.

'Probably as good as any,' I reply, 'which is an improvement for them, bearing in mind that I've given them no chance in the last two rounds.'

'And if they win you'll automatically get tickets for the final, right?'

'Well I'll probably have to queue for them again, but yes.'

'And where are Cardiff in the league?'

'Towards the top.'

'And Barnsley.'

'Towards the bottom. I think they're just about in the relegation zone.'

'Oh dear. There's a lot riding on this then.'

'Quite.'

With fifteen minutes to go, Wembley has all of a sudden become full, save for a dotting of spaces in all of the Club Wembley sections which ring the waist of the stadium. Announcers from both clubs have been collaborating with the main stadium announcer to whip the crowd into a frenzy and we've cheered another video section showing the best goals of the competition so far. An ominous omen is the number one goal was Cardiff striker Jimmy-Floyd Hasselbaink's strike against Wolves in an earlier round.

With ten minutes to go, the club announcers take us through some final 'local' colour. For Barnsley it is another rendition of that Eurobeat-disco muzak that I listened to when I was on hold to the ticket office, for the men from the valleys, it's a Welsh male voice choir knocking out an old favourite.

'What the hell are they singing?' Asks Nick the American with a bemused face.

'Men of Harlech,' I reply.

'Men of Hurlock? Like Terry Hurlock?' Nick's knowledge of obscure eighties hatchet men is impressive if misguided.

'Men of Harlech. Have you never seen *Zulu*?'

With five minutes to go the two teams are led out from the tunnel at the middle of the pitch for the introductions, and this is perhaps the one complaint I have about the new Wembley. I much preferred that long walk around the greyhound track at the old stadium, which heightened the anticipation for the fans and must have had many a players' sphincter twitching.

Dead on four o'clock, we kick off. And it is at this point that my day begins to unravel. What had started badly with the break up of the original Stoneman team selection, then rallied through the easy journey and the fabulous surroundings, all goes awry. I snap no more than a dozen action shots before my super digital SLR camera starts playing up. I check the display on the back of the camera which reveals that I have almost no battery left. I realise that I have forgotten to charge it up overnight. Schoolboy error. I panic and go for my back-up camera, a little point and shoot thing, which immediately starts complaining that its battery is exhausted. I'm fiddling around with both of them, trying to conjure some power, when I hear some panicked squeaks around me. I look up and see a ball bobbling around in the Barnsley box, which is then lofted into the back of the net by a black-shirted Cardiff player. I'm almost overwhelmed by a feeling of nausea. A Cardiff goal. An early Cardiff goal. An early Cardiff goal which I've missed with my power-drained cameras. I can't even get some snaps of the celebrations.

Beside me, Stan has started cheering.

'It's in,' he cries, 'what a goal.'

'Shut up,' I hiss, 'we're in the Barnsley end.' (What is it about Vanessa and her father, that they have to cheer for goals in the wrong parts of grounds?)

'Not a good start,' says Nick.

'Still early,' I grimace.

'Daddy, I don't think Barnsley are going to win,' says Evie, all sweet innocence and seriousness.

'There's still a long way to go,' I say, trying to reassure myself, but the reality is that I've become instantly miserable. Nine minutes in to the semi final and the team I need, not want necessarily, but *need* to win are one-nil down. *And* I've forgotten to charge my camera. Idiot. I pack both of the cameras away in my rucksack and sit back to endure the game.

Out on the pitch, Barnsley have rallied from the early setback, which the giant TV screen tells me was inflicted by Joe Ledley in the ninth minute, and are starting to press the Cardiff goal. The best things are coming from skipper Brian Howard, and the villain of the Southend match Jamal Campbell-Ryce, both of whom are lofting balls into the box to Istvan Ferenczi and Chelsea hero Kayode Odejayi. But whenever the tall strikers win a ball in the box, it either flashes wide, bounces tamely to the keeper, or falls to a Cardiff player.

Up at our end, Hasselbaink and his fellow veteran forward Trevor Sinclair are constant concerns based on their previous reputations rather than any telling possession, although Sinclair pulls a fine reaction save out of Luke Steele in the Barnsley goal. But that chance apart, the Tykes are enjoying the lion share of the game, with Cardiff happy to sit on their one goal lead and try and catch the Yorkshire side on the break. And when each Barnsley attack washes up onto the Cardiff beach and then recedes, I find myself glancing at the TV screen with increasing frequency. The minutes are ticking past at a furious rate.

Every football fan, watching their team trail by a solitary goal, knows this feeling. When you go two down, the tension is relieved slightly, when you let in three, the pressure is off and you can start focusing on moaning and groaning and preparing for the next game. But a single goal deficit is the worst possible situation. You don't want to let in any more, because although this would release you from the current anxiety, you are still in the game. But as each chance passes, each half chance disappears, the anxiety in your stomach ratchets a notch tighter. And the damned clock keeps ticking away merrily.

There is a brief respite at half time. Evie and I go off to queue for the toilets, Nick disappears for some of the overpriced food and Stan heads off for a coffee, leaving the other two girls guarding our belongings in the seats. It takes me all of half time to make it through the queues to the toilet and by the time I return the two teams are already back out on the pitch. None of us have said a single word about the game. We all know that Barnsley have had a *lot* of possession, without making any meaningful in-roads into that miserable one goal deficit, that worst possible start.

The second half kicks off with me thinking that at least if Cardiff score again it will be at the far end of the ground as far as I am concerned, whereas if Barnsley can find a goal it will be right in front of us. I have to wait twenty minutes for that moment. In the sixty sixth minute, the Cardiff back four are caught flat-footed, stepping up for an offside that never comes. Campbell-Ryce slots a ball through the defenders unleashing Odejayi from the halfway line. He has half the length of the pitch to run in on Peter Enckleman in the Cardiff goal. He has so much time to bear down on the goal, that I have time to stand up as all the Barnsley fans around me arise, reach over to Evie, whose sight line is blocked by the people in front, pick her up in both arms and pull her up above the heads of the people in front of me so that she can see the action unfold. I imagine that for Odejayi this same span of time between the halfway line and the goal must seem like an aeon. He knows he has the single, greatest chance of the match, he knows that he has the opportunity to get Barnsley back in the game. His mind will already be calculating whether to go to the keeper's left or right, he will be changing his mind, back and forth, as the angles tighten and Enckleman moves out to face him. He will be debating whether to take another touch or to hit it, as he passes into the penalty area. I've spoken at length in this cup odyssey about the times when matches seem to go into slow motion, where the brain is processing so fast that normal time seems to slow down. I pity Odejayi for the range of emotions that he must be experiencing in those fifty short yards from halfway line to box. He makes his final decision and hits a low drive, to Enckleman's left hand side, and the bottom of the net ripples.

A great roar of relief begins to erupt from my throat, and Evie is lifted higher in my arms, but then the ball flashes out beyond the goal, beyond the net and crashes into the advertising hoardings…

The euphoria welling in my throat is switched off like a light, and a heavy, disbelieving despair fills the void as my brain tries to compute what has happened. He's *missed* it.

I gently lower Evie back into her place and then slump down into my seat, my head in my hands. Right there I know that the game is over. If *I* feel *this* bad, then how do the Barnsley players feel? How will *they* rally themselves after this? And how cock-a-hoop must the Cardiff team be, after all, the half of the stadium dressed in blue is currently celebrating as if they'd scored another.

A gentle quiet descends on the Barnsley half of Wembley. We *all* sit down. The sensation of mass bereavement is appalling. We *all* know that it is over. You just don't miss chances like that and win football games like this. There won't *be* another chance like that.

Four minutes after the Odejayi miss, the first ripples of celebration start to emanate out from the Cardiff City end. A few optimistic individuals ignore the fact that there are twenty minutes to go, because they *know* that the Bluebirds are going to win. I've feared it since the ninth minute. My stomach has been agonising in tight, little knots for over an hour. The belief of the optimists is contagious and more and more Cardiff fans join in the celebrations, their actions mirrored by their players who comfortably frustrate their opponents with some solid defending here, some time-wasting there, the merry-go-round of the substitutions speeding the advance of the ticking clock.

The Barnsley players are misplacing passes, knocking it sideways, failing to penetrate. It is a slow, agonising death. The fourth official refuses to put us out of our misery by showing four added minutes of extra time. The Cardiff fans immediately start whistling to the referee and yet their shrill calls are almost mocking, as it is *me* that wants this game to be over, to call time on the tiny flicker of hope that remains throughout the prolonged half.

Finally he blows and the blue half of Wembley erupts, while the red half, almost silently, just rise to their feet and start heading for the exits. Nobody is speaking. The sudden exodus puts pressure on the exits and a queue forms, halting us in our tracks, so we turn back to look down on the glorious pitch, from these glorious surroundings and raise our hands to clap the devastated red-shirts sat prone on the green turf.

As the exodus eases we make a swift exit from the stadium and hurry to the car. Nobody wants to be caught in a traffic jam getting away from this scene of devastation. We just want to get clear. We mumble phrases of disbelief at the Odejayi miss, but still we aren't really talking, there is none of the analysis from the previous two rounds, against Chelsea and against Liverpool. It's the misery of football that a team can overcome two Goliaths and then get stabbed in the side by just another foot solider.

We drop Nick the American off in Stoke Newington and head through east London towards Essex. Evie starts to feel car sick on the Lea Bridge Road and throws up into the Wembley plastic bag that my matchday programme came in. Then halfway up the M11, with everyone just longing to return to the comfortable confines of our house, my car suddenly loses all power from its engine and glides to a depressing halt by the side of the motorway. I have to call out Green Flag and we stand for a frozen hour by the side of the road waiting for a tow, great lorries rumbling past us.

We finally arrive home at ten o'clock, four hours after leaving Wembley. Vanessa greets us at the door, her maternal concern washing across three generations of her family. She sits us down in the kitchen and produces buckets of tea and mountains of hot, buttered toast.

'Not quite the life-defining moment you were hoping for then?' She asks, with a blend of authoritative irony and compassionate concern. 'This book of yours better sell some copies. What are you going to do for final tickets now?'

Barnsley 0
Cardiff 1 (Ledley 9)

Attendance: 82,752
Money Spent So Far: £678.25
Miles Travelled So Far: 1,945
Winners Receive £900,000

2006
Epiphany Part Three

The third and final event of 2006 which completed my footballing salvation were the World Cup finals in Germany. At the time, Nick the American worked for the internet giant Yahoo, one of the main sponsors of the showpiece event. And one of the terms of Yahoo's sponsorship deal with FIFA was that employees got priority on buying tickets for the games, at face value, ahead of the general public.

The pecking order for the tickets ran down through the company from the executives at the top, through the sales and marketing divisions, so that by the time it reached him – a product manager working on Yahoo Mobile – the real plum ties such as England games or the knockout stages were already gone. But there were still a selection of group matches involving other countries available. He asked me if I was interested in going on a mini tour. I nearly bit his hand off.

As with any major finals, getting a ticket for the game is one consideration, but getting flights and accommodation can be equally as tricky and so it was I found myself at 5am on the morning of June 21st sat at the wheel of my battered, old, green Peugeot 206, by the dockside at Dover, waiting for a ferry to take me to France ahead of a three hundred and fifty mile drive to Frankfurt. Even at that early hour the ferry was chock full of football fans, all making the pilgrimage to soccer's roving Mecca. As it was still the group stages, England were still in the competition, and although playing poorly, there was no reason for alarm just yet, so there was a sense of anticipation which built with every turn of the ferry's propeller screw.

On arrival in Dunkerque I then had a mad dash through four countries; France, Belgium, Holland and finally Germany, to make it to Frankfurt for that evening's game, which offered to be a potential humdinger between Holland and Argentina. In a pre-sat nav era, for me anyway, I made a couple of wrong turns which included one complete revolution of the Brussels equivalent of the M25, so that by the time I reached the outskirts of Frankfurt, the clock was ticking against me and I had to frantically find the hotel, find somewhere to park and then find my friends who were already in the city. Then find a beer.

It was my first experience of the madness, mayhem and majesty that descends on a city when the World Cup is in town. There were people everywhere of all nationalities and colours. Naturally there were a lot of oranges and blues for this particular match, but the spectacle had drawn people from all four corners of the world.

We took a taxi from the city centre to the stadium and marched into an orange and blue, bi-polar cauldron of atmosphere, the like of which I have never seen before. It was magical. One of the people in our party was obsessed by Maradona and spent the first twenty minutes of the game scanning the corporate seating looking for the diminutive genius. With a cry of 'Got him!' he handed around the binoculars that Nick had thoughtfully brought along and we clapped eyes on the fallen idol, bouncing around among the suits like a ten-year-old, wearing a blue and white jersey and whirling the scarf tied to his wrist in time with the uplifting chant of the Argentina fans to our right.

As it turned out the game itself was a fairly mundane nil-nil draw. Both teams were banking on beating the other two in their group to progress and so were happy to play out for a point, but for me the occasion was not so much about the football but about drinking in the rich experience within the stadium. It made me realise that the real power of football is not so much the game itself, but the surroundings. The game is the catalyst for an ever-changing sequence of sensations; the vivid colours, the raucous chants, the mingling smells of grass, liniment and burgers, the press of the crowd and the tastes of victory or defeat. All of the things which the small screen, even the HD-ready widescreen, cannot convey.

A suitably lively night out in Frankfurt followed, although the game didn't kick off until nine o'clock at night so it was midnight before we were back in the city. Then the following morning, Nick and I piled our stuff and ourselves into the Peugeot for a three-hour journey to Nuremberg to take in Michael Essien's Ghana against the USA. It was an afternoon kick off and we made it to the ground with just minutes to spare. Born and raised in New York to an English mother and Armenian father, Nick had some skin in this game, so while I was just happy to savour another occasion, his focus was very much on the result. Unfortunately it did not go the way the Americans wanted and a dubious penalty award meant that Ghana played out a two-one win. I must admit to taking some delight in the result. Having worked for American internet companies for a number of years I have something of a love-hate relationship with those from the other side of the pond, and it's nice to see them occasionally humbled.

We left the ground at around four o'clock in the afternoon and started to make our way back into Nuremberg when we came across one of the Fanfest parks that the Germans had created for those supporters who could not get into the grounds. Dominated by the biggest of big screens on which to watch the matches, the Fanfest parks were like mini-football carnivals. Every style of cuisine, every possible combination of alcoholic refreshment, all catered for in a shanty town of concession stands around the open-air auditorium. It was a balmy, summer's evening and we settled down to experience the atmosphere ahead of a game played out on the screen and under the stars between Brazil and Japan.

When the match finished people started to drift away from the park, but a group of fans had formed a circle and were passing a ball among themselves. Each participant given a handful of touches to perform some keepie-uppie devilment before passing on to the next person. As I stood in the circle awaiting my turn, I counted fourteen different national colours being worn by the players. When the ball finally arrived at my feet, the combination of a handful of lethally-strong cocktails and my general ring-rustiness with a ball led to me reinforcing the continental opinion of the English game being all kick and run and no finesse. However I redeemed myself and the pride of England with a behind the back flick which kept an errant ball in play, although this did lead to a dehydrated groin muscle intimating that I should call it a night. But spending fifteen minutes with that cluster of like-minded, accepting strangers was a magical experience that I will never forget.

With Nuremberg's night life sampled we then travelled the next day to Stuttgart for our final game of the tour. Togo against France. Something of a mismatch with the Togo squad in complete disarray following arguments about player payments and a general lack of talent. France made hard work of it, rather pleasingly, and only emerged ninety minutes later with a fortunate two-nil success. Proudly sporting a yellow Togo T-shirt that I'd had knocked up in a printer's shop off Carnaby Street before the trip, I'd heckled, harassed and harangued the French supporters in true English fashion and also had my picture taken with two Gallic supporters dressed as Asterix and Obelix: *'Hey Obelix, une photo s'il-vous-plait!'*

On the tram from the stadium back to the hotel we were packed like sardines into a Football Special, and forced to listen to a gaggle of Scotland supporters who'd come along to the finals for the ride, slurring their way through a selection of Rod Stewart's back catalogue. It was as though this World Cup had everything but the Saint and Greavesie. Another long night in a Stuttgart grunge bar, where my yellow Togo shirt shone like a beacon among the leather, kohl and black jeans, and then I drove back to Dunkerque for the ferry home.

By the time I reached the port my Peugeot had decided to partly shed its exhaust pipe, which was by then dragging along behind me like a goldfish poo. The French ferryman took one look at the car and told me 'Non. Zere ees no way you are coming on ma ferree dragging zat.' Tired, exhilarated and emotional, I bent down behind the car, yanked the exhaust pipe clean off, stuffed it onto the back seat and with bleary-eyed authority screamed 'Happy now?' He let me on. I guess he figured that in an hour and a half I would no longer be a French problem. Back in England, and with the Peugeot sounding like a tuba, I crawled up the motorway to Essex, to my family, my home and more importantly my bed, and with the rhythmic chant of the Argentinean fans drumming away in my heart and my head. My footballing redemption was complete. They say that Jesus Saves, but in my case, Trochowski, Gerrard and Maradona had combined to tuck away the rebound. (Sorry).

April 2008
Final-ly

There was a certain part of me which was perversely pleased that Barnsley were beaten by Cardiff. It was the journalist. The old hack who I've tried to keep in professional check for so long. The vulture trained to take glee from a bad turn of events. Who *wasn't* horrified by a natural disaster, or a hideous crime, but rather *delighted* that it had happened on his news patch. Not a particularly nice person, I'll grant you that, but the person who knew that the combination of Barnsley failing and my cup final passport evaporating would make a better chapter for the book. If I struggled to obtain a ticket it would all be a bit more newsworthy. If there was anything of my father in me – the accountant – then he would be *horrified* at the turn of events, because it meant that I would probably now need to pay through the nose to get to the final.

Nearly everyone I met in the aftermath of the Barnsley defeat greeted me with the same horrified phrase – '*What are you going to do now?*' – but throughout my cup odyssey I had never really been worried about getting tickets for Wembley. There were just *too* many of them on sale. I had ninety thousand opportunities to get myself into the stadium – not including dressing up as a steward. No, this was only going to be a matter of price.

I had a number of leads to follow.

The first was through my next door neighbour Sheryl. Her sister's husband was a Club Wembley member – this was how I had got a VIP car park ticket next door to Wembley for the semi final. I made an enquiry and was told he had *four* tickets on offer, but that he wanted five hundred pounds a pop for them as a batch. Two grand seemed a bit rich to me, and there was no chance of getting *that* one past Vanessa.

Next up was an intriguing opportunity which followed a chance conversation I had on the day after the semi final. A new guy at work called Clive Baker and I were stood by the coffee machine one Monday morning.

'Did you have a good weekend?' He asked.

'Not really,' I replied. 'I went to the FA Cup semi final between Barnsley and Cardiff yesterday and then on the way home my car broke down. I didn't get in until ten o'clock.'

'Oh dear,' he replied. 'Do you support one of the teams then?'

'No, not really. I *sort* of support Barnsley, but only because I've been following them for a few rounds. You see I've actually been to *all* of the FA Cup games this year, right from the first matches back in August. You know, following the winning team. I was hoping Barnsley were going to win because I've got a season ticket with them and so I would have been guaranteed a final ticket.'

'Oh I see,' said Clive. 'That's actually quite a coincidence because I was at the match yesterday too.'

'Really?' My brain began processing. Clive Baker, nice Welsh lilt to his voice. 'But I thought you were a rugby man?'

'Well yes I am really,' Clive had taken great pleasure in reminding me of Wales' victorious Grand Slam efforts a month or so ago, 'but I got a call on Friday night from a friend of mine who said he had a couple of tickets that he didn't want. Actually he's more of a friend of a friend, that sort of thing, works in the city.'

'Go on.'

'Well he said that he wanted the tickets to go to someone who *really* wanted them, and he knew that I was from Cardiff, and so offered them to me.'

'What sort of tickets were they?'

'Oh good ones. Corinthian Club. Like I said, this fellow works in the city, so they are sort of corporate hospitality ones. He didn't want to go because none of the big clubs were in the semis this year.'

'And how much did you pay for them?'

'Well he didn't really want any money, so we just gave him a case of wine. Naturally I was very pleased with the result, but too bad for you and Barnsley.' I gave him a shrug to indicate that my Tykes persona was already lying in a crumpled heap on the bedroom floor, like last night's discarded clothes.

'So do you think he'll want to go to the final?'

'I don't know. He might be a Portsmouth fan, or he may need them for corporate entertaining. Do you want me to find out for you?'

'Yes please!'

'OK, leave it with me.'

I left it with him.

Next I paid a visit to the same website which connected me with Kenny the Liverpudlian tout. Scanning down the list of offers, there seemed to be no one at that point with tickets for the final, so I posted a 'Wanted' message to see what that would unearth. And a few hours later, I got a call on my mobile phone from a Mancunian character:

'Are you still looking for tickets for the final?'

'Yes.'

'Which team do you support.' I thought for a moment before my reply.

'Cardiff. But I've been following the cup all the way through.'

'OK, well I've got Club Wembley tickets in the Cardiff end, but I can't make it to the final because I've got to go away tomorrow. How much do you want to pay for them?'

'How much do *you* want?'

'I only want face value for them, what did you pay for your semi final tickets?'

'Fifty five pounds. How many have you got?'

'Four. Look if you can get to a bank today and pay the money in for them, I'll get the address changed for the tickets so they get sent out to you. The bank closes in ten minutes so you'll have to get moving.'

'OK.' I took down the bank account details from Manc Man and set off for the nearby branch of Lloyds TSB that he had conveniently *Googled* the address for, but throughout the call my brain had been calculating furiously. I didn't like the way that *everything* he had said had been so accommodating, nor that there had been a ten-minute window to close the deal. So I decided to wait until the bank had closed before calling him back to say that I had been too late. Even before that however he rang me three times to see what was happening, but I ignored the calls until after half past four, then rang him back.

'Sorry mate, the bank was closed before I could get to it.'

'But I've already changed the postal address for the tickets with Wembley,' he bemoaned, pausing for a moment. 'Can you get to the bank in the morning and make the payment then?'

'Yes, of course.'

'You're not mucking me about are you?'

'No!'

'OK, I have to leave tomorrow at one o'clock, but I'll check that the payment has been made before I go, and leave the address on the tickets as it is now.'

'All right,' I replied. He rang off, but I'd already smelt rats, so I used my phone to *Google* the name he had given me for the account details and read report after report from bitter football fans the length and breadth of the country who had been taken in by this character, paid their money and then never seen any tickets.

These included one poor Barnsley fan who had shelled out over three hundred pounds for bogus semi final tickets and never received them.

Equal parts furious and relieved, I composed a measured text message to send off to this "person": '*Hi, I just read some negative stuff about you on the web, so I won't be making the transfer tomorrow – I suggest you call Wembley and change the address for the tickets back. Cheers John.*' Not so much a close shave as common sense, but no doubt there would be plenty of desperate Cardiff or Portsmouth fans who ended up wiring money to that evil bastard.

Meanwhile, the websites and newspapers were filling up with the usual stories of disgruntled fans who were bemoaning the meagre ticket allocations for the two finalists. Cardiff and Portsmouth were both getting just twenty five thousand tickets, some eight thousand less than the club allocations for the semi final. There was *zero* chance of getting a ticket through the clubs, but it made me think. If you took *their* allocations away, and the constant of the seventeen thousand Club Wembley seats out of the equation, that meant that the FA were holding back around twenty three thousand tickets for the final. So who would be getting those? I decided on a spot of research and *Googled* an article from the BBC website which explained the situation. According to the article: '*The twenty three thousand tickets go to groups the FA calls "the football family", which include the ninety two professional football clubs, one hundred and thirty four full member clubs, UEFA, FIFA and county and international football associations.*'

Of course. All of the clubs in the English football pyramid are rewarded for their continuing support of the national game by way of a small allocation of tickets for the showpiece final. A "thank you" to the individuals who turn out in all weathers, shout at each other, kick lumps from one another, swear at the referees and then go out on the lash. I vaguely remembered from my time with Braintree & Bocking United that our manager Tony Child would come into the dressing room after the last match of the season and ask if anyone wanted a cup final ticket. We'd then draw lots to see who would get them. Perhaps my old club could be an opportunity for me here? That's if Tony was still involved with the team. It had after all been eighteen years since I'd last been in touch. But then again he *must* remember my salmon–like leap and headed equaliser in the cup final against Galleywood. Surely that must account for something?

I dug out Tony's details from an old address book and dialled the number. The call went through to voicemail so I left a rather complicated message and then hung up. Miraculously he called me back at around 10pm and said that yes he *was* still involved with the team, yes he *did* remember my cup final equaliser and yes he *probably* would get some final tickets from the Essex FA this year. But if he did, then in the time-honoured tradition it would depend on whether any of the current squad of players wanted them before he would be able to allocate one to me. I said I'd leave it with him.

I waited and waited. With just weeks to go until the final, I was beginning to sweat. But then the Footballing Gods decided to hand me a break. Clive Baker came over to my desk one Monday morning and signalled for me to follow him into a Conference Room.

'OK,' he said, a warm look on his face, 'we're on. That's if you don't mind me coming too.'

'How much?'

'Two hundred and fifty each.'

'For *Corinthian Club* tickets?'

'Yes.'

I could hardly believe my luck. 'These tickets, they do really exist. You're not having me on are you?'

'No, of course not.'

'Right then, you're on.'

I went to the cash machine at lunch time, withdrew the money, and bought myself a cup final ticket for one of the best seats in the stadium, and all the booze I could manage.

Saturday May 17th, 2008:
Final
Cardiff v Portsmouth

I wake up on cup final morning with mixed emotions. The anticipation of reaching the final is tinged with the sadness of conclusion. I jump in the shower my thoughts fixed firmly on the game, clean my teeth with visions of the Wembley arch printed in my mind, and then take my blue, Ware, FA Cup T-shirt out of the cupboard for the very last time.

While Vanessa takes the kids to swimming, I mooch around the house finalising my preparations. I make sure the batteries on my camera are fully charged this time, and pack my reporting kit into my rucksack. I watch snippets of *Soccer AM* on Sky, and stare out at the grey clouds and fine rain which is falling on the back garden. The weather conditions are nothing like I had imagined. I was expecting the bright sunshine which I always associate with cup final day, but the sky is overcast and misty. It's almost exactly as it had been back in August of last year when I travelled to Haringey Borough for match number one on my quest. It seems my nineteenth cup match of the season will be accompanied by a greyness which mirrors my mood.

I have to keep reminding myself that I am supposed to be enjoying this. That I should be excited and happy. I've achieved everything I've set out to do. I've made it to every round, overcome all of the logistical and ticketing hurdles. I'm up to date with my book chapters and I just need to write up today's game come the final whistle to complete it. I've proven all of the doubters wrong. I should be ecstatic. But instead I find myself wondering why I feel so hollow.

It may be that I feel little affiliation to the two teams competing today. I have yet to see Premiership outfit Portsmouth play live in the competition, and apart from a sense of sympathy at Harry Redknapp's twenty five-year managerial quest for a trophy, I can't see myself cheering Pompey on. Championship side Cardiff will obviously be plucking at my underdog-loving heart strings, but the Bluebirds forced me to suffer eighty one minutes of semi final agony, and that wound has not healed. It may also be that I am just *not* as excited about the prospect of a visit to the National Stadium, having already been there six weeks ago. This is the flip side of the argument about keeping the Wembley turf sacred for the final itself. Having visited the magnificent arena in the semis, there is no mystique attached to today's excursion to north London. But probably the most accurate answer is that I simply don't want this journey to come to an end.

At half past eleven Vanessa drives me to Chelmsford Station and sends me on my way. I've decided to take the train to Wembley this time, primarily in anticipation of sampling the hospitality unlocked by the Corinthian Club tickets. I change at Stratford for the Underground and travel almost the entire length of the Jubilee Line to Wembley Park station. It's another ridiculously easy journey as the train is only boarded by a few Pompey fans at Waterloo.

However I emerge from the train into a sea of blue shirts and waves of noise. The Pompey Chimes are ringing out starkly against the softer lilts of 'Blue Army' from the valleys. We are corralled out of the station by police officers, straight into a cascade of rain from the low-lying clouds. I stand on the road bridge outside of the station and look up Olympic Way to the National Stadium. Now one of the long-standing images I have had in my mind's eye throughout this journey has been the expectation of this moment. Of standing on that bridge, staring up at the arch, and seeing the throng of pilgrims marching towards it. The reality is a major disappointment. The stadium is barely perceivable against the misty skies, the arch barely illuminated by its twinkling lights. And the pilgrims aren't marching up Olympic Way, but rather scurrying for cover from the falling rain. I have barely a moment to snap a photo before my camera is drenched, and the photos I *do* get are nothing like the one I had imagined. It means I will have to completely rethink the front cover of the book.

Just then I get a text message from Corinthian Clive telling me that he has arrived and is waiting by the Club Wembley entrance. I holster my camera and set off through the gloom to meet him. We shake hands and I shake off the rain almost directly below the Bobby Moore statue, and then after the mandatory bag search, head up into Corporate Heaven, ascending majestically by way of a series of escalators that zig and zag us through the different levels of Wembley. Two smart hosts meet us at the summit, bedeck us with corporate badges, glossy programmes and an assortment of Corinthian Club bumf, and then guide us to our table for the pre-match meal. At this point I could be in any plush hotel, corporate headquarters or West End restaurant. I scan the bustling crowd of diners expecting to see the good and great of the footballing world but to no avail – not even the

Saint or Greavsie, and we finally take our seats next to a couple who introduce themselves as Dave and Chantelle MacKay. Corinthian Clive knows them from his semi final visit and he introduces me as the Road To Wembleyian that I am.

'I remember someone doing that before,' says Dave, 'a journalist I think.'

'You mean Brian James,' I reply, 'Tividale to Wembley was the book he wrote.'

'Yes that's right. So where did you start?'

'Well I started with Haringey Borough versus Wembley, because the Road To Wembley...'

'...has to start with Wembley,' smiles back Dave. This is all fairly familiar. Ten months ago I had the same conversation with Silver Hair in the Haringey Borough club house. The major difference is that the standard of refreshments has improved immeasurably, as a glass of champagne and fillet steak are placed before me rather than the tea and cheeseburger from Haringey. As we begin to tuck in, a comedian is introduced to the Corporate audience and we munch through our food as the impressionist reels through an amusing skit featuring famous voices from the world of football. It's all very Tarby's Celebrity FA Cup Final Bar, for those readers who remember that FA Cup tradition from yesteryear. And a world away from the pre-match build-up that I have become accustomed to. Just as the remains of the cheese board are cleared away, and a fresh bottle of wine deposited in front of us, an announcement is made that the national anthems will be sung in five minutes time, signaling a mass exodus from the restaurant area into the stadium.

When I had visited Wembley for the semi final, we had taken our seats early, and watched the crowd fill out slowly around us. This time with just a quarter of an hour to go until kick off, it is like walking into a cauldron. The stadium is packed full, the noise is deafening and my eyes gorge on a sea of colour. Wembley is alive with the constant swaying back and forth of thousands of blue and white flags at the Portsmouth end, and blue and yellow flags for Cardiff. The rectangle of brilliant green in front of me is home to the traditional marching band, and a set of podiums, upon which stand Katherine Jenkins and Lesley Garrett. As we reach our seats, the band strikes up and the two ladies belt out a stirring rendition of the Wembley hymn *Abide With Me*. Very moving. Then to an enormous cheer, the two teams are led out from the tunnel almost directly below me, and the FA Cup is placed on a stand in front of them. It is the first time in my life that I have *actually* seen the trophy itself. It sits on its plinth shining with a preternatural luminescence. *The Holy Grail*.

Katherine Jenkins gathers herself together, and to the accompaniment of the band, begins the first bars of *Land Of My Fathers*, launching Corinthian Clive to his feet beside me for his own baritone rendition. Not to be outdone, as Lesley Garrett delivers an accomplished version of *God Save The Queen*, I bellow along beside her. It is a magical moment. The demarcation lines have been set. Pompey to my left and the Bluebirds to my right. No-man's land just the thinnest of white strips across the middle of the green, green grass of Wembley. For the first time that day I get, really, really excited. I will worry later about the gaping void to my existence that the end of the journey heralds. For another ninety minutes, it's game on again. Portsmouth's Nwankwo Kanu rolls the ball forward at the sound of referee Mike Dean's whistle and we get underway.

As the game unfolds I'm surprised to see that the seats to either side of us are still empty. I make that comment to Corinthian Clive and he tells me that a famous TV presenter is the usual incumbent. Obviously the lure of Portsmouth versus Cardiff is not seductive enough for him, and his bank account is buoyant enough not to require selling the tickets on. I find it a shame that these seats are empty, when plenty of deserving causes would relish them, but it does give me the opportunity to stretch out and focus on snapping merrily away with the Nikon.

The opening exchanges are very even, but dominated by the defences, who are both squeaky tight. Portsmouth have height and experience in their back four, Cardiff offer dogged resistance. My problem however is my inability to get overly enthusiastic for two sets of teams who I barely recognise. It is reminiscent of that first Haringey match when I knew neither teams. I try to play the emotion game to see who I want to win, but there really is nothing riding on this match for me. Unlike the previous rounds I don't have a preference for where I go next, as there *is* no next. I can't seem to get excited when Pompey attack, and it looks as though Cardiff lack that cutting edge which will offer them the chance of any goals.

Corinthian Clive, a Welshman from Cardiff, has no problems in that department, and is roaring when the ball roams forward and squeaking when the Bluebirds are in retreat. But I just sit back in the comfortable, padded, (yes padded) seats and let the occasion wash over me. The sights and sounds of ninety thousand people, engrossed in this landmark event.

As we approach half time, I am just mentioning to Corinthian Clive that Cardiff have held their own, not been outclassed, that you wouldn't know which was the Premiership team, when Portsmouth score. It's a scrappy goal. A short cross from the right by John Utaka is fumbled by Cardiff keeper Peter Enckelman into the path of Kanu who thankfully accepts a tap in from a couple of yards out. It is a reprieve for the Nigerian who had early danced around Enckelman only to drill a shot into the side netting beside a gaping open goal. One side of Wembley leaps to its collective feet in jubilation, you can hear twenty five thousand pins drop at the Cardiff end. Corinthian Clive slumps into the padded protection of his seat in dejection. For the Welsh and the neutrals like me it is the worst possible development. We needed Cardiff to score first to make a real game of it. You get the impression that Harry Redknapp will take his team in at half time and ensure that the Pompey defence shuts up shop for the second half. Cardiff's inability thus far to make any serious impression on the Portsmouth goal only compounds this. There is a brief moment of hope in injury time when the Bluebirds actually get the ball into the back of the Portsmouth net, but as the fans to my right erupt, Mr Dean blows for an earlier handball by Glen Loovens and the muted Cardiff celebrations are echoed by the jeers of the Pompey faithful.

At half time we rise to our feet and head back into our allocated tables at Corporate Heaven, picking up a bottle of lager from our hosts on the way. Dave, Chantelle and Corinthian Clive all agree that there is probably no way back for Cardiff, but I know that there will be one more chance. History from previous rounds tells us that there is *always* one last chance.

Almost before we have had time to finish our lagers we are called back to our seats for the second half. The final forty five minutes out of the twenty eight and a half hours of football that I have witnessed on my cup odyssey. I find myself praying for a Cardiff goal, partly to make a game of it but mostly to prolong the ecstacy for as long as possible. Extra time and penalties would eek things out just that fraction longer. Portsmouth under Harry Redknapp are too wiley to get suckered into the *Goliath Complex*, and Cardiff are too blunt up front to deliver the *Siege Engine* patterns of play. Instead you have the veteran Sol Campbell, Sylvain Distin and David James building giant footballing fortifications in front of their goal. It's the reverse of the *Only A Matter Of Time* pattern, in that you know it is only a matter of time until the final whistle, when Portsmouth will be crowned the ultimate victors.

The sands of time tick away for Cardiff and for me. I find myself staring at the giant, electronic scoreboard, whose clock is slowly counting down, measuring out the final few yards of my mythical quest. I can feel that sense of emptiness filling my soul, in place of what I had imagined would be a sense of fulfilled achievement. Is this how everyone feels after achieving their ambitions? Did the great adventurers of history experience this same slow deflation? Was it the same for Odysseus on the return journey to Ithaca? Did Ceasar make triumphant returns into Rome and then think – 'Right then, who've we got in the next round?'

The Portsmouth fans are *willing* the clock to tick faster, the Cardiff faithful are praying for some miraculous breakthrough. I am probably the only person in the stadium who wants this game to continue *ad infinitum*. To be suspended indefinitely while I sit in this fabulous seat, in this amazing arena, watching the one and only cup final I am probably ever going to see... My eyes are glued to the figure of Mr Mike Dean as we play out the added minutes of injury time, and finally, slowly and authoritatively he puts his whistle to his lips and signals the end of play in the 2007/08 Football Association Cup. That last golden chance for Cardiff never really came, Portsmouth are victorious.

The Pompey faithful to my right are in ecstacy. They are dancing, singing and waving their blue and white flags furiously. To their credit off to my right, the Cardiff fans have nearly all stayed behind, to applaud the valiant losers from the lower league for taking them as far as they have. Corinthian Clive is up on his feet applauding. I am standing with my camera to my eye scanning the scenes of jubilation on that green rectangle looking for that final, defining photograph of the cup odyssey. It actually comes to me courtesy of the status of the Corinthian Club ticket. It places me directly beside the pathway on the way down from the royal box. Having been introduced to the footballing dignitaries, led by former England Manager Bobby Robson, first past me come the officials, Mr Dean and his assistants. They are followed by the defeated Cardiff players, clutching their runners-up medals – a coveted momento that nobody *actually* wants. Then, having received the glimmering trophy and raised it to the delirious Portsmouth fans just minutes before, comes Sol Campbell, leading his victorious team. I give Nwankwo Kanu a pat on his sweaty back but decide against ruffling the curly hair of David James. I'm waiting, waiting...

Finally, at the back of the line, smiling from ear to ear and mobbed by well-wishers, comes Harry Redknapp. In his hands are the *Holy Grail*. As he walks past me, and I snap furiously with my Nikon in one hand, the Football Association Challenge Cup is so close to me, I can reach out and touch it...

Cardiff 0
Portsmouth 1 (Kanu 37)

Attendance: 89,874
Money Spent So Far: £928.25
Miles Travelled So Far: 2,055
Winners Receive £1,000,000

May 2008
At The End Of The Day...

So it turns out that football is all about winning or losing. It made no difference to me whether I was on the barren terraces of Wodson Park or in the packed atriums of Wembley; whether park pitch or National Stadium. The minute a game kicks off, it's all about what happens on the rectangle of grass in front of you. A win is a win, and a loss can be heart breaking. The joyful scenes of celebration by the victorious Portsmouth players that I witnessed at the climax of the 2008 cup final were no different from those demonstrated by Non-League Ware when they knocked out Thurrock, or by Barnsley when they put paid to Liverpool or Chelsea. All that was different was location, location, location, and let me tell you, I was far happier with the freedom of those Non-League pitches, than I ever was penned into a seat at the great footballing cathedrals I visited. The exclusive Corinthian Club seats being the exception that proves the rule.

However one thing that the Non-League grounds could never match was the pomp and pageantry of the big theatres and the bigger games. Wembley, Anfield, even to a lesser degree Oakwell, all provided occasions that are burnt into my memory. A sense of belonging to something bigger than the sum of its parts. The colours, the smells, the sounds and the sweating mass of humanity, whose collective emotions can be polarised at the flick of a switch, or rather the flick of a ball into an open net.

My adventures on the 2008 FA Cup odyssey exceeded my expectations. It was truly a quest, with its highs and lows, its adversities to be overcome and its glories to be exalted. I felt honoured to witness the first chink in the cartel of the 'Big Four', long may that last. And what started out as a whim, and developed into an obsession, ultimately delivered a period of my life that I will never forget, and which I will constantly look back on with the fondest of memories. In fact I was almost depressed when it came to an end, and I know that when the 2008/09 fixtures are posted on the Football Association website I will be sorely tempted to sign on for another tour, just as each of the hundreds of clubs — be they big or small — will also throw their names into the hat once again.

As you read this the FA Cup will be at one of its staging posts. If by some lucky chance you are in that brief summer respite between the May final and the August preliminaries, I advise you to lock yourself away in your study, send your spouse out to the shops and make your preparations. The Road To Wembley will be starting soon somewhere near to you, I recommend that you get on it. You can bet that I will be.

www.roadfromwembley.com

Epilogue

I've waxed lyrically about the football resurrection I have experienced over the last few years, and following my cup exploits, I now have a whole new number of touchpoints to look forward to at a quarter to five on a Saturday afternoon when the results start flooding in and I learn the plight of the teams I have come to cheer or hiss. For the record, the 2007/08 seasons of each of my teams finished like this:

Haringey Borough probably had the most successful season out of anyone. They finished second in Division One of the Spartan South Midlands league achieving promotion back to the Premier Division alongside Kentish Town. They also edged home as two-one winners in the Divisional Cup Final against Ampthill Town.

At the time that I encountered *Wembley FC,* the team had high hopes of a return to Step Four of the Non-League Pyramid, but they finished their season in the Premier Division of the Combined Counties league a couple of positions below mid-table and will have to try again next year.

Great Wakering Rovers tenure in Division One North of the Isthmian League is also set to continue for another term after they finished in mid-table.

When *Thurrock* were unexpectedly dispatched from the FA Cup by Ware, their season was looking grim, but the team rallied in the second half and ended up in twelfth spot of the highly-competitive Blue Square South.

Hythe Town's season went right to the wire as they just missed out on promotion from the Step Five Kent League, finishing in fourth spot. Ace marksman Buster Smissen rattling up forty seven goals in all competitions. Unfortunately he could not find the back of the net in their final match of the season, when they lost the Kent League Cup Final one-nil to Erith Town.

The other Kent team that I encounters, *Tonbridge Angels,* finished in the top ten of the Isthmian League Premier, some accomplishment considering they lost their lethal marksman Jon Main to AFC Wimbledon in November. Main's record of fifty two goals in fifty seven matches for the Angels says it all, and he helped the Dons in their successful bid to gain promotion into the Blue Square South.

Kidderminster Harriers were mid-table in the Blue Square Premier when I met them, and finished up in mid-table. 'Bleeding' Harriers.

Their vanquishers, *Dagenham & Redbridge*, were desperate to stave off relegation in their first season in the Football League, and the job was done with a match to spare, as they finished in twentieth position out of twenty four, seven points above the relegation zone.

My love-hate relationship with *Southend United* seems destined to continue. Steve Tilson's side got my hopes up again by securing a League One play-off berth, only to fall at the first hurdle, when after a nil-nil draw at Roots Hall, they were comprehensively beaten five-one in the return at Doncaster.

Liverpool's season was one of hope and promise in the summer, as they tried to close the gap on the Premiership's top three, but once again their weaknesses were exposed as they continue to hold the mantle of fourth best team in the country. After the FA Cup misery against Barnsley, they also suffered Champions League heartache at the hands of Chelsea.

Over at Stamford Bridge, *Chelsea* famously took the Premiership title right down to the last afternoon following a storming run of results at the back end of the season. But the championship was never in their control thanks to Manchester United's superior goal difference, and the Blues could only draw on the last day, while United secured yet another league title. The Chelsea disappointment was compounded by defeat to United in Moscow in the Champions League on penalties.

Ultimately you can only applaud the achievement of *Cardiff* in reaching the final. I'm sure that if you had offered them an FA Cup runners-up medal at the start of the season, they would have bitten off your hand. But due to the nature of the giantkilling cup this year, and bearing in mind the slim margin of defeat, I'm sure there are plenty of Welshmen thinking what if Loovens' handball-goal had been allowed? In the league the Bluebirds consolidated their mid-table finish with another win over Barnsley on the last day of the season.

What more can you say about Harry Redknapp's current tenure at *Portsmouth*. Having saved them from apparent Premiership oblivion, he has built Pompey into a top ten side and now clasped his hands on his first managerial trophy. Europe now beckons for one of east London's favourite sons.

Having become my favourite team north of the Watford Gap, *Barnsley* put the disappointment of the semi final defeat behind them and shored up their

Championship status which had begun to look a tad fragile. They ended the term three points clear of the relegation zone although survival was clinched before the last match of the season.

Throughout the season as the frequency of the FA Cup matches abated, I continued to pay the occasional visit to Wodson Park, or if they were playing at a nearby away match, to see my newly-beloved *Ware*. I would always nod to Lensman and stand maybe fifty paces to the left of the Ware Travelling Support. On the pitch, the Wodson Aces managed to make the Isthmian Division One North play-offs but fell at the first knockout hurdle to Redbridge in monsoon-like weather conditions. Ware boss Glen Alzapiedi summed it up on the Herts 24 website: 'We have achieved all the targets we set. We got to the play-offs, first round of the FA Cup and reached two county cup finals. As a season we have been very good and played some attractive attacking football. As far as that's concerned we have done very well. The problem has been finishing it off at the end, that's the big disappointment.'